The
EMPERORS

The
EMPERORS

HOW EUROPE'S RULERS
WERE DESTROYED
BY THE FIRST WORLD WAR

GARETH RUSSELL

AMBERLEY

To Charles and Kathryn,
On the occasion of their marriage

All images from the plate section are courtesy of the Library of Congress

First published 2014

Amberley Publishing
The Hill, Stroud
Gloucestershire, GL5 4EP

www.amberley-books.com

British Library Cataloguing in Publication Data.
A catalogue record for this book is available from the British Library.

ISBN 978 1 4456 3433 3 (hardback)
ISBN 978 1 4456 3439 5 (ebook)

Typesetting and Origination by Amberley Publishing.
Printed in the UK.

Contents

Acknowledgements

The majority of this book was written in Belfast, the regional capital of a section of an island that lies on the western edge of the continent that was buffeted by the storms of the global tragedy of the First World War, but it was completed in New Haven, Connecticut. I would like to extend my thanks to the Linen Hall Library in Belfast, the Bodleian Library in Oxford, and the Berkeley College Library at Yale for providing atmospheres so conducive to work and for their wonderful resources which made writing this book both a challenge and a pleasure.

I very much appreciate the help and encouragement offered by so many people including Nicola Gale, my editor at Amberley, and my parents Ian and Heather, as well as Lauren Browne, Antonia Ede, Claire Handley, Catherine Maxtone-Parker, Dr Hannah McCormick, Rose Morgan, Eric Spies and Tom Woodward, with whom the idea for this book was first discussed. This book was made possible by the many excellent works of scholarship that have been undertaken in the century since the outbreak of the war, particularly in recent years, as well as the publication of key primary texts by the printing presses at the universities of Oxford, Cambridge, Yale, Harvard and Stanford. All historians stand on the shoulders of giants and this book is no exception; to thank all the academics who have dedicated their lives to making these subjects so wonderful to study would take many pages, men and women such as Professor John C. G. Röhl, who has spent decades unearthing and publishing so many of the vital documents concerning Wilhelmine Germany.

However, one more in particular bears special mention – having served as a lieutenant-colonel in the Allied occupation of Vienna after 1945, Gordon Brook-Shepherd befriended several members of the Hapsburg family, who had been active in opposing the Nazi annexation of 1938. His acquaintanceship with the Crown Prince Otto brought him into the company of the Dowager Empress Zita, widow of the First World War's Emperor Karl. Over the course of several decades, Brook-Shepherd persuaded the Empress to commit her memories to paper, as well as to sit through several interviews about the events in Vienna and Budapest during the First World War. Thanks to this, we have access to the personal thoughts and recollections of one of the war's principal royal figures – memories that might otherwise have been lost. Although Zita's versions of events were not infallible, all historians studying her husband's reign must be indebted to Gordon Brook-Shepherd's diligence and tact in recording them.

Prior to the October Revolution, Russia used the Julian calendar, which was thirteen days behind the Gregorian calendar employed by the West. Hence why the revolution that overthrew the monarchy in 1917 is sometimes referred to as the February Revolution and, less frequently, as the March Revolution. For clarity's sake in a book that attempts to set the Russian monarchy in its international context, I have given all the Russian dates in the New Style.

Monarchy is very much the grand synthesis of the personal and political and I have attempted where possible to balance both threads as best I can. Spellings and titles are up to the reader or author's discretion in a book written in English about subjects who spoke German and Russian as their first languages. I have gone for the more Germanic Franz Josef, Karl and Wilhelm rather than Francis Joseph, Charles and William for the Austrian and German emperors. Both the traditional titles used for emperors in Germany and Russia, *kaiser* and *tsar*, derive from the Roman *Cæsar*, but all three monarchies used the French or English translation of *emperor* as well. I have mostly referred to Wilhelm II by his most familiar title of Kaiser, the Austrian monarchs as emperors and Nicholas II as the Tsar. I have stuck to referring to Wilhelm's wife as the Empress, rather than the slightly more unusual sounding *Kaiserin*, and like most of their courtiers I have moved between referring to Alexandra as Tsarina and Empress. Most of these courtiers capitalised their sovereign's title when referring to them in the specific and I have followed suit where possible. I have opted for Hapsburg instead of Habsburg and Romanov over Romanoff. Where there was room for doubt I have tried to use titles that are more familiar to an English-language audience, hence why Nicholas II's son is referred to as the Tsarevich rather than *Tsesarevich* and his daughters as grand duchesses rather than *tsarevnas*, in keeping with how many of their tutors and retainers addressed them.

Russians are traditionally given a second name in reference to their father's name. Nicholas II was Nicholas Alexandrovich, meaning Nicholas, son of Alexander. Nicholas's third daughter was Maria Nikolaevna – Maria, daughter of Nicholas. For princesses who converted into the Russian Orthodox faith, like the Empress Alexandra, it was customary to give them the patronymic second name of Feodorovna, if their father's name did not translate into Russian.

Gareth Russell
New Haven, CT
Holy Week, 2014

It may seem to you of this present generation a page of history you have heard about in rather a vague way as belonging to an era before you were born. The Second World War, and the upheavals resulting from it, have pushed the events of the 1914–1918 War into the background. I consider therefore that perhaps it comes as not amiss that you young people should know something of the tragedies in the lives of us old ones, and what we underwent during those fateful years.

Princess Marie Louise of Schleswig-Holstein (1872–1956)

Prologue

'Oh, George, is the news very bad?'

I remember quite well thinking when I was seventeen that I could never be happy again. I mean everybody was unhappy. Because one knew so many people. Every day somebody was killed, you see. It was a real holocaust. It was horrible. I remember that feeling quite well.
  Lady Elizabeth Bowes-Lyon (1900–2002), later Queen Consort
        to King George VI and mother of Queen Elizabeth II

Every Sunday during the First World War, Princess Marie Louise of Schleswig-Holstein would join her parents and sister for lunch at Windsor Castle with her cousin, King George V. By the summer of 1918, Marie Louise was a handsome lady in her late forties with her sympathies firmly on the British side of the conflict. During tea with the exiled Dowager Empress Eugénie of France, who had been granted asylum in England years earlier, Marie Louise said that if half the stories about the Kaiser's activities were true then he deserved to be deposed, to which Eugénie replied, 'My child, no one who has experienced a revolution would wish even their worst enemy to undergo all the horrors that it entails.'

The vehemence of Marie Louise's opinions was all the more remarkable given that the emperor in question was her first cousin. In that regard, Marie Louise's position was comparable to dozens of European princes and princesses in the war years. Her style as a princess of Schleswig-Holstein was Germanic, her father, Prince

Christian, was German, while her mother Helena was a princess of the United Kingdom and a daughter of Queen Victoria. Her godfather had been the late Emperor Franz Josef of Austria, whose empire now fought on the same side as Germany, while her ex-husband, Prince Aribert von Anhalt, was a German. Yet Marie Louise could also count among her first cousins King George V of the United Kingdom of Great Britain and Ireland, and the Tsarina Alexandra of Russia, who was currently living under house arrest with her family following the revolution of 1917.

Devoted to the British royal family, Marie Louise had suppressed all pre-war emotional ties to Germany and Austria. She felt great sympathy for her cousin George at the burden he carried as the war progressed and the death toll mounted into the millions. Sunday lunches at Windsor in wartime were often silent or morose affairs as the King, weighed down by news of the latest casualty figures, appeared 'very tired and worried', in Marie Louise's words. One afternoon, as the other family members assembled to stand and greet the King and Queen as protocol demanded, the sovereign entered looking 'so grave and distressed' that Marie Louise's mother Helena cried out, 'Oh, George, is the news very bad?' Standing next to her, Marie Louise later claimed she was bracing herself for even worse news from the trenches on the Western Front, where a recent German offensive had caused terrible casualties with almost no tactical gain.

The King replied, 'Yes, but it is not what you think. Nicky, Alix, and their five children have all been murdered by the Bolsheviks at Yekaterinburg. I have ordered that the awful news should not be released to the Press until I have had time to let Victoria know.' The burden of duty fell on Marie Louise, who was due to go to the Isle of Wight the next day to spend some time with her cousin Victoria, the Marchioness of Milford Haven, who was the late Tsarina's sister. The King penned a letter informing the marchioness of 'this ghastly tragedy' and Marie Louise agreed to deliver it, recalling later, 'I have often had to face difficult situations that have needed both tact as well as courage, but never anything so terrible as to inform someone that their much-loved sister, brother-in-law and their five children had all been murdered.'[1]

On the Isle of Wight, the marchioness took the letter and read it in private. Afterwards, Marie Louise remembered that hardly anything at all was said about its contents. Nobody knew what to say about 'a subject too poignant and too sacred' and instead the two cousins spent a few days in each other's company gardening, reading and sewing shirts, scarves, hats and gloves for the troops. 'I realised that the only thing that could in some measure lessen her agony and sorrow was to employ every moment of the day with definite hard work,' Marie Louise wrote in her memoirs, and it was only after she returned to London that she 'received a truly wonderful letter from her, in which she thanked me for my silence which had helped her to get a grip on herself and her emotions which she could not have done had we discussed at length the details of the tragedy and what she was suffering'.

In many of the royal households of Europe, silence descended over the disappearance and death of the Romanovs. It was in many ways the Rubicon moment of the war, symbolising, as perhaps it was intended to, the death of the old world; no matter which side won the war, the golden age of monarchies which had preceded it had vanished, rendered irrecoverable by the events of four short and terrible years.

1

The Russian, German and Austro-Hungarian Monarchies in 1913

'The Old World in its Sunset'

In 1815, the forces of the great powers of Europe descended on Paris as their alliance ended the career of Napoleon Bonaparte, the Corsican commoner who had made himself Emperor amid the dying chaos of the French Revolution. Bonaparte was banished and Louis XVIII restored to the throne of his ancestors. In the century that followed, Europe became the uncontested master of the globe. Its empires expanded, the growth of its economies and population was unprecedented in recorded history, and its self-confidence seemed limitless as the invention of the railways, the telegraph system and rapid advancements in medicine, industry and technology revolutionised the way people lived.

At the centre of 'Europe's century' were the monarchies, the greatest of which had wrought the ruin of Napoleon in 1815 and then held a victors' congress at Vienna, the chief aim of which was to solidify the political status quo. For nearly a century, the congress's legacy remained intact. Conflicts like the Crimean War or Prussia's wars which led to the unification of Germany as a new empire in 1871 were either confined to small or distant parts of the Continent or so short in length that they fed the growing consensus that a prolonged war between the great powers was no longer possible. The duration and savagery of the American Civil War between 1861 and 1865 was often dismissed as nothing more than the growing pains of a faraway republic not yet a century old and few Europeans took heed of the disturbing developments in military technology that had helped make America's war so bloody.

By 1900, Europe's leading nations were so wealthy, so powerful and possessed of such impressive armies that a popular view emerged which held that the sheer enormity of the continent's global influence was in itself the guarantor of peace. The empires balanced each other, acting as one another's deterrents, and their increasingly complex alliances that by the first decade of the twentieth century had grouped the major nations into two distinct camps were all part of the Concert of Europe, the exhausting diplomatic dance which had safeguarded the long peace. Looking back on the seemingly halcyon days of the pre-war world, Winston Churchill, a monarchist to his core, said, 'Nations and Empires, crowned with princes and potentates, rose majestically on every side, lapped in the accumulated treasures of the long peace. All were fitted and fastened, it seemed securely, into an immense cantilever. The two mighty European systems faced each other glittering and clanking in their panoply, but with a tranquil gaze ... The old world, in its sunset, was fair to see.'[1]

Imperial Russia
In 1913, the Russian imperial postal service found itself confronted by a highly unusual problem in the field of employee relations. A set of stamps showing all the rulers of Russia since the election of the first Romanov Tsar in 1613 had recently been issued to mark the 300th anniversary of the dynasty's accession. However, a backlog in mail delivery arose when numerous postal officials refused to imprint the postmark on any stamp bearing the face of one of the Romanovs. Described by foreign journalists as 'loyal and eminently respectable scruples', the clerks' insistence that they would do nothing to besmirch an imperial visage, even one printed on the apparently innocuous form of a postal stamp, resulted in the commemorative portraits being withdrawn.[2] Four years later, the monarchy was swept away by revolution and a year after that, the

last Romanov Tsar, his wife and their five children were murdered and buried in an unmarked grave.

Explaining why the euphoria of the tercentenary gave way so quickly to the murderous depravity of the Red Terror is no easy task. For many years it was thought, and it is a view still taught in many schools, that tsarist Russia was a society so arcane and unjust, so innately backward and hopelessly corrupt, that its demise in 1917 was an inevitability: a question not of why but simply of how. In reaction to what they saw as the desecration of Russian national spirit under Soviet rule, Russian nationalists painted a very different picture, in which the Romanov empire had been brought to ruin by nothing more than bad luck and political conspiracy. Stories such as those in Nobel Prize winner Alexander Solzhenitsyn's series of novels *The Red Wheel* promoted the idea that Imperial Russia had been a society far more benign than sinister and certainly infinitely more compassionate than the Soviet regime that eventually replaced it. In this version of events, 1913 was not so much an Indian summer as a sign of the progress that would have remained unchecked if the First World War had not intervened.

As in so many things, the truth is more complicated even than saying that it rests in the middle of the two contrasting views. Few things in history can be counted as an inevitability and the implosion of the Russian monarchy in 1917 is certainly not one of them. Up until the very last minute, it could have been saved. It had faced a far more serious threat to its survival in 1905, when the myth of Russian military invincibility was shattered by a wholly unexpected and equally humiliating defeat in a war with Japan.[3] Catastrophe in the Far East collided with growing working-class unrest at deplorable conditions in the factories and the after-effects of the recession of 1902, causing widespread rioting. When one large demonstration, led by a priest and fiercely protesting its monarchist zeal, marched on the Winter Palace in Saint Petersburg to petition the Tsar for better living standards for the capital's poor, the guards panicked and opened fire, killing hundreds. That Nicholas II had been miles away at the time and the palace all but deserted made little difference in the ensuing outcry. The Tsar's uncle Sergei, one of the pillars of Russia's ultra-Right, was assassinated by a nail bomb as his carriage drove out from the gates of the Kremlin in Moscow; his widow, hearing the blast, dashed out into the blood-soaked snow and, finding no trace of her husband, had to help recover pieces of his body while the assassin was hauled into police custody.

All over Russia, servants of the imperial bureaucracy were targeted. Hundreds of assassinations and a wave of strikes brought the government to its knees. The Tsar accepted that peace would have to be bought. The autocracy of his ancestors, so cherished by his late and colossal father, would have to go. Nicholas's Danish mother, the Dowager Empress Marie, offered sage advice where so few others had or could and asked her son to listen to the proposals being put forward by his father's Minister of Finance, Sergei Witte. She begged, she cajoled, she entreated; when she felt the situation called for it, she threw herself at her son's feet, pleading with him to see reason. She urged him to listen to Witte, who, in her own words 'certainly is a man of genius, energetic and clear-sighted'.[4] In his time as Alexander III's Finance Minister, Witte had already wrought miracles by securing unheard-of levels of foreign investment in Russia and rapid subsequent industrialisation.[5] For this, the godfather of Russian capitalism was hated as much by the ultra-conservatives, who saw peasant agriculture as the soul of Russian nationhood, as he was by the Left, who blamed him for the ills endured by the urban proletariat.

Witte had already shown himself capable of making tough short-term decisions in order to secure long-term goals. He knew that the acceleration of the Industrial Revolution in Russia would bring with it great unrest, but equally he knew, or believed, that it was only through weathering this that Russia could guarantee prosperity and stability for its future generations. In 1905, he advocated that the dynasty make equally difficult decisions. Autocracy must be replaced by some kind of constitutional monarchy. Such a concession would split opponents to the crown and thus divide the protesters among themselves. Faced with unprecedented unrest, the Tsar acquiesced and signed the October Manifesto, which granted the empire's subjects the right to freedom of conscience, assembly, speech and religion and, crucially, made provision for the creation of an elected legislature, known as the Duma. Nicholas shuddered but he signed. 'From all over Russia they cried for it,' he said in a letter to his mother, 'they begged for it, and around me many – very many – held the same views ... There was no other way out but to cross oneself and give what everyone was asking for. My only consolation is that such is the will of God, and this grave decision will lead my dear Russia out of the intolerable chaos she has been in for nearly a year.'[6]

But while the October Manifesto did achieve the intended result of splitting the liberals from the radicals – one former Marxist-turned-liberal, thirty-five-year-old Peter Struve, had been so appalled by the violence of 1905 that he captured many a liberal mindset when he exclaimed, 'Thank God for the Tsar, who has saved us from the people!' It did not, to the Tsar's shock and fury, bring about an immediate end to either the rioting or the revolutionaries' bombing campaigns. The Bolsheviks co-ordinated an armed insurrection of factory workers in Moscow, while Leon Trotsky emerged as the prominent leader of the Soviet of Workers' Deputies in Saint Petersburg, which aimed to create a political alternative to the monarchy. As police authority collapsed, mutinies swept the armed forces and panicked governors in the provinces wrote of peasants ransacking and looting aristocratic estates, Nicholas wrote to his mother, 'More and more voices are heard protesting that the time has come for the Government to take matters firmly in hand – which is a very good sign indeed ... The old headless Liberals, always so critical of firm measures on the part of the authorities, are now clamouring loudly for decisive action.'[7] Horrified at the continuation of violence and galvanised by the fact that even liberals were now 'clamouring' for a clampdown on the revolutionaries, the imperial government struck back at the beginning of 1906. Even as preparations were underway for the creation of the electorate and the Duma, the ultra-monarchist Peter Durnovo was appointed Minister of the Interior. A brilliant political tactician with nerves of steel, Durnovo helped co-ordinate the government's response to the riots and, in the words of one of his colleagues, he did it 'systematically, even ruthlessly'.[8] Mass arrests, suppression of the strikes, the use of the army and the reassertion of government control over the railway and telegraph networks saw the revolutionary movement lose co-ordination, confidence, momentum and finally support. By the time the first Duma was officially opened by the Tsar in a glittering ceremony at the Winter Palace in April, the putative revolution had collapsed.

Yet the birth of his brainchild did nothing to salvage Nicholas's faith in Witte as Prime Minister. As far as the Emperor was concerned, he had been duped into signing the October Manifesto by a man who was evidently nothing more than a self-aggrandising career politician. 'I have never seen such a chameleon of a man,' he wrote. 'That, naturally, is the reason why no one believes in him any more. He is absolutely discredited with everybody ... Durnovo, the Minister of the Interior, is doing splendid work. I am very pleased with him.'[9] Nor was Nicholas's opinion of Witte an isolated one; even many of his former supporters felt that Witte had badly underestimated the threat posed by revolutionaries in 1905. His departure and eventual replacement with Peter Stolypin, one of the few provincial governors who had kept his nerve during the violence, was not widely mourned. If Witte had been the Russian monarchy's Necker, Stolypin was its more successful Breteuil.

Tall, well-educated and dynamic, with a dark beard and dark eyes, Stolypin was to go down in history as the last great statesman of Imperial Russia. He was robust, in his early forties, a member of the gentry and a brilliant public speaker. His policies for preventing a repetition of 1905 were simple – economic reform coupled with political retrenchment. If this makes his premiership sound like a glorified form of the carrot and the stick then that is because such an assessment is not too far from the truth. Widespread land reforms were introduced to alleviate the financial strains on the peasantry; the *kulaks*, a wealthier class of peasant, were given government assistance to buy their own farms, rather than simply to rent them; legislation was also enacted to provide health insurance for urban workers and Witte's policy of attracting foreign investment to Russia was continued. The economy boomed, as for the first, and so far the last, time in her history Russia was able to efficiently make use of her vast natural resources.

Nicholas, still uneasy at the fact the Duma existed at all, seemed by and large far happier with Stolypin than he had been with Witte. For most of the period between 1907 and 1914, the Tsar moved between his natural conservatism and tentatively attempting to make the new semi-constitutional monarchy work, and in this he was suited to a premier like Peter Stolypin, who was a pragmatist but also a sincere monarchist. Nicholas supported the decision to gut the October Manifesto of most of its more radical provisions, although he agreed that it would be impossible to undo it completely. He agreed to the redefinition of the electorate in 1907, ensuring that it was now weighted in favour of property owners, and he opposed any attempt to divide up aristocratic estates among the peasantry, noting in the margin of a government report on the issue, 'Private property must remain inviolable.'[10] As the economy flourished and political stability was restored, Stolypin also won much approval for his policy of treating revolutionary activists as nothing more than glorified criminals and killers. Shortly after the October Manifesto, Stolypin's home had been hit by a revolutionary bomb in an attack that destroyed the building, killed twenty-seven people and left two of his children, fifteen year-old Natalia and her three-year-old brother, severely injured. In a letter to one of his colleagues, Stolypin told of how he had scrambled through the ruins of his house to search for survivors: 'When I carried out my daughter from under the wreckage, her legs hung like stockings. My son has one knee broken and his head is injured. He is all crumpled up.'[11] More than most, Stolypin therefore understood the revulsion many Russians felt towards the revolutionaries after 1905. Between 1906 and 1909, hundreds of revolutionaries were arrested, tried and executed. The evidence against most of them was overwhelming but the number of executions saw to the hangman's noose being dubbed 'Stolypin's necktie' by an unimpressed member of the Duma. Stolypin was so outraged that he challenged the gentleman to a duel; an apology was issued, the duel avoided and the nickname flourished from the publicity.

There were significant problems that Stolypin tried to resolve but which were ultimately beyond the power of any one man, chief among them being reforms in the countryside. Tensions there remained unabated and mutual distrust defined relations between most of the nobility and the peasantry. Alcoholism – to numb the pain of a truly terrible existence – and hatred of the social hierarchy were rampant in Russia's factories, but the situation for the millions who still lived in agrarian communities was more complicated than that suggested by the popular image of a starving peasantry ground under by callous aristocrats and the Cossacks' whips. At the turn of the century, the Russian peasantry as a collective generated over half the empire's income while paying about a fifth of its taxes, the diet of the average Russian peasant in the first two decades of Nicholas II's reign was roughly the same as that enjoyed by the population of capitalist West Germany in the middle of the 1950s, while the independent peasant farms, which became increasingly common in the Stolypin era, were producing far more food than the farms located on large aristocratic estates. Tensions arose not just from peasant resentment at the wealth and privilege jealously guarded by the aristocracy, but also because more and more Russian noblemen, seeing their chief sources of income lose out in productivity, were attempting to run their estates on Western capitalist lines, introducing sweeping reforms in how they planted and harvested, and in the process aggravating rural conservatism and contributing to a widespread view of the nobility as absentee *de facto* foreigners with little to no regard for the true sons of the Russian soil.

Yet, jibes about neckties notwithstanding and with certain problems still left unresolved, Peter Stolypin's political career was more successful than otherwise.[12] Conservatives were pleased to see membership of the recently legalised trade unions drop from 300,000 in 1907 to just over 40,000 in 1913. Millions of peasants became property owners, despite lingering aristocratic opposition as resentment over the violence seen in 1905 saw the aristocracy digging its heels in to become even more indifferent to the concerns of the rural peasantry. Five consecutive years of beautiful summers and comparatively mild winters led to bumper harvests; education reforms and increases in teachers' salaries improved the prospects for Russia's next generation to continue the capitalist dream nurtured by Stolypin's government and plans were put in place to have completely eradicated illiteracy in the empire's young by 1922. Russia's railway networks and steel mines broke records with how quickly they expanded. Coal production doubled. Industrial productivity in general increased by 125 per cent in five years. Government income rose sharply and by 1914 the empire had outstripped the United States as the major global exporter of grain.

But the death he had avoided in 1906 caught up with Stolypin in 1911 when he attended a performance of the opera *The Tale of Tsar Saltan* in Kiev. The Tsar was in the audience, accompanied by his eldest two daughters, the fifteen-year-old Grand Duchess Olga and fourteen-year-old Grand Duchess Tatiana, when a young revolutionary called Mordka Bogrov approached the Prime Minister during the second interval and shot him twice in the chest. The Tsar, who had just left the imperial box, came back to investigate the strange noise: 'Women were shrieking and directly in front of me in the stalls Stolypin was standing. He slowly turned his face towards me and with his left hand made the sign of the Cross in the air. Only then did I notice that he was very pale and that his right hand and uniform were bloodstained … People were trying to lynch the assassin. I am sorry to say the police rescued him from the crowd and took him to an isolated room for his first examination.'[13] The Grand Duchess Tatiana was hysterical as the imperial suite was rushed from the theatre in case the Prime Minister's murder had simply been the opening act. The Dowager Empress described herself as 'distressed and indignant' about Stolypin's 'horrible and scandalous' murder.[14] Tatiana's mother did not quite share her daughter or mother-in-law's distress. She had never forgiven Stolypin for criticising her beloved spiritual confidante, Rasputin, and she wrote to the new Prime Minister, Count Vladimir Kokovstov, 'Life continually assumes new forms … the Lord will help you. I am sure Stolypin died to make room for you, and all this is for the good of Russia.'[15] Tact was never one of Her Imperial Majesty's virtues.

Two years later, when the dynasty led the nationwide celebrations to mark the tercentenary of Romanov rule in Russia, Stolypin's legacy meant there was room for great confidence among the empire's many monarchists. The opulent festivities of 1913, which saw the Tsar and his family undertake a sort of dynastic pilgrimage to Kostroma, where, in 1613, sixteen-year-old Mikhail Romanov had emerged as the Tsar chosen to end a generation-long trauma known as the Time of Troubles, evoked scenes of widespread rejoicing. But even as Moscow and Saint Petersburg were lit up with fantastic light displays and portraits of all the Romanovs from Mikhail to Nicholas were hoisted in public buildings throughout the empire, there were still issues that needed to be tackled. The revolutionaries may have been scattered by exile, broken, divided and increasingly despondent about there being any chance for a revolution in their lifetime, but the Duma and the court were frequently at odds with one another. The high court nobility clung tenaciously to the view that regardless of their views of the rest of the upper classes, the rural peasantry were inalienably devoted to the Tsar and that all demands for further political reform came only from the urbanised bourgeoisie, whose heads had been turned by a lot of silly Western liberal nonsense. The Duma, not unfairly, accused the court of disregarding educated public opinion at every available turn. The alliance of mutual interests which had bonded the two together in 1905 had weakened by 1913 and the Tsar's coterie did not help matters by heaping a dozen petty humiliations on the politicians' heads during the tercentenary. The delegates were usually given the worst seats at any of the public functions, they had to make their own travel arrangements and, unlike the courtiers, they had to pay their own way as well. Far from evoking joy at the success of the partnership between the Duma and the throne, the public celebrations surrounding the tercentenary only served to reinforce the ultra-conservatives' delusion that the last seven years had been a blip – an aberration from the grand narrative of Russian history, which to them was indisputably a tale of the Tsar tied by unalterable bonds of love and affection to his people. The Tsarina expressed this lacuna better than anyone when she told one of her ladies-in-waiting, 'Now you can see for yourself what cowards these state ministers are … we need merely show ourselves and at once their [the people's] hearts are ours.'[16]

Like her husband, Alexandra Feodorovna was not actually stupid and she was marginally less blind than many of her critics suggested. However, it was ironic that she of all people should have articulated that the key to the imperial family's popularity was their visibility. The personalities and private lives of the Tsar and his family will be discussed at length later, but for now it is suffice to say that by 1913 they had all but retreated from public view. There were several reasons for this. The first was the Tsarina herself. The birth of five children in relatively quick succession had destroyed her already fragile health and she was plagued by heart palpitations and sciatica which left her confined to her bed or her chaise longue for days at a time. She was also extremely shy and uncomfortable in large crowds. The aristocracy of the capital chose to interpret her behaviour as wanton rudeness and detested her accordingly. Meriel Buchanan, the daughter of the British ambassador to Saint Petersburg, witnessed the Empress's panic attack first hand when the Tsar and his wife attended a performance at the theatre one evening. Within minutes, Alexandra began to shake and fan herself compulsively, 'the diamonds which covered the bodice of her gown [began] to rise and fall, flashing and trembling with a thousand uneasy sparks of light. Presently, it seemed that this emotion or distress mastered her completely, and with a few whispered words to the emperor she rose and withdrew to the back of the box, to be no more seen that evening. A little wave of resentment rippled over the theatre.'[17]

The last great imperial ball, the traditional zenith of social interaction between the monarchy and the high nobility, was held in 1903. After that, Alexandra refused to host any more and the cavernous ballrooms at the Winter Palace went largely unused. At almost every available opportunity, it seemed as if she was going out of her way to antagonise the aristocracy. Most of her favourite ladies-in-waiting, women like Lili Dehn and Anna Vyrubova, were members of the bourgeoisie. When her eldest daughter Olga turned sixteen in 1911, Alexandra organised the traditional coming-out ball for the girl to mark her formal entry into the world of high society. But even here, there was a sting. The Grand Duchess's ball was held at Livadia, the imperial family's summer home 1,500 miles away from Saint Petersburg, rather than at any of the Romanovs' numerous palaces in the capital city as was customary.

By 1913, both Olga and her younger sister Tatiana should have been regular fixtures in the capital's social calendar, but to the vast majority of the upper classes the imperial children remained as strangers. The Duchess of Saxe-Coburg, visiting Russia for a family wedding in 1914, was incensed by Alexandra's failure to introduce her daughters to life among their peers. When Olga and Tatiana did appear at functions, the Duchess noticed, 'As the girls know nobody in society, they simply hopped around like provincial demoiselles without anybody being presented to them and they were never made to talk with any of the ladies young or old ... Now fancy Grand Duchesses who perhaps will soon marry and perhaps leave the country not being properly introduced into the Petersburg society! ... the whole of the old and good etiquette has been abandoned.'[18] It was left to the Dowager Empress to arrange a debut ball for Tatiana in Saint Petersburg, which she also used as an opportunity to rectify the error of hosting Olga's in the Crimea – the ball at the Anichkov Palace was given in honour of both girls. Alexandra managed to stick the party out for an hour and a half before leaving early to yet another wave of whispering and contempt; Nicholas stayed on until half past four in the morning, unable to tear his exuberant daughters away from the merriment. Wracked by ill health, crippled by shyness and shunned by an aristocracy whose members she regarded as frivolous, self-indulgent, immoral and gaudy wastrels, the Empress Alexandra was the chief cause for the imperial couple's estrangement from the empire's elite.

The second reason for the Romanovs' isolation in the final decade of their rule was the haemophilia of Nicholas and Alexandra's only son, Alexei. Born in 1904, during Russia's disastrous fracas with Japan, Alexei was named after Nicholas's favourite ancestor, the seventeenth-century Tsar Alexei the Gentle. A variation of Salic law, which prohibited inheritance of the throne by a woman, had operated in Russia since 1797 and the birth of four daughters in 1895, 1897, 1899 and 1901 had been marked by progressively diminishing levels of enthusiasm. Alexei's birth in August 1904 had therefore been the cause of rejoicing tinged with relief and when Pierre Gilliard, the grand duchesses' French tutor, met the Tsarina with her young son for the first time he described Alexandra as 'transfused by the delirious joy of a mother who had at last seen her dearest wish fulfilled. She was proud and happy in the beauty of her child. The Tsarevich was certainly one of the handsomest babies one could imagine, with lovely fair curls, great grey-blue eyes under the fringe of long, curling lashes and the fresh pink colour of a healthy child. When he smiled, there were two little dimples in his chubby cheeks.'[19] Six weeks after the birth, the heir began to haemorrhage from the navel. Alexandra's uncle Leopold and her little brother Friedrich had both lost their lives to haemophilia, a rare disorder in which the blood does not properly clot or coagulate.[20] The child's first bleeding stopped and Alexandra temporarily relaxed as she told herself, hope of hopes, that it had been something unrelated to the terrible hereditary disease. Then, as their son began to crawl, she and Nicholas were forced to confront the truth. Alexei was covered in angry bruises from the slightest tumble; the baby screamed in pain as the blood beneath the bruise would not clot and instead transformed into excruciating swellings.

Respecting the etiquette which stipulated that poor health in members of the imperial family should never be disclosed until they were *in extremis*, and consumed by guilt that she as the female carrier had 'given' her son his life-threatening illness, Alexandra insisted on a wall of secrecy circling the imperial household, forming a barrier that increasingly did not just prevent information from getting out but also sound advice from getting in. So total was Alexandra's protection of her only son that some of Nicholas's relatives had no real idea of what was wrong with Alexei, neither did Peter Stolypin, and as a result they found Alexandra's near-hysterical dependence on the wandering holy man Rasputin even more puzzling and upsetting.

As Alexandra's health collapsed further under the strain of looking after Alexei and monitoring his every move, she gave herself over even more to religion and tried her best to ignore the public's speculation. Everyone knew something was wrong with the heir, they had seen it with their own eyes when during one of the tercentenary processions he had been so ill he had to be carried by one of his sailor-guardians. A year earlier, Alexei had fallen at Spala, the imperial family's hunting lodge in Poland, injuring his groin as he boarded a small rowing boat. The damage done was sufficient to warrant the Last Rites being administered as a bulletin announcing the Tsarevich's death was prepared by the court's grand chamberlain. At the eleventh hour, Alexandra telegrammed Rasputin, who assured her that the child would not die, and the next day the swelling began to decrease, although it was months before Alexei was able to recover his former fitness, hence the need to have the child carried during part of the tercentenary. The miracle at Spala convinced the Empress of Rasputin's closeness to God, and even doubters within the family's shrinking circle of intimates, like Nicholas's youngest sister, the Grand Duchess Olga Alexandrovna, were hard-pressed to explain how the boy had recovered. But few outsiders knew any of this and as the rumours flourished and Alexandra's dependence on Rasputin grew, the gulf between the Romanovs and their subjects deepened.

The third and final reason for the Romanovs' removal from regular view was more mundane: security. After the spate of assassinations in 1905 and 1906, fears that an enterprising anti-monarchist would carry out a successful attack on the Tsar or another member of his immediate family prompted increased protection for the Romanovs. When Nicholas and Alexandra visited their relatives in Britain for the Cowes week regatta in 1911, the future King Edward VIII was 'astonished at the elaborate police guard thrown around his every movement'.[21] It was only with the tercentenary celebrations that the obsessive cloistering of the imperial family was temporarily relaxed and it showed, as Alexandra noticed, what wonders their public presence could still achieve. Observing the outpouring of patriotic pride in 1913, *The Times'* Russian correspondent wrote, 'Nothing could exceed the affection and devotion to the person of the Emperor displayed by the population wherever His Majesty appeared. There is no doubt [of] this strong attachment of the masses'.[22]

However, the tercentenary did not play as well in other parts of an empire that by 1900 covered one-sixth of the world's land surface. The Romanovs ruled over a population with multiple ethnicities, faiths and languages, yet the last half-century or so of imperial rule saw a sustained and insensitive drive to enforce the values of Mother Russia on the entire empire. Officials and even teachers were banned from using any language other than Russian, towns were renamed and attempts to revive architecture from the bygone days of medieval Muscovy received government backing, causing predictable and understandable feelings of outrage among the Poles, Letts, Finns, Lithuanians and Estonians who were also subjects of the Tsar, however unwillingly, and who found the policy that was subsequently dubbed 'Russification' to be offensive and galvanising. Nicholas's mother attempted to counsel him against the policy, particularly in Finland, but her words went unheeded as Nicholas chose to continue the programme put in place by his father, whose government had rested squarely on the tripartite mantra of Orthodoxy, Autocracy and Nationality. Russian nationalist fervour had an even less attractive manifestation when it interacted with centuries of religious bigotry to produce some of the most terrifying outbursts of anti-Semitic violence in Europe prior to the advent of Nazism. Pogroms against the empire's sizable Jewish communities, like those during the chaos of 1905 and 1906 which had left thousands dead or wounded, were usually the result of local unrest rather than deliberate governmental planning, although the civic authorities in Kiev and Moscow treated the Jewish population of the city abominably by ordering their mass expulsion in 1886 and 1891 respectively. The imperial government did absolutely nothing to counteract anti-Semitism and Nicholas II's father had even defended it by pointing out that Christians were entitled to feel hatred towards the group who were historically responsible for the martyrdom of the Messiah.

The picture that emerges of Russia in 1913 is that of a vast empire, the second largest in human history, experiencing a sustained period of rapid economic expansion and led by a monarchy that had recently proven its ability to weather the harshest of storms. There were still political tensions between a conservative-nationalist court and a parliament which felt more needed to be done to guarantee a peaceful and prosperous future, but the more significant problems lay in the resentment of the empire's many minorities at the tactless nationalism of the central government, tensions between landowners and peasants in the countryside, and a revolutionary movement in recession but not yet totally extinguished. None of these problems were necessarily unmanageable and if the tsarist empire could not have existed for much longer in the way that it did in 1913 there is nothing to suggest that the collapse of the monarchy itself was in any way inevitable or even likely until Russia came into conflict with the two empires on its western borders.

Wilhelmine Germany

On 23 May 1912, Kaiser Wilhelm II attended the launch of the *Imperator* at the Bremerhaven shipping yard in northern Germany. The creation of the vessel was surrounded by a significant amount of media excitement; at the time of its maiden voyage a year later, the *Imperator* was the largest moving object in human history, a 52,000-ton luxury liner with room for 4,500 passengers in four different classes. That the launching ceremony took place only five weeks after the *Titanic* disaster did not seem to unduly faze any of the attendees or dampen the German press's enthusiasm for the new wonder-ship. The *Imperator*'s enormous size would snatch back the accolade of the world's largest vessel from the British liner *Olympic*; when news leaked that a forthcoming British ship, Cunard's *Aquitania*, would be longer than the *Imperator*, the *Imperator*'s owners responded by sticking an enormous crowned eagle on the prow. The eagle, its claw surmounting a globe with the words *Mein Feld ist die Welt* ('My Field is the World'), was a monstrosity and a liability. It added the requisite length to beat out the *Aquitania*, but it proved impossible to sustain and eventually, after it had been battered by the Atlantic storms, it had to be removed.

Nonetheless, the eagle's proud boast captured the mindset of many Germans by 1913, particularly in the military and at the court. The creation of the Second Reich in 1871 had been achieved primarily through military success, with Prussia's victories in short wars against Denmark, Austria and France providing the impetus for unification. The northern state of Prussia's subsequent primacy within the empire was not universally popular and the second largest of the German communities, the southern kingdom of Bavaria, particularly resented it. Bavaria was the bastion of southern Catholicism to Prussia's proud Protestantism; it saw itself as a centre of the arts and derided what was widely perceived as the boorish militarism of the Kaiser's homeland.

Wilhelm II, who inherited the throne from his father in 1888, was not the most tactful of men. With his heroically absurd moustache and penchant for theatrical military uniforms, Wilhelm struck many of his contemporaries as ridiculous, when he was not malign. (During one visit, the Archduke Franz Ferdinand of Austria worried that he looked foolish in one of his uniforms before telling himself that no matter how bad he looked he was bound to benefit by virtue of comparison because Wilhelm 'always dressed himself up in the worst possible taste.')[23] Even many of his fellow royals were at best ambivalent about 'Cousin Willy'. His first cousin, Empress Alexandra of Russia, detested him, one of the few opinions she held in common with her mother-in-law, the Dowager Empress Marie, who described the Kaiser as 'vulgar and detestable'.[24] Even his beloved grandmother, Queen Victoria, who was nursed by Wilhelm on her deathbed, was concerned about her grandson's political instability. After Alexandra married Nicholas II in 1894, Victoria wrote frequent letters to the young Tsar, whom she liked very much, warning him against listening to any of Wilhelm's advice, particularly on the subject of Britain. Nicholas, whose imperturbable politeness was often mistaken for gullible quiescence, particularly by Wilhelm, who wrote him numerous letters holding forth on his numerous opinions on everything that was wrong with the world, thanked Victoria for her warning.

In the years after Germany's defeat in the war, the criticism of Wilhelm's relatives seemed mild when compared to descriptions of him as a depraved anti-Semitic war criminal who had plunged Europe headlong into catastrophe and whose authoritarian regime and passion for colonialism had paved the way for Nazism fifteen years later.[25] Yet Wilhelm, while certainly gifted with more than his fair share of faults, was not by any stretch of the imagination a war criminal, nor did the monarchy of the Second Reich have much in common with the terrifying monstrosities of the Third. Wilhelm II's main problem was not a predisposition towards viciousness but rather his chronic and bombastic inconsistency. At times, he seemed dazzled by Britain, his mother's homeland, praising its industry, sometimes mimicking its aristocracy's tweedy sense of country fashion and raising toasts on family holidays to the memory of long-dead British war heroes like Horatio, Lord Nelson or Richard, Earl Howe; then he would turn on a sixpence, uttering bitter denunciations and showing a fevered sense of competition. In foreign policy, he swung on whether Germany's alliance with Austria-Hungary, signed in 1879, should be maintained or jettisoned. He repeatedly undermined his foreign ministers in making overtures to Russia by attempting to convince Nicholas II that an alliance between their monarchies was morally superior to an alliance with a republic. Nicholas, concerned that Germany might encourage Austria-Hungary to behave more aggressively towards the Slavic kingdoms in Serbia and Montenegro and forewarned about the quality of Wilhelm's advice, continued to prefer the existing alliance with France to any mooted pact with Germany.

Attempts to split Russia away from her alliance with republican France struck a particularly disingenuous note when Wilhelm himself toyed with the idea of ending Germany's generation-long animosity with its neighbour. He claimed, not always convincingly, that he had 'no hatred towards the country that is widely known as the hereditary enemy of my empire'.[26] He encouraged his widowed mother to holiday in France, hoping that her presence would ease French animosity toward the German empire. The plan, like so many of Wilhelm's, backfired when the French press expressed outrage at the fact that the Dowager Empress was being housed near the site of some of Germany's most resounding victories against France in 1870. For all his love of imperial expansion, Wilhelm apparently at one point considered abandoning Germany's colonisation of Africa if it would lead to improved relations with Britain.[27] One of his courtiers, Chlodwig, Prince zu Hohenlohe-Schillingsfürst, wryly noted, 'It seems that His Majesty is recommending another new programme, but I don't take it too tragically; I have seen too many new programmes come and go.'[28]

The Prince's comment is contained in a letter to Wilhelm's great favourite, Count Philipp zu Eulenburg. Between them, Eulenburg and Hohenlohe led one of the most powerful factions at the Kaiser's court. Eulenburg was a brilliant courtier, who provided the friendship and affection painfully missing from Wilhelm's life and who also knew how to rein in some of the Kaiser's more emotional impulses. His letters bounce between charm and forcefulness, balancing the enjoyable ephemera of high society gossip with the more serious issues of national and international politics. He cleverly refused to see Wilhelm too often, avoided taking an office in the palace and instead confined many of their interactions to social events, thus maintaining the air of a friendship unsullied by the drudgery of day-to-day government. He guided Wilhelm through several clashes with his ministers and arranged the appointment of some extremely influential ambassadors and administrators. He championed the monarchy's right to assert its influence in government, but he understood that it needed to be practised cleverly. Count zu Eulenburg's homosexuality and the closeness of his relationship to the Kaiser has caused ongoing speculation about Wilhelm's own sexuality and the suggestion that the two men were in fact lovers rather than simply close friends has been postulated many times, beginning with Marcel Proust and continuing right the way down to the present.[29] One of Wilhelm's sons, Augustus Wilhelm, was almost certainly what we would now recognise as gay, but his father's sexuality is not so easily understood.

The Kaiser's robust preference for his own gender in every other field of his life was obvious. He nearly causing a diplomatic incident when he slapped both the Tsar of Bulgaria and the Grand Duke of Mecklenburg-Strelitz on their behinds in public, and he organised several cruises on the imperial yacht *Hohenzollern* that were male only, which certainly added fuel to the speculative fire, but finding proof of any same-sex liaisons that went beyond homoerotic banter and close emotional dependence is almost impossible. Admittedly, Wilhelm's first Chancellor, Otto von Bismarck, coyly suggested that the nature of the Kaiser's relationship with Eulenburg was 'not to be confided to paper', but in contrast to that we have ample proof of various heterosexual flings, including one in his twenties with a high-class call girl with the rather gloriously unsubtle working name of 'Miss Love'. On the subject of Wilhelm and Philipp zu Eulenburg, Wilhelm's most recent biographer Christopher Clark convincingly points out that although nothing is provable there is no 'need to postulate such a relationship in order to explain the character of the connection or its political significance'.[30]

Eulenburg smothered Wilhelm II with the affection he felt had been missing in his childhood. During his birth, the attending doctors incorrectly assumed that the baby was a stillborn and tore him from his mother's womb in an attempt to save the Crown Princess's life. In the process, the nerves at the top of Wilhelm's left arm were permanently damaged and he may have suffered minimal perinatal brain damage, which might help explain his occasional balance problems and outbursts of slightly manic bad temper. However, a diagnosis of at-birth mild brain damage is not the only possible explanation for these, because both problems could also have been caused by what happened afterwards. Agonising medical treatments that look faintly like torture to the modern eye were used to try to correct what could not be corrected; despite the Crown Princess's unease at their tactics, medical experts from Berlin were brought in to try a variety of cures including minor surgery, binding the toddler's arms to his side as he learned to walk, electroshock therapy, an arm-stretching machine, placing his arm inside the carcass of a freshly slaughtered hare so that his limp limb could absorb the vitality of the dead animal's warm blood, and strapping him into a leather and metal contraption that covered most of his torso. Crown Princess Victoria wrote to her mother in England that 'to see one's child treated as one deformed – it is really very hard … Doctors are so odd sometimes, they don't mean to be unfeeling I am sure but they appear so'.[31] Perhaps unsurprisingly Wilhelm was to remain self-conscious about his injury for most of his life and in adulthood dark humours would take over as he thrashed about in violent mood swings, as if he could find no other way to deal with emotional or political restrictions than to scream, rage and shout.

As he grew up, his relationship with his liberal and Anglophile parents suffered as he adopted the politics of his militant and conservative grandfather, Wilhelm I. This produced a fairly miserable home life and by the time Wilhelm became Emperor in 1888 following his father's ninety-nine day reign, cut short by laryngeal cancer, his relationship with his mother was one of suspicion and mutual resentment. His father had died apparently deeply disappointed in his eldest son, a feeling which neither he nor Victoria did anything to hide and which she, in her grief and reproaches, may quite possibly have exaggerated. In this context it was easy to see how the *bonhomie* and unwavering affection of men like Philipp zu Eulenburg would have such an effect on the Kaiser. For fifteen years, he was one of the most powerful figures in the Wilhelmine monarchy.

However, over the course of 1906 and 1907 six high-ranking members of the German army committed suicide when they were blackmailed with exposure of their homosexuality. That some of them may have been romantically involved with Eulenburg, or that he at least knew why they had taken that terrible final step of suicide, cannot be discounted; either way the net was tightening around him as thinly veiled speculation ran rampant. In April, a journalist called Maximilian Harden, writing for the liberal newspaper *Die*

Zukunft, published an article hinting at an affair between Philipp zu Eulenburg, 'leader of a sinister and effeminate camarilla', and Count Kuno von Moltke, a member of a prominent military family who was also one of the Kaiser's adjutants and the military commander for Berlin. Harden's intentions were primarily political – he hoped to discredit a man who was known to support semi-absolutist monarchy, but the case rapidly became a media free-for-all.

Homosexuality had been criminalised in Germany by legislation enacted in 1871 and the recent wave of suicides in the upper echelons of the army showed how much damage it could do to a reputation. In an atmosphere of panic and repression, zu Eulenburg and von Moltke made a terrible mistake when von Moltke decided to sue for libel and Eulenburg took the stand – the legal question of whether or not Harden had libelled them turned on the question of their alleged homosexuality. The ensuing court cases were Germany's equivalents of Britain's Oscar Wilde trial, with politically damaging evidence being submitted about how some of the men in the Kaiser's entourage addressed him as *Liebchen* ('sweetheart' or 'honey bunch') when in private. Members of the extended imperial family were named by eyewitnesses as having been seen sipping champagne at intimate all-male parties with Kuno von Moltke. The police apparently had a list of hundreds of names of German homosexuals with successful careers – the list vanished, although the defence hunted frantically for it; the possibility of its discovery was a sword of Damocles hanging over the head of 'many of the most brilliant names of Court circles'. Countess von Moltke, preparing for a divorce, testified that her husband had only slept with her twice during their marriage, although she later seemed to regret what she had done and declined to give evidence at a subsequent hearing. Men who had done nothing more sinister than advise the Kaiser on wine, champagnes, brandies and tobacco had their reputations torn asunder in the courtrooms when they were named by witnesses who were asked questions about von Moltke's and zu Eulenburg's social circle, there were more suicides and some of those named as homosexuals, like Johann von Lynar, scion of one of Prussia's most ancient aristocratic families, were sentenced to years of hard labour for violating Paragraph 175 of the Criminal Code which prohibited homosexuality in the German empire.[32]

For those critical of Wilhelm II's government, the scandal was a goldmine. Cartoons appeared showing the semi-naked figures of zu Eulenburg and von Moltke, replacing the two figures that traditionally stood on either side of the Hohenzollern family's coat of arms, caressing one another in deliberately effeminate styles. The implication was clear – two homosexuals on either side of the Kaiser. Nor was the nationalist press, broadly supportive of Eulenburg's political agenda, exactly quiet; when Dr Magnus Hirschfeld, the world's leading expert on human sexual behaviour and homosexuality in particular, a man later nicknamed 'the Einstein of Sex', was called upon to give evidence by Harden's defence team he caused a sensation by stating that in his professional opinion, even if he had never actually followed those desires to have sex with another man, it was quite clear that Kuno von Moltke was a homosexual, prefixing his testimony with the assertion that homosexuality was a natural, healthy and inescapable manifestation of human sexuality. That Dr Hirschfeld was Jewish prompted the right-wing press to scream that Eulenburg was being destroyed by a shadowy Jewish conspiracy and accuse the doctor of promoting homosexuality in a strategy that would corrupt the morals of the empire's youth. The main result of the court case, apart from a huge surge in newspaper sales, was that Eulenburg could not prove that Harden had been libellous in suggesting that he and von Moltke were not heterosexual and as a result Eulenburg himself only narrowly missed being tried for perjury. His health collapsed, his influence at court evaporated and his reputation never fully recovered. From necessity, Wilhelm had to keep him at arm's length for the rest of his life.

After Eulenburg's demise, the influence of Wilhelm's wife, Augusta Victoria of Schleswig-Holstein, grew considerably. Lauded for her commitment to charity and her sincere patriotism, Augusta Victoria had added to the masculine aura the dynasty was so keen to project by giving birth to six sons, as well as their youngest sister, the lovely Princess Victoria Louise, the apple of her father's eye. However, Augusta Victoria's success as *materfamilias* and Lady Bountiful was not matched when it came to her role as her husband's confidante. The historian John Röhl thought that the Empress's letters 'to her husband during her marriage are one of the most depressing sources that a historian of the Hohenzollern family is obliged to read'.[33] Unlike Eulenburg, who had attempted, in his own words, 'to battle against [the Kaiser's] English antipathies', Augusta Victoria was firmly sympathetic to the most jingoistic elements of the German military and they counted on her support.[34] She was virulently hostile to Britain and for all her sincere and laudable projects to encourage a spirit of Christian philanthropy in her husband's empire she was also small-minded, bigoted and stubborn. When Wilhelm's younger sister Sophia converted to Orthodoxy shortly after her marriage to Crown Prince Constantine of Greece, Augusta Victoria told her bluntly that she would burn in hell for abandoning the Protestant religion. Sophia told her that it was none of her business and the then-pregnant Augusta Victoria worked herself up into such a tantrum that her son Joachim was born prematurely, a situation which she and Wilhelm blamed on Sophia. The Empress carried her religion to the point where she refused to employ any Catholics, and as the crisis of the war loomed, Augusta Victoria's closeness to the German Right was to acquire a new political significance.

Public respect for the Kaiser was weakened even further in the wake of the Eulenburg affair when he gave a disastrously tactless interview to Britain's *The Daily Telegraph* in 1908, in which Wilhelm managed to insult the British by calling them 'mad, mad as march hares'. The same stood for sections of his own people by stating that he was the mastermind behind a German foreign policy that had maintained friendly relations with Britain despite most Germans' resentment of it. He also claimed that he had previously given the British army tips on military strategy. What made him say things that were by turns incendiary and untrue is unclear and it fuelled fears within the government that the Kaiser had, at best, a tentative grasp on reality. When the interview was published, the Reichstag was incredulous, with a Social Democrat delegate speaking of the 'legitimate rage and deep shame among the German people' at their Emperor's indiscreet and embarrassing remarks.[35] The ensuing parliamentary debates became a critique of Wilhelm's leadership and the powers of the monarchy. The press was harsher still in its pronouncements and even Wilhelm's Chancellor, Prince Bernhard von Bülow, distanced himself from the Emperor when he issued a statement insisting that he had not seen the text of the interview before it went to publication. The implicit point being that no one with any political sense could possibly have thought it was a good idea to see such nonsense printed.

Part of the essential problem facing the German monarchy was not so much incidental – namely, the current Emperor's capabilities – so much as institutional; after studying the Kaiser's life, the acerbic George Bernard Shaw thought Wilhelm had dealt well with a 'part which was not only extremely difficult but to a great extent imaginary and flatly impossible'.[36] For most of the nineteenth century, Prussia had oscillated between liberalism and conservatism and the tensions had not eased with unification. Added to that was the imperfect nature of unification itself. The Kaiser was not Emperor of Germany but German Emperor, a legal nicety designed to illustrate the fact that the King of Prussia, as Emperor, was only first among equals, with the kings, grand dukes and princes of pre-unification Germany retaining their titles, wealth and, to varying degrees, their local influence. In practice, it did not always work like that and resentment, particularly from the Bavarian court, at the House of Hohenzollern's imperial pretensions was never far beneath the surface. The constitution drafted to make the new Reich work had created a semi-constitutional monarchy with an electorate and a bicameral legislature, but the old debate over the merits of authoritarianism versus wider participatory democracy was still evident in the constitution's deliberate ambiguities over the extent of the monarchy's power in relation to the Reichstag's. Under Imperial Germany's constitution, the Emperor could, if he felt called to it, dissolve the Reichstag, and he alone had the right to hand select the cabinet and the chancellor, Germany's equivalent of a prime minister. The government in Imperial Germany was therefore separated from the legislature. The Kaiser was also the supreme authority when it came to foreign affairs, the only arena in which there were no formal checks on his power, which is perhaps why Wilhelm II, who loathed restrictions in any way, seemed to focus so much of his attention on it, as well as matters pertaining to the military, a necessary state of affairs given the high command's condescending revulsion for elected politicians. The armed forces' influence was significant because their role had never been clearly defined and they were the effective leaders of German nationalist sentiment, a movement which the Hohenzollern monarchy had tied itself to with great success in the previous generation.

However, it was the power of ministerial appointment in particular which often showcased the widening gulf between the nationalist forces, who looked to the monarchy and the army as their political touchstones, and the country's working classes, who were growing in number thanks to the expanding German economy and who were more and more likely to vote for socialist parties, such as the Social Democrats (SPD), who won thirty-five Reichstag seats in the first federal elections of Wilhelm's reign and 110 in 1912, the last elections before the war. Although they never won an outright majority, their rise in support, as well as the middle and upper classes' unease at what that meant, highlighted the social, economic and political tensions in Wilhelm's Germany. Wilhelm himself had come to the throne appalled at what he saw as the inhumane conditions faced by many of his working-class subjects and he clashed with Chancellor von Bismarck over his sympathy for the miners' strike of 1889, but Wilhelm's support for social welfare was paternalist rather than socialist. The cabinet remained staffed primarily by aristocratic gentlemen who were by no means incompetent but who often shared some variation of their Emperor's world view. Cabinet, army, monarchy and parliament were thus often pursuing slightly or radically different agendas in a constitutional set-up that had inadvertently made it possible for at least one to be pitted against the other. The result being that for most of Wilhelm II's time as Emperor, the German political scene was one of regional rivalries, a growing disconnection between the elite, uncertainty caused by the political position of the army, which had been left deliberately vague in the constitution drawn up in 1871 and political reforms that were either blocked, never fully implemented or, at the opposite extreme, rushed through by the Reichstag without proper analysis.

Wilhelm tried to remedy the latter problem by pushing through small initiatives of his own. He supported wide-reaching reforms of Prussia's secondary school system by encouraging proposals that it adopt a less rigid and anti-scientific curriculum. He also offered value imperial encouragement to Christian societies' successful attempts to advance German medical practice and open state-of-the-art public hospitals, old people's residential homes and doctoring and nursing training academies. He sponsored the creation of groups designed to promote scientific research, technological advancement and the arts, and made generous endowments to Prussia's Academy of Sciences, setting up, as philanthropists are ever wont to do, a prize and fund in his own name. He made grand speeches, sometimes echoing the desire for peace among the nations which he had expressed in his first speech to the Reichstag after his father's death, but was always careful to praise the army and his beloved navy, and to pay homage to Germany's manifest destiny as a great power.

The nationalism that Wilhelm II seemed to be by turns entranced and unsettled by increasingly looked outwards. Military nationalism had birthed the Reich in 1871, it therefore followed as a matter of logic that the same force would carry Germany's greatness further into the arena of becoming a global imperial power. This interpretation of Germany's destiny, brilliantly captured by the slightly terrifying eagle placed on the prow of the *Imperator* in 1913, was one which increasingly put her at odds with her neighbours, especially the United Kingdom. Germany's territories in Africa were small in size and even smaller in their strategic worth; by the time Imperial Germany tried to win a global empire for herself the other European powers had long ago beaten her to it. By the 1890s there was not much left to grab. Regardless, huge amounts of money and energy were poured into Germany's military and naval expansion, the latter particularly riling Britain, who felt that Britannia alone should rule the waves. Similarly unimpressed reactions came from Paris and Saint Petersburg. In 1892, Tsar Alexander III ditched nearly half a century of tsarist opprobrium for French republicanism (until then it was illegal to even play 'La Marseillaise', with its glib lyrics about lynching aristocrats, in Russian territory) to sign a mutually defensive alliance with France. Nicholas II continued to view his father's French alliance as the cornerstone of Russian foreign policy, despite Wilhelm's best efforts to persuade him otherwise and in 1907 Britain was added to the entente, with all three promising to defend each other if they were attacked by an aggressive, unnamed but hardly unknown, power.

Back in Germany, the palace and the army's ebullient

self-confidence in the country's future appeared justified by sustained and impressive economic expansion. Turn-of-the-century Germany was one of the world's most prosperous states. With plenty of fertile agricultural land, huge natural reserves of coal and iron ore, and population growth aided along by an increasingly excellent healthcare system, by the middle of Wilhelm II's reign Imperial Germany stood at the forefront of new industries like electrical engineering, steel production and chemical production. Her railways and her fleet of ocean liners, of which the *Imperator* was simply the latest and largest in a long line, were among the best in the world. Germany's public education system was superior to those in Britain, France or America, while working conditions for her urban working classes and the development of a sophisticated welfare state meant that a German factory worker's average life expectancy was about five years longer than that of their British equivalent and nearly two decades longer than that of a Russian.

In 1913, when the *Imperator* set sail on her maiden voyage with a vast portrait of the Kaiser glaring down at first-class passengers on their grand staircase, European royalty was converging on Berlin to attend the sumptuous wedding of the Kaiser's only daughter, Princess Victoria Louise, to the Duke of Brunswick, a Romeo-and-Juliet-style wedding, since the two families had hitherto detested each other for years and Victoria's eldest brother threatened not to attend. There was room for confidence, as indeed there was everywhere else in monarchical Europe. It was the Kaiser's Silver Jubilee year and he could legitimately claim to rule over a prosperous empire that was, in many ways, one of the envies of the world. Yet the belligerency of Imperial Germany's foreign policy, the enthusiasm of her highest ranking generals for a war, the uncertainty that the Kaiser both felt and caused, as well as concerns that Germany could force Austria-Hungary into making a hasty decision when it came to the Balkans, had all helped create an international climate that was both distrustful and perpetually vigilant of the Hohenzollerns and their empire.

The Dual Monarchy

The great Czech historian František Palacký once said that if the Hapsburg Empire had not existed, it would have been necessary to invent it. Its heartland of the Danube basin was the great intersection between east and west in Europe and it was often in Hapsburg territory that the decisive battles of European history had been fought. For centuries, it had been the leadership provided by the monarchy which prevented the region's many competing ethnic groups and cultures from turning on each other and it was necessity's proverbial role as the mother of invention which shaped the Hapsburg dynasty's extraordinary journey and their longevity.

The family had first risen to greatness in the thirteenth century, providing them with a pedigree that made the Romanovs to the east and the Hohenzollerns to the north look positively *parvenu*. The Hapsburgs often preferred to make love where others made war. Royal marriages and dynastic bloodlines resulted in the family being left to inherit kingdoms when there was nobody else left to assume the mantle – that was how Hungary and Spain came into their orbit. By the fifteenth century, one of their emperors had adopted the acronym of the vowels AEIOU to signify how he and his kin saw their future – *Austria Est Imperare Orbi Universo* ('It is Austria's destiny to rule the world'). By the following century, this maxim seemed to be halfway true – the marriage of a Hapsburg prince to the heiress to the Spanish throne meant that their son, Charles V, ruled over an empire that included most of central Europe, the Netherlands, Spain, Naples, Sicily, Sardinia and huge swathes of the Americas. One ambitious prince of the line came up with his own familial motto, *Orbis Non Sufficit* ('The world is not enough'), a declaration so bombastic that in 1963 it struck the author Ian Fleming to have it placed beneath the crest of the family of his fictitious British spy James Bond.[37]

Christian Europe was increasingly obsessed with the fear of an Islamic invasion spearheaded by the expanding power of the Ottoman Empire, based mostly in what is now Turkey. This fear was not as paranoiac as it seemed. In 1453, the Ottomans had overthrown the last remnants of the Byzantine Empire, the Christian empire in the East, and they were expanding their borders in southern Europe. Increasingly, the Hapsburgs came to be seen as the first line of defence. In 1571, they and their allies defeated the Ottoman navy at the Battle of Lepanto in a victory so resounding that it was accredited to the intercession of the Blessèd

Virgin Mary, prompting the Vatican to institute a festival to Our
Lady of Victories on 7 October.[38] It was after another Hapsburg
victory, the defeat of the Ottoman armies as they laid siege to
Vienna in 1683, that the Turkish threat to western Christendom
was judged to have vanished.

Just as Europe had looked to the Hapsburgs to counteract
the threat posed by the Ottomans, they also looked to them to
thwart the ambitions of France, a role that they gladly undertook,
increasingly in conjunction with the British. As the eighteenth
century wore on, the rise of the Protestant kingdom of Prussia
in northern Germany and the Orthodox empire of the tsars
resulted in many central- and eastern-European Catholics looking
to the Hapsburgs for protection. There were setbacks even as the
enormous and beautiful Baroque palaces and cathedrals sprang
up in Vienna and Salzburg as tributes to the empire's inimitable
self-confidence. The Spanish branch of the Hapsburg clan died
out in 1700 after generations of inbreeding. This was never as
much of a problem with their less insular Austrian cousins, and
it is almost entirely to the Spanish side of the family that we owe
the popular stereotype of royalty as habitual inbreds. That point
has been both overstated and misunderstood. It is worth noting
that in the medieval and early modern period what we would now
recognise as inbreeding or incest was not uncommon. In an age
when very few people left the village, town or county where they
had grown up, inbreeding across the course of several generations
was inevitable, regardless of one's social class. Royalty could no
more marry outside the sacred confines of their class than most
of their subjects could marry outside the limits of their locality.
However, even in that context, the Spanish Hapsburgs, with their
fanatical preoccupations with Catholicism and the sanctity of
royal blood, had taken it too far. Philip II and Philip IV had both
married their nieces.[39] After Carlos II's death in 1700, the War of
the Spanish Succession ended in defeat for the heartier side of the
family in Austria, who had to endure the humiliation of a French
prince being installed on the Spanish throne. In the 1740s, to the
general astonishment of the Austrians, the upstart Protestants from
Prussia used the accession of a woman to the Hapsburg crown
as an excuse to seize the prosperous county of Silesia, inflicting a

sizeable defeat on 'happy Austria'. Then in 1793, Emperor Franz II proved unable to stop the execution of his thirty-seven-year-old aunt, Marie Antoinette, at the height of the French Revolution.

The revolution that took Marie Antoinette's life spread outwards, as she had predicted in the years before her death. It nurtured a new creed of nationalism, the idea that one's country and its national identity were paramount, and in the process trounced the old notion of the divine right of kings upon which the Hapsburg monarchy was based. Their belief that a monarchy was supranational, above ideas of patriotism or regional identity and thus superior to any sense of locality, was no longer in step with the *modus operandi* of European politics. In 1806, the armies of Napoleon toppled the Holy Roman Empire, a millennium-old political construct covering most of modern-day Germany and retrospectively referred to as its First Reich, and with its collapse, the Hapsburgs' centuries-long dominance over Germany went into sharper decline. In Austria, they regrouped themselves into what was now called the Austrian Empire. In the hearts of the imperial family, it remained the Hapsburg Empire. Refusing to believe that the nineteenth century's love affair with nationalism was any more than a passing fad, the Hapsburgs set their faces to the past. Until 1846, Latin remained the official language of the empire's government and bureaucracy, rather than any of their subject people's mother tongues. As the court saw it, they were not tied to any one nation; they served them all by claiming to favour none.

For the twenty years following the defeat of Napoleon in 1815, the Hapsburg way of doing things seemed to be back in the ascendant. Guided by their brilliant Chancellor, Prince Clement von Metternich, the Austrian emperors embarked upon a policy of political stagnation. The Metternich period also happened to be one of economic progression and what the government lacked in enthusiasm for political change it made up for in its knack for backing the right horse economically. However, try as they might, the genie of national pride would not go back into the bottle and the empire, along with much of the rest of Europe, was caught up in the wave of unrest produced by economic downturn in 1848. Riots swept the Austrian Empire and particularly in areas like Budapest and Milan these riots were anti-Austrian and pro-nationalist.

By that point the throne's incumbent was Emperor Ferdinand I, a politically imbecilic introvert who was nonetheless utterly adored by the vast majority of his subjects. Mothered by his loyal and long-suffering wife Maria Anna of Savoy, the plump Ferdinand was famous for once going on strike as monarch when his concerned physicians banned him from eating any more of his beloved dumplings. Cut off from his favourite delicacy, it was tools down for the Emperor, as he regally proclaimed, 'I am the emperor, and I want dumplings!' Such behaviour seemed delightful to the *bon vivants* Viennese. Even as the riots of 1848 worsened in the capital, few of the protestors could bring themselves to criticise Ferdinand directly. Blame for all the country's ills was heaped squarely on his pernicious aristocratic advisers, especially von Metternich. When brought news of the riots, Ferdinand allegedly asked, 'But are they allowed to do that?'

Faced with the fact that the entirety of the old government had been compromised, mass resignations took place in the hope of quelling the riots and the clean-sweep started at the top, with Ferdinand abdicating in favour of his eighteen-year-old nephew, Franz Josef. The abdication took place in the archiepiscopal palace in Olmütz. As the new Emperor knelt before the old, Ferdinand whispered, 'God bless you. Be brave. God will protect you. It was done gladly.'[40] In his diary entry for that night, Ferdinand noted, 'The function ended with the new Emperor kneeling to his Emperor and master, that is to say me, and asking for a blessing, which I gave by laying my hands upon his head and making the sign of the Holy Cross. Then I embraced him and he kissed my hand. And then my dear wife embraced and kissed our new master, and then we went away to our room.'[41] The ex-Emperor and his wife heard Mass afterwards and then spent the evening packing their things. Life in honourable retirement was not too onerous for Ferdinand I and he died in Prague at the age of eighty-two.

Franz Josef, who became Emperor in the chaos of 1848 and died in the chaos of the First World War, is remembered as he was at the end – warm eyes, white whiskers and military dress, 'the Last Cavalier', 'the dear old gentleman in the Hofburg'. When he came to the throne upon his uncle's abdication, however, he was an energetic and virile young man who loved to dance, hunt and ride. Otto von Bismarck, who subsequently came to detest him, met him four years after he became Emperor and wrote that Franz Josef had 'the fire of the twenties, coupled with the dignity and foresight of riper years, a fine eye, especially when animated and a winning openness of expression, especially when he laughs. The Hungarians are enthusiastic about his national pronunciation of their language and the elegance of his riding.'[42] Tsar Nicholas I was even more impressed, writing to his wife, 'The more I see of him, the more I listen to him, the more I am astonished by his intellect, by the solidity and correctness of his ideas. Austria is lucky indeed to possess him.'[43] It is to Franz Josef's first Prime Minister, Prince Felix zu Schwarzenberg, that we owe the best assessment of the Emperor's character and capability. Even at this young age, Schwarzenberg articulated the qualities that enabled Franz Josef to shoulder the great burden of ruling for sixty-eight years but also the personality traits that made so many people, including some of his closest relatives, regard him as a cold and detached bureaucrat.

The Emperor sees the magnitude and difficulty of his task and his will is firmly set to meet it. His intelligence is acute, his diligence in affairs astonishing, especially for one of his age. He works hard for at least ten hours a day, and nobody knows better than I how many ministerial proposals he sends back to be revised. His bearing is full of dignity, his behaviour to all exceedingly polite, though a little dry. Men of sentiment – and many people in Vienna lay claim to kindliness – say that he has not much heart. There is no trace in him of that warm, superficial goodheartedness of many Archdukes, of the wish to please, to strive for effect. On the other hand he is perfectly accessible, patient, and well disposed to be just to all. He has a rooted objection to any kind of lie and is absolutely discreet. But the quality that is most valuable to him in his present position, above all at a time like the present, is his courage. I have never seen it fail for an instant, even in the most difficult situations of whose peril he is entirely aware. Physically and morally he is fearless, and I believe the main reason why he can face the truth, however bitter, is that it does not frighten him. Time will make him more self-reliant: I do my best to assist that good work; then the country will have in him what it needs above everything – a man.[44]

For the first twenty years of his very long reign, Franz Josef supported the plan that to recover from the upset of 1848 the empire must create a centralised unitary state with as much as possible being controlled from Vienna, recapture the lands lost in northern Italy because of 1848, establish its dominance over Germany, and find allies in Europe who could sustain the empire's position as the dominant central European power. As Edward Crankshaw in his beautiful history of the empire's final century noted, it was 'a dream of the highest-vaulting kind, and, as dreams go, not absurd.'[45] In every single one of these goals, however, Austria was to fail, and by the turn of the century these setbacks had led to many regarding the collapse of the empire as nothing more than a matter of time.

To begin with, the Italian lands were never recovered and attempts to get them back were as expensive as they were embarrassing. Austria then committed a catastrophic bungle when it failed to send help to Tsar Nicholas I when Russia was opposed over her actions in the Crimea. Nicholas had sent valuable military aid to the Austrians during the crises of 1848 and he greatly admired Franz Josef; most of Russia's foreign policy had hitherto been determined by the Tsar's determination to uphold the cause of monarchism in Europe. By alienating her one-time ally, Austria created a powerful enemy and one that could cause great problems for Vienna if it chose to intervene with the Slavic communities currently living in the southern and eastern parts of the Austrian Empire.

In 1854, Franz Josef married one of the great beauties of the age, Princess Elisabeth of Bavaria. Tall and svelte with alabaster skin and a hauntingly lovely face, Elisabeth looked like a fairytale princess. Franz Josef shared his people's adoration for her and the couple produced four children – Sophie, Gisela, Rudolf and Maria Valerie. Yet like many a princess before and since, Elisabeth struggled to adapt to her new homeland; she found it impossible to escape the critical attention of her mother-in-law, the Archduchess Sophie, or the Archbishop of Vienna, Cardinal Rauscher, who thought she was insufficiently pious. Most unhappily of all, try as she might, she could not reciprocate her husband's passion.

Dazzling in public, Elisabeth increasingly became a nightmare in private. Her beauty regimen became an obsession – what nature had given her, Elisabeth would perfect. She would take three hours to dress her hair every morning, specialists were brought in to treat it in all-day sessions involving eggs, brandy and meticulous combing, raw meat was allegedly applied to her sleeping mask to firm up her skin, she gave up pillows because she believed they would affect her skin and posture. At various stages in her life, she was in the grips of what would now be recognised as a severe eating disorder. She was disgusted by fat people and her desire to maintain her own eighteen-and-a-half-inch waist bordered on the maniacal. Even in middle age, the Prince of Hesse called her 'almost inhumanly slender'.[46]

Keen to escape Vienna, Elisabeth initially attempted to enjoy some private time at home in Bavaria, but any attempt at anonymity was blown out of the water when she arrived at the train station in Munich to find the entire siding decorated with white lilies and her cousin, King Ludwig II, waiting to greet her formally in full Austrian military dress uniform. Despite this, she was particularly close to Ludwig. Like her, he fixated on beauty and elegance, a desire to escape from ugly reality into a world of art and sentiment. The two royals took moonlight cruises on Lake Starnberg, reciting Schiller and Shakespeare to one another as the silvery light bathed the decks of Ludwig's private yacht, *Tristan*, named for one of the heroes in the romance of Tristan and Isolde. Ludwig wrote of 'feelings of sincere love and reverence and faithful attachment to you which I have cherished in my heart since early youth'.[47] Such was their closeness that the cousins were eventually accused in some unkind and gossipy circles of carrying on an adulterous liaison, but, unknown at the time, Ludwig's diary kept a meticulous record of his struggle with his homosexuality.[48] His chaste adoration for Elisabeth is set alongside his self-loathing every time he felt a romantic or sexual desire to one of his own gender. One entry from September 1877 sees him describe himself as being 'terribly near the brink of a complete fall' because of his infatuation for one of his courtiers, while agonised phrases like 'From henceforth nevermore!!!' litter the pages.[49]

Like her cousin, Elisabeth's struggle against her own nature caused increasingly bizarre and disconcerting behaviour, be it day-long exercise, eight-hour walks, suddenly developed phobias, or sustained spells of melancholia during which she was bedridden. In the 1860s, she finally found an outlet for her talents. The Empress was intellectually gifted, with a particular aptitude for languages, in adulthood she picked up Magyar and ancient Greek, and her sympathy for the Hungarians meant that she was especially popular in that part of the empire. As demands grew for the Hungarians to be granted parity of esteem with the Austrians, Elisabeth threw herself into supporting their cause.

The Empress's support, the rise in unrest in Hungary and the advice of many of his courtiers finally persuaded Franz Josef to pass the Ausgleich of 1867, which restored Hungary's independent parliament with significant internal powers and effectively created a dual monarchy, under which the dynasty united the two political systems of Austria and Hungary. Franz Josef would be Emperor of Austria and King of Hungary and at his and Elisabeth's subsequent coronation in Budapest the ecstatic crowds seemed to be cheering more for Elisabeth and the new era she was partly responsible for than for her husband. As part of the coronation festivities, the Hungarian nation gifted the royal couple with the eight-winged palace of Gödöllő, subsequently Elisabeth's favourite residence.

Not everyone in the empire was sold about the long-term prospects of the Dual Monarchy. It had bought peace in Hungary but kicked a hornet's nest in the rest of the empire. There was a split within the empire's elite over what the future of the empire and specifically Hungary should be. There were those even within the imperial family, like the Emperor's nephew Franz Ferdinand, who sympathised with the accusation that the Ausgleich had freed the Hungarians to treat Croats and Slavs within their territory in a deeply unfair way. While Franz Josef worked hard to undermine popular anti-Semitism and pan-German nationalism in Austria, there was little he could do about ethnic resentments in Hungary, which generally defended its parliament's right to introduce whatever actions it saw fit. Querying why Hungary had been given rights denied to the rest of them, other groups under Hapsburg rule were now agitating to be given equal status to the Magyars, something which Budapest opposed at every turn, guarding its newly won sovereign prerogatives like a tigress. Franz Josef, by nature an ultra-conservative more devoted to preserving stability than pursuing dreams of reform, was Budapest's best ally because had no intention of embarking upon another grand constitutional reform like the Ausgleich. By the turn of the century, there were therefore many who thought the multinational nature of the Hapsburgs' empire meant that its collapse was unavoidable. In her private diary, Franz Josef's youngest daughter expressed her 'lack of belief in Austria's survival', while in Russia in 1913, one of Nicholas II's courtiers wrote, 'His Majesty spoke of the disintegration of the Austrian Empire as a mere matter of time. The day, he said, would come when we would see a Kingdom of Hungary, a Kingdom of Bohemia, and the incorporation of the German provinces of Austria into the German Empire, while the southern Slavs would be absorbed by Serbia and the Rumanians of Transylvania by Rumania. Austria, His Majesty held, was at present a source of weakness to Germany and a danger to the cause of peace.'[50]

Yet the Hapsburg monarchy's preoccupation with internal stability produced a flowering of the arts in Vienna as the waltzes of Strauss, father and son, floated from ballrooms over the waters of the Danube and Art Nouveau flourished in the capital's academies and salons; Otto Wagner, Gustav Klimt and Sigmund Freud set to work in a cosmopolitan and secure environment with no censorship and an appreciation for the novel and the beautiful. Vienna at the turn of the century was a centre of the arts no less than it had been in the days of Mozart and the glory days of the Hapsburg monarchy, and the atmosphere of peace and elegance which the court was keen to promote played no small part in making that possible, despite the Left-leaning views of many of the empire's most celebrated artists. Nor was the empire's political system as backward or inept as usually thought – all the empire's communities were enabled to send representatives to the parliament in Vienna and Franz Josef had the typical conservative's support for specific changes to resolve specific problems in the hope of avoiding any more significant or seismic unrest.[51]

Franz Josef took his vocation as guardian of this ticking clock very seriously. He awoke before dawn, ate sparingly and worked throughout the day, meticulously inspecting every paper put in front of him. By 1900, he was an old man who had formed an obsessive attachment to his rigid schedule. This was not just due to his religious interpretation of his duties, but also because of the tragedies that had befallen him in the years since 1867. In that year, his younger brother Maximilian was executed by Mexican revolutionaries after a disastrous attempt to create a European-style monarchy in the Americas ended in failure. Maximilian's widow, the heroically loyal Carlota of Belgium, suffered a complete nervous breakdown and spent the rest of her life in seclusion. Five years later, Franz Josef's redoubtable mother passed away. In 1889, he was shattered as the monarchy was rocked by the suicide of his only son, Rudolf. The troubled and thwarted Crown Prince arranged a murder-suicide with his teenage mistress at the Mayerling hunting lodge, which was subsequently turned into an abbey by Rudolf's grieving parents. It survives to this day. Seven years after that, Franz Josef's brother Karl Ludwig died of typhoid, and two years later Empress Elisabeth was murdered on a holiday to Geneva by a young Italian anarchist called Luigi Luccheni, who had vowed to kill the first royal he encountered. Elisabeth was stabbed as she and a lady-in-waiting prepared to board a steamboat, politely thanking in German, English and French all who were trying to help her even as she lost consciousness. Her assassin, grinning from ear to ear when photographed in custody, justified himself later with what one journalist contemptuously described as only 'the animal virtue of courage' by saying 'I came to Geneva to kill a sovereign, with object of giving an example to those who suffer and those who do nothing to improve their social position; it did not matter to me who the sovereign was whom I should kill.' His diary, recovered after his arrest, expressed his desire to 'kill someone important so it gets in the newspapers'. At his trial he appeared with his moustache immaculately waxed and gave the jury a polite bow before telling them later, 'My doctrine is that no one who does not work should be allowed to live.' He did himself even fewer favours when he told them, with chilling seriousness, 'Human suffering is the motive of my act.'[52]

As Franz Josef went about his mind-numbing daily routine in the aftermath of Elisabeth's assassination, an adherence to a schedule through which he believed he could impose order on to chaos, there were many who began to regard 'the Old Gentleman' with a great deal of affection but many more who thought that the Hapsburg Emperor was crossing the 'T's and dotting the 'I's while the problems created by the Ausgleich and conflicting nationalisms throughout his empire went unanswered.

2

Sarajevo, 28 June 1914

'Terrible shock to the dear old Emperor'

People never knew quite what to make of the Archduke Franz Ferdinand. Zita, his niece by marriage, described him as 'a very powerful and determined personality but also a devoted family man'.[1] Most of his uncle's courtiers regarded him as a dangerous liberal, while sections of the European press presented him as a foaming-at-the-mouth reactionary. Tall and broad-chested, but pale from a bout of tuberculosis in adolescence, he had the large blue eyes of the Hapsburgs and the prematurely thinning hair of his uncle the Emperor, which he attempted to fight with numerous cures of dubious efficacy. Often frigid in public and given to outbursts of spiteful bad temper, he nonetheless was quick to apologise when in the wrong and he had a real zeal for the truth, even if he did not want to hear it. Passionate about the military, one of his greatest talents in life was horticulture and the man who almost never smiled in crowds would often wander through the crowds who had come to inspect his gardens, chatting enthusiastically with them about their shared interests.

Born at the Palais Khuenburg in the southern Austrian city of Graz in 1863, he was the eldest son of Emperor Franz Josef's younger brother. At the age of seven, he lost his lovely but fragile mother to tuberculosis. Luckily, maternal affection was soon supplied by his Portuguese stepmother, the Archduchess Maria Theresa, whom Franz Ferdinand adored. His education was heavy on religion and languages, the former leaving him with a lifelong devotion to Catholicism. At the age of twelve, he inherited one of the largest art collections in Europe when he was nominated as the heir to the recently deceased Duke of Modena. At the age of twenty-five he came into a much more troubling inheritance when his childless cousin Rudolf committed suicide at Mayerling. The subsequent death of Franz Ferdinand's father meant that he became heir in Rudolf's place. Grief-stricken and distrustful, the Emperor could never quite bring himself to give Rudolf's old title of Crown Prince to the newcomer. Franz Ferdinand, who revered the Emperor and the monarchy, never publicly complained, but the uncle's unease with his nephew worsened as the years passed.

After a few youthful dalliances, Franz Ferdinand began to consider getting married. As the future Emperor, duty required a consort and a family. The problem was, with his passion for cheap romance novels, the Archduke did not just want to marry, he also wanted to be happy. He did not want someone too young and he certainly did not want anyone too stupid. Looks were a secondary condition and the right type of ancestry even less so. His aunt the Empress Elisabeth, speaking from sad experience, gave him revolutionarily simple advice on the subject: 'Only marry the woman you love.'[2] Despite his reluctance, rumours abounded that he might marry one of the Prince of Wales's daughters or a cousin of Tsar Nicholas. Pushy royal parents, like the Count of Paris, arranged excruciatingly obvious run-ins with their daughters in the hope of sparking an attraction. One of the most persistent of the would-be matchmakers was the Archduchess Isabella, Duchess of Teschen, a rotund matriarch and fixture of the Vienna social scene. The Archduchess had the biblical-sounding tally of seven unmarried daughters, ranging from nineteen-year-old Archduchess Maria Christina to her five-year-old sister, the Archduchess Maria Alice. Isabella's hopes naturally fixated on the eldest of the girls, but with the best laid plans often going awry, the numerous invitations designed to bring Franz Ferdinand into Maria Christina's orbit also served to bring him regularly into the company of one of Isabella's ladies-in-waiting, the daughter of a former diplomat from Bohemia, Countess Sophie Chotek. The Archduke asked Sophie for a dance at a masquerade ball at the Larisch Palace in Vienna in the spring of 1894. He never forgot that 'so wonderful' night and by summer, romance had blossomed.[3]

Fury thundered forth from the thwarted Archduchess, who apparently discovered the truth of what was going on when she found Franz Ferdinand's pocket watch after one of his visits and opened it to discover that it contained a photograph of her lady-in-waiting, rather than her daughter. The entire household was summoned to watch Isabella's humiliating and vicious verbal attack on Sophie, after which the poor woman was fired. Carrying her woes to the Emperor, Isabella raged that her family had been terribly insulted by Franz Ferdinand's deception. When he spoke to his nephew about the situation, Franz Josef was aghast as Franz Ferdinand told him that he wanted to marry Sophie. Isabella retaliated by telling everyone that Sophie was the Archduke's mistress and that, having lost her virginity outside of marriage, she was clearly a worthless woman. As with Anne Boleyn centuries before, Sophie was surrounded by hostile rumour – no one seemed to believe in the power of coincidence and human luck. Sophie, they insisted, must be a near-clairvoyant mistress of the art of manipulation. She must, so the gossips claimed in the ballrooms and dinner parties of the capital, have set out to get the heir apparent and she had now whipped him up into such a frenzy that only she could satisfy him.

Franz Ferdinand's behaviour did nothing to counteract society's suspicions. When Sophie attempted to end their relationship rather than cause any more trouble, he was distraught. Her critics claimed this move must therefore have been nothing more than a feint, cleverly designed to increase his ardour. When the Emperor pointed out that marriage to Sophie would violate the Hapsburg Family Statutes, which mandated that members of the dynasty only marry their social equals, Franz Ferdinand was so upset that he threatened to kill himself. Faced with the prospect, however remote, of a second heir committing suicide, Franz Josef gave his permission with supreme reluctance and numerous caveats, the chief of which was that the marriage would be morganatic, by which Sophie would legally be Franz Ferdinand's wife but she would not be eligible to share his title, neither would any future children be permitted to hold imperial titles or stand in line to inherit the throne. On 28 June 1900, in a ceremony at the Hofburg Palace, presided over by the Archbishop of Vienna and the Primate of Hungary, Franz Ferdinand swore on the Bible that 'neither our wife nor the children which with God's blessing may come from this marriage nor any of their descendants can lay claim to those rights, honours, titles, coats of arms, or privileges that would be accorded to wives of equal rank with their Archducal husbands and the children of such an Archducal union of equality in accord with the statutes'.[4]

A euphoric honeymoon followed, but in its aftermath Franz Ferdinand was appalled at the lengths his uncle's court would go to in order to punish Sophie for marrying above her station. Handsome rather than beautiful, superbly dignified, soothing, elegant and a devout Roman Catholic, Sophie Chotek was in many ways an ideal bride for royalty. She certainly proved her mettle by behaving impeccably throughout the court's decade-long vendetta. Even the Emperor's speech at the time of her marriage had begrudgingly conceded that Sophie 'descends, it is true, from noble lineage'.[5] Her family had been ennobled by the Hapsburgs in the sixteenth century, they had a long history of exemplary service to the empire and the Choteks were one of the elite few among the nobility who could boast sixteen quarterings on their crest, advertising at least four unbroken generations of aristocratic descent on all sides of her great-great-grandparents' families. Still, she was an outsider who had no business marrying a Hapsburg because she was, to use a phrase that no one would have used to describe her unless she had married a prince, a commoner, and the court never let her forget it. At family dinners, if she was invited at all, she was served last and seated at the bottom of the table. She was forbidden from accompanying her husband to any state functions. She could not stand near him if the national anthem was playing. They could not even sit in the same box at the theatre. At balls, she had to enter last, behind every other female member of the imperial family. Both doors at the ballroom's entrance were opened for the archduchesses' entrances; one of them was closed just before Sophie stepped in to further highlight her inferiority. On only one occasion did Sophie crack by abruptly fleeing a ball when she realised that the court's lord high chamberlain, Prince Alfred de Montenuovo, had purposefully failed to arrange for a man to give her his arm. Refusing to suffer the mortification of entering a packed ballroom alone, Sophie chose to go home instead.

Franz Ferdinand had an encyclopedic memory for insults and the wounds inflicted upon his wife led to him regarding many members of his uncle's government as enemies. Although the couple had full use of the magnificent Belvedere Palace in Vienna, they rarely used it, instead spending their early married life travelling with their three children, Sophie, Maximilian and Ernst, all born between 1901 and 1904. After an obligatory stint in Vienna for New Year's, usually the time of the purgatorial Hapsburg supper humiliations for Sophie, the family took a large suite at the Alpine resort of St. Moritz, for the Archduke's skiing. Time would then be spent back at Konopischt, a twelfth-century castle thirty miles from Prague which the Archduke bought for the 2014 equivalent of about 40 million pounds sterling and where, with a resident staff of fifty-five, he oversaw a series of renovations that turned the castle from a gothic monument into one of the most comfortable and well-equipped homes in the empire.[6] It was there that Franz Ferdinand's passion for horticulture gave rise to the castle's famous rose garden, where two hundred varieties of rose bloomed in perfectly manicured displays. The garden became famous throughout Europe and Franz Ferdinand eventually opened it on special days to the public, during which time he would wander among the visitors.

After a brief springtime cruise in the Adriatic, the family usually celebrated Easter in Trieste before spending a few weeks at Artstetten Castle in Austria, a beautiful home with spectacular views of the Danube river and where Franz Ferdinand had spent much of his own childhood. It was here, in Artstetten's chapel, that the Archduke wanted to be buried, since he knew that Hapsburg etiquette would be inexorable even in the grave and Sophie would be forbidden from resting alongside him in the family's crypt in Vienna. In July, the family might spend a few weeks at a seaside resort in Belgium, before decamping back to the empire to reside at Chlumetz, a pretty manor house that Franz Ferdinand planned to bequeath to his youngest son, Ernst. Throughout the autumn, they travelled again, living mostly in a series of hunting lodges where Franz Ferdinand, an excellent shot, could indulge his passion for his favourite sport. According to his own meticulously kept diary, over the course of his adult life the Archduke killed 247,889 animals. Surprisingly, this is not such an unusually high number in a generation that had turned mass hunting into a staple part of any aristocratic get together.[7] The couple's family life was exceptionally happy. Despite his rather gruff reputation, the Archduke was a very affectionate and loving father and unlike many upper-class parents in the Edwardian era, he and Sophie saw a lot of their children, taking breakfast with them, meeting throughout the day when they were not at lessons, saying their bedtime prayers with them and taking dinner *en famille*, when there were no guests to entertain. In a letter to his stepmother Maria Theresa, Franz Ferdinand wrote, 'You don't know how happy I am with my family and how I can't thank God enough for all my happiness.'[8] A further sign of the Archduke's desire to modernise the dynasty came when he chose to send his two sons to study at a school, rather than be educated at home by tutors like most of the Hapsburg children. The two boys were sent to Schottengymnasium, a boarding school in Vienna run by the Benedictine order of monks and modelled on elite private schools like Eton, Harrow and Winchester in England. There, they were taught alongside members of the nobility, including their kinsman the future Prince of Liechtenstein, but also the sons of factory owners, wealthy bankers, prominent politicians and generals.

Attitudes to Franz Ferdinand's marriage eventually began to thaw as the Viennese court's pettiness had the opposite of its intended effect, in that it generated sympathy for Sophie. Knowing of the Archduke's sympathy for the Slavic people of the empire and touched by the romance of his marriage, the intelligent and rigidly self-disciplined King Carol I of Romania and his colourful German wife, Queen Elisabeth – a lady who published quite lovely poetry under a pseudonym, penned plays about Anne Boleyn and verses about Sappho, published anthologies of Romanian folk-songs, encouraged her own nephew to marry a non-royal like Franz Ferdinand and at one point briefly considered herself a republican – invited the couple to spend a few days with them on a private visit to the King and Queen's magnificent new home at Peleş in the Carpathian mountains. The castle was the King's pride and joy, and by couching the invitation as one extended purely on a personal level to the Archduke as a man rather than as the Hapsburg heir, Carol was able to circumvent Vienna's attempts to prevent Sophie receiving the approval of foreign courts. A private visit to London to attend the Chelsea Flower Show, a must for the creator of the Konopischt rose garden, saw the couple take a suite at the Ritz and spend a weekend with the Duke of Portland, President of the Royal Horticultural Society and an enthusiastic hunter to boot. Knowing that the heir to the Austro-Hungarian thrones was in the city, the British royal family invited them both to lunch at Buckingham Palace, where they were given a tour by the King's widowed mother, Queen Alexandra. Sophie made a very good impression and she was nothing like the *arriviste* horror that Alexandra or her daughter-in-law Queen Mary had expected. The couple were invited back in an official capacity the following year, during which the King and Queen tactfully did not request the presence of any of the other British princesses in order to avoid making Sophie feeling uncomfortable over questions of etiquette or precedence. Queen Mary told her son, the future King George VI, that she found the couple 'both extremely nice and easy to get on with'.[9] The Belgian royal family often joined Franz Ferdinand, Sophie and their children when they holidayed there in the summer and the Kaiser, after worrying that meeting them might imply he approved of *mésalliances,* finally swallowed his scruples and upon making her acquaintance he was so charmed by Sophie that he chivalrously bowed over her hand, in a gesture that produced bile in the Hofburg and breathless excitement in European gossip columns. An emperor had bowed to the interloper. After nine years of marriage, Franz Josef finally decided to grant his nephew's wife a title. Although he would sooner die than make her an archduchess, he did make her Duchess of Hohenberg and a year later he declared that she could now be addressed as 'Your Highness', still a step below her husband's 'Imperial Highness', but a significant step nonetheless.

A happy home life was not matched by political fulfilment for the future Emperor. The press's depiction of him was both unfair and inaccurate. Because of his support for the modernisation of the army and the imperial navy, he was often described as a warmonger, when in fact his opposition to war was so strong that it ended his friendship with Count Conrad von Hötzendorf, the Austrian Chief of Staff who was constantly agitating for a war against Serbia. When his alleged politics were not being criticised, the heir's personality was often traduced. He was portrayed as cold, vicious and spiteful. Although he did hold a grudge, he was not tyrannical and he certainly was not stupid enough to shun a good man for telling an inconvenient truth. As the first decade of his marriage progressed, he also grew in confidence and began to have ideas of his own that increasingly pitted him against the men surrounding his uncle. Tensions had already risen about how the court had treated his beloved Sophie, but the feud between the Belvedere and the Hofburg became entrenched as Franz Josef and his advisers realised how far Franz Ferdinand intended to go with his reforms once he became Emperor. As a young man, he had travelled widely and he returned from the United States both unsettled and inspired. He was appalled by what he saw as the chimera of the American Dream, which promised so much but which had nonetheless created a society that, to Franz Ferdinand, was far more unequal and uncaring than any of the old world empires. However, the federal structure of the American republic had given him food for thought and he increasingly came to the conclusion that only by implementing a similar system in Austria-Hungary could the monarchy's many problems be resolved. It would give all the empire's subject peoples an opportunity to deal with local matters to their own satisfaction, while simultaneously solidifying the throne's position as the force that brought unity, guidance and stability. Such a move would be deeply unpopular in Hungary, but Franz Ferdinand intended to press on regardless.

On the last weekend in June of 1914, the Austro-Hungarian army was planning to hold a two-day manoeuvre of just over 20,000 soldiers in the hills around Sarajevo to demonstrate new tactics and some of the modernisations that Franz Ferdinand had been so keen on. The provinces of Bosnia and Herzegovina were the most troublesome in the Hapsburg Empire, in ways that draw numerous parallels to the situation regarding mainland Britain and Northern Ireland for most of the twentieth century. Bosnia and Herzegovina were divided internally by sectarian and ethnic tensions, with the Serbian population wanting the provinces to leave the empire and unite with the independent kingdom of Serbia to the south. A united Serbia was something strongly opposed by most of Bosnia and Herzegovina's Islamic and Catholic Croat communities, who felt they would be discriminated against in a Greater Serbia and therefore looked to Vienna to protect them. The problems posed by a divided region of the empire that lay adjacent to a country with a strong popular movement for unification were added to by a powerful international backer in the form of Imperial Russia, whose people and government often took a highly sympathetic view towards 'little Serbia' and her struggle for Slavic unity. Terrorist organisations like the Black Hand, with its shadowy initiation rituals that included keeping vigil in the presence of skulls, had dedicated themselves to expelling the Austrians from Bosnia and Herzegovina; powerful sections of the Serbian government supported them, both morally and financially.

Small wonder then that Oskar Potiorek was decidedly less than thrilled to be appointed Governor General of Bosnia and Herzegovina in 1911. Leading an embattled administration that could do nothing without offending at least one of the competing sides in the province, Potiorek badly wanted some sign of imperial approval that would cement his political credibility with the region's local elites. The army manoeuvres constituted a perfect excuse for him to invite the heir – the Emperor was sick with bronchitis, but Franz Ferdinand took a great interest in the army and he had never been to Sarajevo. The invitation was sent and the Emperor agreed that it was a good idea to bolster loyalty to the throne in the region.

Franz Ferdinand did not agree with his uncle's assessment and neither did several high-ranking officials in Sarajevo, including the chief of the Sarajevo police, who was stunned to discover that the Archduke would be entering the city on the feast day of Saint Vitus, a festival dear to Serbian Orthodox Christians and the anniversary of a medieval Serbian victory long associated with the expulsion of an oppressive foreign power. Nobody in Vienna seemed to be aware of the significance of the date, but that was because Oskar Potiorek, desperate for the visit, did not enlighten them. Usually sanguine about threats to his personal safety, even Franz Ferdinand shuddered at the risks involved in visiting such a turbulent region. However, the Emperor had said yes on his behalf and there was no way to back out without losing face.

Shortly before the visit, the Archduke went on a hunting weekend with some friends and repeatedly confessed his unhappiness at having to go to Sarajevo. The pro-Serbian press was already in a ferment, describing the Duchess as 'a monstrous, filthy Bohemian whore'.[10] For her part, she was determined to accompany her husband despite his objections and this gave rise to the ludicrous story, repeated later even in histories by men as esteemed as A. J. P. Taylor, that Sophie was the driving force behind the visit because she knew etiquette in Bosnia-Herzegovina would be less stringent than in Austria and she could therefore bask in the approval denied her in the empire's heartlands. The idea that 'for love did the Archduke go to his death' is arresting, but it seems to bear no relation to what actually happened.[11] Sophie's niece, the Comtesse de Baillet-Latour, later told Queen Mary, 'Aunt Sophy was always haunted by the idea that some day an attempt might be made to take his life, and she never ever left him.'[12] Sophie was terrified of her husband putting himself in danger and she did not want to leave him to face it on his own. To increase the couple's security, the decision was taken to house them at Ilidže, an upper-class holiday resort a few miles from Sarajevo, which would hopefully make them easier to protect and more difficult to reach. Despite the precautions, the Archduke's feelings of dread did not seem to lift and the day before he set off he gave his desk keys to his devoted valet, Franz Janaczek, a Czech peasant who had risen to become head of the Archduke's household. Janaczek was given instructions on what to do with his employer's papers if something happened in Sarajevo.

At the same time, at a cabinet meeting in Belgrade, the Serbian Prime Minister Nikola Pašić let slip to his colleagues that there were plans to assassinate the Archduke when he arrived in Sarajevo.[13] For years, controversy raged about the extent of the Serbian government's involvement in the plot, but it now seems clear that Austria-Hungary's accusations, so crucial in starting the war, actually erred on the side of charity. The would-be assassin, a nineteen-year-old high school dropout called Gavrilo Princip with a depressingly predictable passion for Nietzsche and experience in one of the Black Hand's training academies, was planning to murder Franz Ferdinand in a move co-organised with his former flatmates, Trifko Grabež and Nedeljko Čabrinović. Princip's youthfulness and his undoubted love for his country have caused many writers to romanticise him as a passionate young idealist driven to commit a lone and terrible act through sheer desperation. But such an assessment does Princip a disservice. He was far more Marat than Corday. His real radicalisation took place not in occupied Bosnia but when he emigrated to nearby Serbia; it was in Belgrade that the slight young man gave himself over to the nationalist cause with a fervour that bordered on the ecstatic. It was the grand love of Princip's life and he was subsumed utterly by it. Not once did he express remorse for his actions, even when he saw that it had unleashed the First World War, and before embarking on his mission to Sarajevo, he stated his confidence in using terror to achieve the dream of a united Serbia.[14]

Nor were his views confined to a small band of revolutionaries, rather they were shared by many of the most powerful figures in Serbia, including Colonel Dragutin Dimitrijević, who was simultaneously both the chief of Serbian intelligence and one of the leaders of the Black Hand. It was he who gave Princip the four revolvers and six bombs needed to kill the Archduke, and vials of cyanide to kill himself once he was captured. It was he who arranged for Serbian custom officials to smuggle the three young men across the border, back into the Austro-Hungarian Empire, it was he who spoke with military attachés at the Russian embassy in Belgrade to see how deep Russia's commitment to Serbia would run if Serbia happened to get herself into difficulty with Austria and it was he who tried to smooth things over with the Black Hand's central executive committee when they tried belatedly to stop the attack, fearing that the Archduke's murder would bring the full wrath of Austria-Hungary down upon the tiny kingdom of Serbia. Justifying his actions after the war, Dimitrijević said, 'Feeling that Austria was planning a war with us, I thought that the disappearance of the Austrian heir apparent would weaken the power of the military clique he headed, and thus the danger of war would be removed or postponed for a while.'[15] How the head of Serbia's intelligence gathering could possibly have believed that Franz Ferdinand commanded a clique agitating for war when he had consistently lobbied for peace is difficult to fathom. In fact, Dimitrijević knew that Franz Ferdinand was planning to grant significant political concessions to the people of Bosnia and Herzegovina once he became Emperor and if those concessions were granted then the dream of a Greater Serbia would become far harder to mobilise into a reality. The impetus might fall away. Franz Ferdinand died not because he was a monstrous reactionary, but rather because he was an heir apparent whose plans would have pulled the rug from under some of the most dedicated nationalists in Europe.

The Duchess of Hohenberg arrived at Ilidže by train on 25 June. One of her ladies-in-waiting, Countess von Wallenburg, kept her company while the Archduke cruised to join them on the *Viribus Unitis*, one of the flagships of the Austro-Hungarian navy. A private yacht brought him ashore, where he tactfully addressed one of the welcome committees with a few sentences in Croatian. Large crowds of Muslims and Croats gathered to cheer his arrival and he said he was 'deeply moved' by their welcome.[16] When he arrived at Ilidže, he cabled his daughter to tell her how pretty their rooms were and how beautiful the weather was.

The first few days of the trip continued in a similarly positive vein, soothing the imperial couple's fears of an attack. They went in to Sarajevo to pay a visit to Elias Kabiljo, the merchant who had decorated their rooms at the hotel back in Ilidže, because they wanted to thank him personally. After that, a visit to the city's bazaar, where they were thronged by Muslim and Croat well-wishers. Shadowing them in the crowd was Gavrilo Princip, who later claimed that he did not shoot then because he never intended to kill Sophie and at the bazaar she was standing too close to her husband. (One of his fellow conspirators, Nedeljko Čabrinović, contradicted him when he said that the conspirators had been given bombs and if they could not get the Archduke when he was on his own they had all agreed that 'we would sacrifice her and all the others'.)[17] At the weekend, the Archduke went off into the hills to watch the army manoeuvres, which were judged a success, while Sophie went back in to Sarajevo to visit churches, orphanages, schools and mosques. One of her visits brought about a reunion with a priest called Father Anton Puntigam, who had once been the Archduke's private confessor and who now worked at a convent school in Sarajevo run by the Augustinian order. Sophie went to the school and met some of the students and teachers, before travelling back by train to Ilidže, where she telephoned her eldest son Max to wish him good luck in his final exam of the academic year.

The night the imperial army's manoeuvres ended, Princip left his colleagues drinking in a local tavern while he made a lonely pilgrimage to the tomb of Bogdan Zerajic, a member of the Black Hand who had shot himself four years earlier when his plan to murder the Austrian governor general had failed. Princip laid a wreath on the grave. Back at Ilidže, the Archduke and the Duchess were hosting a forty-three person dinner party for local dignitaries and members of their suite. Conversation initially centred on the Kaiser's recent visit to see the rose garden at Konopischt and the success of the visit to Sarajevo thus far. During the dinner, news arrived from Vienna that Max had passed his exams, prompting applause and a round of toasts in his honour. After dessert, a few members of the Archduke's entourage raised the issue of Saint Vitus's Day – now, too late, made known to them – and suggested that given that the rest of the trip had gone so well, it was senseless to tempt fate any farther; they should cancel the next day's itinerary and go back to Austria a day early. The Archduke seemed receptive to the idea, but Oskar Potiorek, who was sitting at the table, raised so many objections that eventually he agreed to carry out the next day's engagements as planned.

The next day dawned bright and cheerful. It was the fourteenth anniversary of Franz Ferdinand's oath at the Hofburg that had made it possible for him to marry Sophie and the couple spent most of the morning in prayer together. After that, they boarded the train for the short journey back to Sarajevo. They were greeted at the station and taken to the local barracks for a brief inspection of the garrison. The Archduke wore the uniform of an Austrian cavalry general: a blue tunic with red pipes and gold epaulettes and a helmet adorned with peacock feathers; the Duchess wore a white silk dress with a rosebud corsage, a wrap, a large white hat with a veil, and a matching parasol. As the sun rose higher in the sky, the Duchess removed the wrap.

As the car made its way towards an official reception at the town hall, Nedeljko Čabrinović picked up one of his bombs and hurled it at the passing motorcade. Leopold Loyka, the Archduke's chauffeur, noticed the activity out of the corner of his eye and slammed his foot on the accelerator. The bomb missed the car by a few feet and bounced into the buildings on the other side of the street. Twenty people were injured in the blast and a tiny piece of shrapnel hit the Duchess in the back of the neck but there were no fatalities. In between shouting 'I am a Serbian hero!' Čabrinović tried to swallow his cyanide capsule, but it did not work and members of the crowd swarmed forward, trying to lynch him. He was rescued by the police and, watching from a distance, Gavrilo Princip tried to shoot him to stop him implicating the Serbian government under questioning. However, as with the incident at the bazaar a few days ago, he could not get the shot and Čabrinović was dragged away. Heartbroken that their plan had failed, Princip wandered aimlessly to a nearby café.

Meanwhile, the Archduke arrived at the town hall and interrupted the mayor by screaming, 'What kind of greeting is this? I come to Sarajevo and I am greeted with bombs! It is outrageous!' Sophie stepped forward and spoke gently to him. Her words had their usual soothing effect. The heir took a deep breath and apologised for his outburst. He allowed the official speeches to continue and in his reply he even referred to the province as a 'magnificent region' and Sarajevo as its 'beautiful capital city'.[18] The Duchess went upstairs to host a reception for wives of local Islamic politicians, who could unveil themselves in her presence since she was a fellow lady, while the Archduke mixed with the men downstairs. To the embarrassment of the other guests, his black temper returned and he goaded Governor Potiorek constantly for organising a visit that had resulted in a bomb attack. To evade other would-be assassins, it was decided that after lunch the motorcade would not adhere to the pre-planned route through the city, but nobody relayed this news to the Archduke's driver.

As the convoy left the town hall, Franz Ferdinand tried to persuade Sophie to travel back privately but she was so shaken by the attack that she did not want to leave him: 'No, Franzi,' she said, 'I am going with you.'[19] In the car, Count Franz von Harrach, a forty-three-year-old member of the Archduke's entourage, placed himself in front of the couple, intending to use himself as a human shield if they were attacked again. The car moved through streets that were still tense from Čabrinović's earlier bomb attack and it was only at this point that Governor Potiorek realised that their chauffeur was not taking the new route. Leaning forward to tell him that he was going the wrong way, Potiorek caused Loyka to stop, pull the handbrakes and prepare to turn the car in the new approved direction. As the car was turning, Gavrilo Princip emerged from the café to find himself standing three yards from Franz Ferdinand. He instinctively pulled out his gun and began firing. He later claimed that because of the adrenalin of the moment he had no idea how many he fired. The Duchess turned to see if her husband had been hit; both she and von Harrach saw the same thing – a trickle of blood spilling from Franz Ferdinand's mouth. Sophie screamed and collapsed, while members of the crowd and the imperial entourage hurled themselves at Princip, preventing him from swallowing the cyanide.

In the car, Franz Ferdinand hunched over his wife, begging her to stay alive for their children's sake, apparently insensible to his own wound. The bullet had hit just above the Archduke's collarbone and he was losing a lot of blood. Count von Harrach, assuming that the Duchess had fainted with shock, began screaming instructions at the traumatised driver, who moved with admirable speed given the circumstances. Trying to keep the heir upright, von Harrach went over to sit next to him and pressed a handkerchief on the wound. As chaos reigned around them, von Harrach shouted, 'Is Your Imperial Highness in great pain?'[20] The Archduke shook his head and kept trying to cradle his wife. 'It is nothing,' he replied. He repeated it until he lost consciousness.

When they reached the governor's residence, the staff who had been waiting to greet the couple with gifts and speeches were instead confronted by scenes of horror. Doctors and priests were summoned as Franz Ferdinand and the seemingly unconscious Duchess were dragged out of the car and carried into the residence. Sophie was taken into Potiorek's private rooms, where her lady-in-waiting laid her out on his bed, waiting for the arrival of a surgeon from the loyal garrison they had visited earlier. The Archduke was taken into the Governor General's study and set down on a chaise-longue, where his aide-de-camp, Baron Andreas von Morsey, cut him out of his tunic. Blood was spilling thick and fast from the

Archduke's mouth, spraying the clothes, hands and faces of the men trying to save him. Baron von Morsey was clutching him in his arms and still desperately trying to get him to speak when one of the hastily summoned doctors said quietly, 'His Highness's suffering is over.'[21] As the others wept and crossed themselves, the baron reached into his pocket and took out a small crucifix and some rosary beads. He wrapped them in Franz Ferdinand's hands while from the other room Countess von Wallenburg began to scream as she undressed the Duchess for the doctor's examination. One of Princip's bullets had pierced her inferior vena cava, causing massive internal bleeding. She had died in the car. Father Puntigam, the confessor who only a few days earlier had shown the Duchess around his new school, arrived to pray over the bodies. Countess von Wallenburg spoke for many in the room when she wrote of 'this grief that went right down to the deepest marrow of my soul.'[22]

As the padre prayed, the empire's telephone and telegraph lines were swiftly shut down to ensure the news reached the relatives first. The Duchess's younger sister Henrietta told the dead couple's children after dinner – the youngest, ten-year-old Ernst, was reportedly gripped by a grief so severe that he behaved like a madman, while the eldest, twelve-year-old Sophie, showed that she was very much her mother's daughter by issuing a statement requesting prayers for her departed parents and thanking everyone for their kind wishes. One of the kindest telegrams they received was from the Kaiser who, referring to his visit to their father's rose garden a few weeks earlier, wrote: 'We can hardly find words to tell you children how our hearts bleed, thinking of you and your indescribable misery! Only two weeks ago we spent such lovely hours with your parents, and now we hear of this terrible grief that you must suffer. May God protect you and give you the strength to bear this blow! The blessing of your parents reaches beyond death.'[23]

The Emperor received the news while on holiday in his pretty summer villa at Bad Ischl near Salzburg. Accounts of how he took the news vary; one particularly awful version, which can be neither proved nor discounted, claimed that he suggested after a few minutes that the assassination had been part of God's plan to correct the damage Franz Ferdinand had done in marrying Sophie.[24] Perhaps the most reliable account comes from the Emperor's youngest daughter, the Archduchess Maria Valerie, who saw him shortly after he received the news.[25] She knew that relations between the men had been strained first by Franz Ferdinand's marriage and then by his politics, and she was honest enough to admit that her father was unlikely to be personally devastated by the death of a man whom he had disliked and distrusted. However, she said that the Emperor had tears in his eyes when he spoke of the sorrow that must be afflicting the three children at Chlumetz.

Before the telegraph systems were reopened for the public, the news was also sent to Franz Ferdinand's nephew, the Archduke Karl, who was likewise on holiday. Taking advantage of the gorgeous weather, the twenty-six-year-old Archduke and his Italian wife Zita had decided to lunch in a little wooden chalet in the grounds of their villa when a servant arrived with a telegram addressed to Karl. Glancing down at the envelope, Karl was mildly surprised to see that it was from Baron Rumerskirch, one of Franz Ferdinand's aide-de-camps and one of the men who had been present in the room when he died. 'That's odd,' Karl said, 'why him?' The telegram read:

> Deeply regret to report that His Imperial Highness and the Duchess were both assassinated here today.

On the opposite side of the table, Zita noticed that 'though it was a beautiful day, I saw his face go white in the sun. We hurried back into the house. The first thing was to get confirmation, and in those days there was no radio or television to switch on. The only sure source would be the Emperor himself, who was at his regular summer residence at Bad Ischl. My husband got through on the telephone and spoke to one of the palace staff on duty there. The dreadful news was true, and the Emperor was returning at once by train to Vienna. My husband was to meet him there at Hietzing, which was the nearest station to the Schönbrunn Palace. The short drive they took together in an open carriage that afternoon, from the station to the palace, where I was already waiting, was the first time my husband had appeared in public as heir to the throne. The crowd, he told me, lined the pavements in stunned silence.'[26] Zita herself had only recently come out of mourning for her elder half-sister, Princess Maria Immaculata, who had suffered from learning difficulties and passed away in May at the age of thirty-nine. Now the Archduchess had to change into a deeper form of mourning and prepare for Franz Ferdinand's funeral.

Back in Sarajevo, Austrian newspapers reported pogrom-like scenes as the assassination tripped the wire of ethnic hostilities and Croats and Muslims vented their fury on the local Serbian community. Reports of widespread public, and even official, rejoicing in Belgrade did nothing to quieten the mood and it heightened feelings of outrage in Vienna. Whatever the wider public may have thought of Franz Ferdinand, there was genuine shock that a lady had been killed alongside him, as well as a feeling that the entire empire had been insulted by Princip's attack. Nobody believed that Serbia was not somehow complicit in the assassination and while attention was temporarily distracted by unhappiness at how the couple's funeral was organised, with Sophie's coffin being slanted down from her husband's to reaffirm her inferior social status and gloves placed atop the bier as was traditional for a lady-in-waiting, once the mourning was over and the bodies had been taken to rest at Artstetten, public opinion swung rapidly behind the hawks whom Franz Ferdinand had opposed in life, but who now insisted that his death mandated vengeance against Serbia. One Austrian nobleman spoke of 'tears in my eyes, tears of sorrow, of terrible rage and fury! Oh, the misery of it, he, our future, our leader, who was to be the strong man, he to whom we all looked to in the future as our saviour out of all the long-past years of ineptitude ... How can one bear such felony and must not every civilised creature on earth stand up and pray for damnation and God's fire of vengeance on that vile, murderous country, Serbia!'[27]

Those who had known Franz Ferdinand and his wife attempted to move on with their lives, but it proved impossible for most of them, and not simply because no murder in human history has ever had more wide-reaching consequences. Count von Harrach, the courtier who had planned to shield the couple from harm, was haunted by the events at Sarajevo for the rest of his life: 'I stood on the wrong side,' he said years later. 'If I had stood on the right side instead of the left, I would have taken the bullets and would have saved their lives.'[28] Fewer things in history offer a more tantalising 'if' than the death of Franz Ferdinand and his wife. As it was, Gavrilo Princip's gunshots set off a chain reaction that tore down the monarchy Franz Ferdinand had dedicated his life to saving and began a process that would destroy the stability of Europe and end or destroy the lives of millions.

conversation
however, her
out. She bit he
network of di
The 'blaze
the jewellery
about to tak
that Berlin v
of the Russi
manner, was
to everybody
twenty-four
Serbian gove
Germany pr
compelled tc
intended, me
wanted a wa
death would
The seco
was that A
confrontatic
government
Conrad vor
could proce
that lay on
Count von
was finishe
and allow
empire wou
lingering H
Belgrade.
That ult
Serbia on
which poin
Serbian fro
condemn
that called
Vienna wo

3

The Early War Years in Austria-Hungary and Germany

'Go to the churches, kneel down, and
pray for help for our soldiers'

In his diary, King George V lamented the assassination of his former guests as 'a terrible shock to the dear old Emperor'.[1] With the exceptions of Serbia and Montenegro, similar reactions occurred in nearly every other royal court in Europe. In Knightsbridge in London, the Dowager Empress of Russia interrupted her granddaughter's honeymoon to tell her the news. She arrived at Irina's flat, accompanied by her sister, the British Queen Mother, and threatened an Ethiopian servant with her umbrella when he mistook her for a casual caller and would not let her in to see the newlyweds. King Carol and Queen Elisabeth of Romania ordered official mourning for a month and in Rome the Pope spoke publicly of his 'sharp pain for the loss of such a wise and enlightened prince' and of his 'deep anger against the perpetrators of such a despicable attack.'[2]

However, despite revulsion at the assassin's act, the summer of 1914 proceeded, at least initially, very much as planned. The Dowager Empress saw no reason to cut short her trip to her sister in England and the two women soon set off for Sandringham in time for the start of the grouse hunting season in August. The Kaiser personally authorised the dispatch of the customary birthday telegram to the King of Serbia on 11 July, on the grounds

that not to
in the Balk
of Finland
on the fort
of France.
situation b
Even so, N
war over
luncheon
Tsar discu
Maurice F
war in th
Berlin. W
upon Aus
its own a
Germany
knew hin
theatrical
century I
'a dazzli
of diamc
blaze of
a review
joined b
a rare p

Throu
decision
distress
climate.
suggeste
honour
next, R
and th
Preside
in his
was 'a
tiara o
still pl

any high-profile individuals known to have engaged in activities harmful to the Austro-Hungarian monarchy – once that list was received the Serbian government must dismiss these people from public service. Explanations were to be provided as to why certain other officials had given interviews to the press in which they expressed clear hostility towards the Austro-Hungarians. Serbia must bring to trial all those who had been involved in plotting Franz Ferdinand's assassination, including the customs officials who let Princip and his co-conspirators cross the border. Austro-Hungarian representatives must be allowed to come into Serbia to oversee these arrests and to see if the promised suppression of the Black Hand and its sister organisations was carried out.

It was that last clause that was the most controversial, because the Serbian government believed, or claimed to believe, that this was only a prelude to an Austrian invasion and the reduction of the Serbian government to nothing more than a satellite of Austria-Hungary. Within a few hours of receiving the ultimatum, Crown Prince Alexander of Serbia argued that to comply with it would rob Serbia of all vestiges of its honour. A line of reasoning that might have carried slightly more weight if his government had not just helped arrange the murder of his Austrian counterpart. However, Alexander's view was shared by many politicians across Europe, even those previously sympathetic to Austria-Hungary. Winston Churchill, then serving as First Lord of the Admiralty, thought the document was 'a bullying and humiliating ultimatum to Serbia, who cannot possibly comply with it'.[8] Today, knowing as we do the full extent of the Serbian government's complicity in, and knowledge of, the murder of Franz Ferdinand and Sophie von Hohenburg, the Austro-Hungarian ultimatum might not seem so excessive. However, it struck many at the time as an act of wanton belligerence, particularly in light of the unsavoury impression created by so many of Franz Ferdinand's former opponents using his death as an excuse to pursue a policy that he had always regarded as lunatic.

As the international mood darkened, talk in Saint Petersburg, both in the press and high society, turned increasingly towards a mobilisation of the army. Some, like the Tsar's cousin Grand Duke Nikolai, who would probably receive the position of the army's

Commander-in-Chief in the event of a war, hoped that full or partial mobilisation might persuade Germany and Austria-Hungary to reconsider.[9] Others, like Nikolai's wife Anastasia, a princess of Montenegro by birth, which had been one of the few countries that had actually celebrated Franz Ferdinand's death, actively hoped for a war. At a dinner party during the French visit, the Grand Duchess and her sister, the Grand Duchess Militsa, were holding forth on their hopes for the rest of 1914. 'There's going to be a war,' she told the French ambassador. 'There'll be nothing left of Austria … Our armies will meet in Berlin. Germany will be destroyed.' Then, noticing that the Tsar had overheard her and seemed displeased, she whispered, 'I must restrain myself. The Emperor has his eyes on me.'[10]

When a rumour circulated that Serbia had agreed to all the terms, there was surprise and disappointment in Berlin. Albert Ballin, the Jewish business genius responsible for the creation of the *Imperator* and her sister ships, was shocked at how some of his friends in government lamented that Serbia's acquiescence had robbed them of an excuse to go to war. At Ballin's suggestion that the Kaiser ought to be called back from his summer cruise on the North Sea, the Foreign Minister replied that if the Kaiser returned early to Berlin he would be in a much better position to stop the war and nobody wanted that. When news leaked through confirming that Serbia had no intention of allowing Austrian officials to have any say in an internal investigation, the mood in Berlin lifted.

On 28 July, Austria-Hungary declared war on Serbia. A day later, the British government communicated to Germany that although she hoped to remain neutral, she could not do so if Germany violated any previous peace treaties guaranteeing the neutrality of countries like Belgium, which Britain had vowed to protect under the Treaty of London. Given that the treaty had been signed seventy-five years earlier there were many in the German cabinet who thought the British were bluffing; they could not possibly consider going to war over a country in which they had no territorial interest. Neither Britain nor France wanted a war, that much was true. Up until the very last moment, there were those in London who were arguing that neutrality was the logical course to take. However, a series of German miscalculations, culminating in

Count von Mensdorff, recalled to Vienna at the outbreak of hostilities, King George V blamed the Crown Prince and his allies far more than he did the Kaiser: 'I don't believe Wilhelm ever wanted war, but he was afraid of his son's popularity. His son and his party made the war.'[15] The Kaiser may not have wanted the war, but he did want to see France defeated and humbled. Unlike the Tsar, he neither liked nor trusted a republic, least of all the French. Once, while reading an account of the last days of Marie Antoinette, Wilhelm had worked himself up into a rage at how she had been treated and he felt that even the distance of a century had not removed the taint of French republicanism's blood-soaked birth. That France's last experiment with monarchy had ended as recently as 1870 thanks to his grandfather's invasion of France was a point that seemed to have missed Wilhelm entirely. All he saw was a troublesome and untrustworthy republic to the west. However, he was not an annexationist. He wanted no German empire in France or Belgium and he wanted more than anything to avoid a war with Imperial Russia. In short, he was confused and, as with so much of that terrible summer, any number of outcomes were possible with Wilhelm.

On 1 August, the hawks got their way: Germany declared war on Russia, citing their recent mobilisation as justification. A plan devised with this eventuality in mind by the recently deceased Count Alfred von Schlieffen now swung into action. Russia had larger armies and she also had an ally. Dealing with one meant crushing the other. Germany must not have the nightmare scenario of a war on two fronts. She would invade France as she had in 1870, once again securing a lightening victory that would knock the republic out of the war and allow Germany to turn east to deal with Russia. The plan assumed that given the vast size of the Russian empire and her comparatively underdeveloped railway system, she would need about six weeks to mobilise, the same amount of time allowed for a German victory over France. To avoid entanglements with any French lines of defence, the German plan was to march through Belgium. The young King of the Belgians, Albert I, had already refused permission for one neighbour to use his country as a base to invade another, but on 3 August the Germans declared war on France and Belgium was invaded. King Albert assumed personal command of his armies and although Belgium stood no chance of victory, they managed to slow German progress. Within days of the war opening, the Schlieffen Plan that had promised such a quick victory had already failed. The British had every intention of honouring the Treaty of London and by September the French and British armies had arrived in Belgium and the north of France, digging themselves into trenches to face their German opponents. The Western Front, the theatre of war in which millions of lives were lost and grotesque advancements in military technology were pioneered, had opened.

The declarations of war brought jubilant crowds on to the streets of the European capital. Photographs of that joy and confidence in a swift victory have since become iconic images of a society's blind arrogance and the pre-war world's ignorance. However, in many ways these photographs are misleading – many people in 1914 were surprised that continent-wide war had started and concerned for what it would mean. Europeans' belief that their continent had become the dominant region in global politics because their superior powers of reasoning had produced centuries of progress that enabled them to technologically and economically outpace the rest of the world now seemed shaken by a war within the club, as it were, and one which could on multiple occasions have been prevented. The Kaiser had all of these misgivings and more. As pro-war crowds surged through Berlin's boulevards to gather outside the Stadtschloss, Wilhelm's principal residence in the capital, the Kaiser appeared on the balcony and gave a speech devoid of his usual jingoistic bravura:

A momentous hour has struck for Germany. Envious rivals everywhere force us to legitimate defence. The sword has been forced into our hands. I hope that in the event that my efforts to the very last moment do not succeed in bringing our opponents to reason and in preserving peace, we may use the sword, with the help of God, so that we may sheathe it again with honour. War will demand enormous sacrifices by the German people, but we shall show the enemy what it means to attack Germany. And so I commend you to God. Go forth into the churches, kneel down before God, and implore his help for our brave army.

Oskar, commanded the King Wilhelm I Regiment on the Western Front and received the Iron Cross, First Class, for valour when he led his men into the charge at the Battle of Verdun and only stopped when he collapsed and had to be carried off the battlefield.

South in Austria, Cecilia's anguish was exceeded by the anguish facing the new heir's wife, the Archduchess Zita. Like Cecilia, Zita of Bourbon-Parma had many relatives on the other side of the trenches, some of whom had been holidaying with her when war was declared. In her case, she had to beg Franz Josef to let her two brothers, Sixtus and Xavier, leave Austria to join the Belgian army. The Archduchess was understandably distraught that her husband and brothers would be fighting in opposite camps, but Karl told his brothers-in-law that 'just as it was his duty now to join the army, so it was our duty to return'.[19] Permission was granted in the last week and the two princes were brought to the border with Switzerland. At the same time, the friend who had given Zita away at the altar in 1911 was taken out of the empire under armed escort because he had fought in the Russian armies in their war against Japan in 1904.

On 16 August, the day after the Feast of the Assumption, a holy day of obligation in the Catholic calendar, Karl set off for the Eastern Front. In her husband's absence, Zita was invited to move with her two children into the Schönbrunn Palace to live with the Emperor. Sometimes seen as the Hapsburgs' riposte to Versailles, the Schönbrunn was a magnificent Baroque extravagance dating from the reign of the eighteenth-century Empress Maria Teresa and, like Versailles, it was famed for its wonderful gardens. Zita moved there with two-year-old Otto and his baby sister Adelheid, where they were with the Emperor to receive news of several promising Austrian victories in the autumn.

With her husband gone, Zita spent much of her mornings visiting military hospitals; in August 1915, she was award the service medal of the Red Cross. As the new first lady of the Hapsburg court, she was also expected to accompany the octogenarian Emperor as hostess for any official functions, which as the war progressed included, to her chagrin, increasingly frequent visits from Kaiser Wilhelm. Cracks were already beginning to appear in the alliance as the war came to be seen more as Germany's than

Austria-Hungary's. After all, it was Germany who had caused Britain, France and Belgium to become involved in a conflict that was initially to have concerned nobody bar Austria-Hungary, Germany, Serbia and Russia, at the very most. Visits by Wilhelm and his entourage also accentuated the old tensions between the Austrians and the Prussians, highlighting what the former saw as the charm of the south against the aggressive bad manners of the north. Interestingly, given her future attempts to break the Austrian alliance with Germany, Zita seemed even at this early stage to bristle at the arrival of the Prussians in Vienna. It was a view that, she felt, was shared by Franz Josef. 'One felt there was never any real contact between them,' she wrote later. 'The atmosphere was never relaxed; there was always electricity in the air and an awareness that Wilhelm II somehow represented a different attitude to life, almost a different culture.'[20]

On a personal level, Zita found Wilhelm II tiresome and she did not warm to his sense of humour. Once, at a dinner party, the Kaiser 'told some jokes at table which did not seem to me to be in the best tastes; so I pointedly did not laugh'. After dinner, Zita worried that she might have been rude and that for manners' sake it would have been better to laugh politely at Wilhelm's slightly risqué banter. 'I mentioned it to the Emperor afterwards,' she remembered, 'in case it had been a *faux pas*. But he thoroughly approved: "Quite right. One is not obliged to laugh at everything." The Emperor never uttered one word of direct criticism against his fellow-sovereign. But little incidents like that showed that they could never hit it off together and it always seemed to me that this reflected a broader gulf between the two peoples.'[21]

Every afternoon, the Emperor would call to Zita's apartments to spend some time visiting her and the children – a third child, the Archduke Robert, was born in 1915 and the Emperor's happiness was visible at the christening. During his visits, he would talk to Zita with a candour he rarely displayed with anybody else. Zita was a sympathetic listener with a soothing manner and in her company Franz Josef began to reflect on his long and extraordinary life. He told her how, in his heart, he had never recovered from 1848, the year his uncle Ferdinand abdicated in his favour and he had been given the throne to save it from the trauma of the uprisings. All of to help people but also to dominate them. With her devotion and inability to form a thought independently of the Empress, let alone to criticise her, she was exactly what Alexandra was looking for, although from time to time even she seemed to find her adoration a touch suffocating. Nicholas was fond of Anna, but he found her habit of bringing all gossip great and small to the Empress's attention in the hope of winning her approval extremely irritating. 'You, for your part, must not allow Anna to bother you with stupid tale bearing that will do no good,' he told her, 'either to yourself or to others.'[2]

When she arrived at the Alexander Palace that evening, Anna was taken through to the Empress's rooms, all of which were kitted out in furniture ordered from English catalogues, to the general revulsion of the nobility, who thought the Tsarina's interior decorating at Tsarskoe Selo a never-ending crime against good taste. Shown into Alexandra's all-mauve boudoir, Anna excitedly told her what she had seen in the city. Alexandra stared at her blankly and then said she must be wrong; the only units that were on the move were near the Austrian frontier. When Anna insisted that she had seen the posters confirming mobilisation, the Empress rushed from the room and went to her husband's study. For half an hour, Anna could hear them quarrelling on the other side of the door, as Alexandra discovered that Nicholas had deliberately kept the news from her because he was worried about her health. Storming back in to Anna, Alexandra collapsed on her couch. 'War!' she said, breathlessly. 'And I knew nothing of it. This is the end of everything.' When the Tsar called over to take his usual evening tea with his wife and her ladies-in-waiting, the tea hour, normally a time for friendly conversation, passed in torturous silence. Anna wrote later that for the next few days, 'The depression of the Empress continued unrelieved. Up to the last moment she hoped against hope, and when the German formal declaration of war was given she gave way to a perfect passion of weeping.'[3]

Alexandra's horror was shared by some of those who had once been close to her husband. Sergei Witte, the financial wizard who had been shunted off into the political wilderness for mishandling the crises of 1905, tried to use every connection left to him to stop a conflict. He thought it was fundamentally wrong to go to war on Serbia's behalf, because after what had happened to Franz Ferdinand they were only going to 'suffer the chastisement they deserved'. When someone suggested that a victory might bring an increase in Russia's size, Witte snapped, 'Good Heavens! Isn't His Majesty's empire big enough already? … And even if we assume a complete victory, the Hohenzollerns and Habsburgs reduced to begging for peace … it means not only the end of German domination but the proclamation of republics throughout central Europe. That means the simultaneous end of Tsarism … we must liquidate this stupid adventure as soon as possible.'[4] His words showed that he had lost none of his powers of perception. The fact that he said them in the company of the French ambassador, representative of Russia's main ally, showed that he had lost none of his powers to annoy.

All doubters were silenced by the outburst of patriotic zeal which greeted the beginning of the war. So complete was faith in Russia's destiny that after years of struggle for constitutionalism the Duma quite incredibly voted to voluntarily suspend itself until the war was over so that the entire nation could rally behind the throne with no division of loyalties or focus. When the Tsar and Tsarina appeared on the balcony of the Winter Palace in Saint Petersburg, a crowd of tens of thousands was waiting for them. It spontaneously burst into a chorus of 'God Save the Tsar'; as flags waved, Nicholas bowed before his people, and cheers erupted for a war in defence of Holy Mother Russia. The explosion of nationalism that Franz Josef feared to be running the war was evident in Russia from the very beginning, and nationalism's inherent tendency towards xenophobia even more so when the Tsar backed a proposal to change the capital city's name from Saint Petersburg to Petrograd, its Russian translation. So far the same sentiments had not turned on Nicholas's German-born wife, but it was only a matter of time.

Alexandra, determined to be useful, contacted the Red Cross and set about training as a student nurse, while she also financed the building of a state-of-the-art military hospital in the grounds of Tsarskoe Selo. Where many other upper-class women were patrons of charities, Alexandra wanted to actually work for one. When she passed the course, she wrote happily to her sister Victoria, living in England, 'We passed our exams and received the Red Cross on to Himself. I was as usual with him in the morning and more than an hour in the afternoon.' She was not, to her distress, there when the young man passed away. Earlier in the day, he had told one of the nurses that he was a little bit uncomfortable but that it was nothing too serious. Ten minutes later, the same nurse came back and said he took a few deep breaths before gently passing away. 'Olga and I went to see him,' Alexandra wrote that night. 'He lay there so peacefully covered under my flowers I daily brought him, with his lovely peaceful smile – the forehead yet quite warm. I came home with tears ... Never did he complain, never asked for anything, sweetness itself – all loved him and that shining smile ... I felt God let me bring him a little sunshine in his loneliness. Such is life. Another brave soul left this world to be added to the shining stars above.' She was distraught and could not stop writing about it at length to Nicholas: 'It must not make you sad, what I wrote,' she apologised, 'only I could not bear it any longer.'[12]

The suffering that Alexandra and her two daughters witnessed were caused by Russia's mounting problems with the war. The economic growth of the last two decades, coupled with the country's pride in its military, meant that very few Russians had seriously considered the possibility of defeat. The memories of the Crimea in 1855 and Japan in 1905 had been shunted to one side. Nationalist propaganda preferred to summon up the ghosts of Saint Alexander Nevsky and the glorious medieval past or Alexander I and the triumph against Napoleon. This optimism had not been completely misguided. With its enormous army, in a short war Imperial Russia could match its enemies. However, the economic growth experienced under Nicholas II and his father was too recent and thus too shallow to sustain a long-term war of attrition, a fact that was horribly exposed in the war's first year. So much has been written about tsarist Russia's failure in the war that it is easy to imagine that there were never any successes. There were victories, particularly in the campaigns against Austria-Hungary, but defeats, when they came, came at a truly terrible cost. At the end of the first month of the war, the Germans lost approximately 5,000 men in their victory over the Russian Second Army at the Battle of Tannenburg. The Russians lost 78,000, with a further 90,000 captured. At that battle, the flower of the Russian aristocracy's fighting men vanished in the course of four days, cut down as the nobility of a cavalry charge was shown to be no match for the modern world of machine guns and heavy artillery. In the opening few days of the siege of the Austro-Hungarian fortress at Przemyśl, 40,000 Russians were killed. News of the slaughters and the thousands of bereaved families began to rapidly erode enthusiasm for the conflict.

At home, the empire's agricultural and transport systems were unable to cope with the huge demand that the war placed upon them and with so many of the railways being used to supply the war effort, it often took longer for food to reach the cities from the countryside. The imperial government's main success was in ensuring that Russia's plentiful food supplies were moved efficiently enough that the army did not suffer any food shortages.[13] Even so, other supplies rapidly diminished – winter boots were not available for most of the soldiers by 1915 and diseases like cholera, typhus, typhoid, scurvy and dysentery had increased by 1916. Lack of ammunition and equipment greatly increased casualties on the front line, while the factories back home struggled to produce the guns and ammunition that the government needed for the army. With so many men of fighting age off to the front, the Russian economy was running on less manpower when it needed to be at its most productive.

By March 1915, it was clear that a munitions crisis was facing the Russian army and at military headquarters, known as *Stavka*, its highest-ranking leaders were blaming each other or the civil servants at the Ministry of War, but never themselves. Having voted itself temporarily out of existence in a gesture of solidarity with the court in 1914, the Duma began agitating to be recalled and Nicholas acquiesced in the summer of 1915. A faction emerged known as the Progressive Bloc, a loose but powerful coalition consisting of about two-thirds of the members of the Duma who were committed to significant legislative changes once the war was over but who also wanted to form a pressure group of sorts that would have a say in ensuring that competent ministers were appointed until that peace was won. Despite what the Tsarina and several of her friends believed, they were not an anti-monarchist lobby, but the fact that they existed at all was proof of a lively concern within the empire's educated elite about what would happen now that the government had finally decided to intervene in the ineptitude on display at *Stavka*.

Grand Duke Nikolai would have to go as Commander-in-Chief. The Empress distrusted his charisma and his wife's ceaseless attempts to promote her husband in the public's affection at the Tsar's expense. The Grand Duchess's sly insinuations about Alexandra's German heritage did not help matters, nor did the fact that the charismatic and clever Grand Duke, the looming giant of the Romanov family at six feet six inches in height, now appeared to be on the verge of a breakdown due to the strains and nightmares caused by so many catastrophic defeats. Yet to replace the Grand Duke was no easy business. A Romanov could not be supplanted by a commoner or even a nobleman without it being interpreted as a calculated assault on his honour. The Tsar decided to replace Nikolai himself. It would lead to a neater merging of the civilian and military branches of the government as well as enabling Nicholas to purge the army of those men who had been associated with the worst mistakes of the early war effort. Purge, in a tsarist sense, had a very different meaning to the same word in the USSR. There were no gulags here and Nikolai's Chief of Staff, the unpopular General Yanushkevich, was simply dismissed from active service. Nicholas hoped that by appearing at the front more regularly he would provide inspiration to the soldiers, that he would have a clearer idea of what was going on, and going wrong, and that it would convey the impression that the monarchy cared about what was happening to its subjects. In the words of his prime minister at the time, Prince Ivan Goremykin, 'His Majesty considers it the sacred duty of the Russian Tsar to be among the troops'.[14] Nicholas was also sufficiently self-aware to know that it was not his job to actually direct strategy and that in this arena delegation was his most important skill. He replaced Yanushkevich with General Mikhail Alekseev, who never overcame the disasters being thrown his way by the economic problems back home but who at least directed the armies more prudently than they had been before 1915. Dominic Lieven, one of Nicholas's best modern biographers, defends the decision, saying that 'the Emperor's decision to assume the supreme command was not only courageous and irrevocable but also correct'.[15] Initially it certainly seemed to have been a wise move. True, Nicholas rejected a proposed deal with the Progressive Bloc that might have bound the Duma and the crown closer together at a crucial juncture, but a series of Russian victories helped stabilise the front and make the war effort look less like a rout.

And yet for all its merits, Nicholas II's decision to become Commander-in-Chief of the armies in 1915 was arguably the biggest mistake of his life, with the possible exception of his abdication in 1917. When he informed his Council of Ministers, they were aghast. They begged him not to go: it would put the throne in the spotlight for blame for every subsequent defeat. The monarchy and the military might achieve a perfect symbiosis, much as they had in Muscovite myths and tales of medieval Rus, but the Tsar's gamble would only pay off if Russia won. Until now, public opinion had often criticised individual ministers or leadership at *Stavka* for the thousands of body bags needed at the front, henceforth the focus of that misery would be the Tsar and all the opprobrium caused by a brutal war would be heaped upon his head. Equally damaging was the fact that the wisdom of appointing General Alekseev as the new of Chief of Staff was not matched by installing Alexandra as Regent in the Tsar's absence.

The Tsarina had a terrible working relationship with most ministers, her shyness made her uncomfortable even in the presence of men who shared her views, her suspiciousness now bordered on paranoia because she chose to see the formation of the Progressive Bloc as a prelude to a treasonous usurpation of monarchical authority, a second coming of the Tennis Court Oath, and she was a German. She would not have described herself as such and indeed to all intents and purposes Nicholas II was married to an Englishwoman: the daughter of an English princess, raised in a house built on British lines with British furniture, cared for by English nannies and sent to spend most of her time under the care of her grandmother Queen Victoria after her mother died nursing her children through the diphtheria epidemic of 1878; even after twenty years of marriage Alexandra's ladies-in-waiting noticed that 'she spoke Russian with a strong English accent'.[16] She also detested the Second Reich and distrusted her cousin Wilhelm. However, to the wider public all that mattered was that the Tsarina had been born in a city that was now part of Germany and the nationality of *Nemka*, 'the German woman', became a focus for speculation as the Tsar chose to leave the day-to-day business of government in the hands of a foreigner. Added to the problem of her nationality was Alexandra's dependence on Grigori Rasputin, a wandering Siberian *moujik*, an itinerant self-styled holy man, with atrocious levels of personal hygiene and, if rumour was to be believed, even filthier morals.

They had first been introduced a decade earlier when the Grand Duchess Militsa, who changed spiritual fascinations like other people changed outfits, brought him to the Tsarina's attention. He was a confident man with a mystical and earthy bent; his unashamed, and possibly slightly exaggerated, peasant mannerisms made him an exotic oddity in the salons of Petersburg society. He claimed to have seen visions of the Virgin Mary, to have wandered as far as the enclosed Christian community at Mount Athos in Greece on pilgrimage and have the power to heal. Always an admirer of his rustic Christianity, Alexandra had become infallibly convinced that he was truly a man of God when he seemed to heal Alexei via telegram in 1912.[17] The miracle was repeated in 1914, when Alexei badly sprained his ankle in the same week that Franz Ferdinand was murdered and Alexandra feared that he might die from the internal bleeding. Another telegram brought another last-minute recovery. In January 1915, Anna Vyrubova was severely injured in a train crash and the doctors expected her to die. Rasputin took one look at her in her hospital bed and announced that she would live, but remained partially crippled. It was a slight over-statement. She was not crippled, she simply needed a stick for walking for the rest of her life, but she did live when everyone but Rasputin thought she would die. At exactly the same time as she achieved her greatest political significance, the Tsarina Alexandra was certain that Grigori Rasputin was 'Our Friend', a man sent by God to cure her son and convey the will of Russia's loyal peasantry to her husband.

5

Total War and the Marginalisation of the Kaiser

'His Majesty has no understanding of the seriousness of the situation'

The Grand Duchy of Luxembourg went more quietly into a German occupation than her Belgian neighbours. The reigning Grand Duchess, twenty-year-old Marie-Adélaïde, protested the Second Reich's invasion of her country, but she was pragmatic enough to realise that there was very little she could do to stop it. Unlike Belgium, Luxembourg had no powerful friends ready to leap to her defence. The young lady's previous two years on the grand ducal throne had been spent trying to remedy what she saw as growing social inequality and she had been very popular as a result. Whether she was as pro-German as her critics claimed when they forced her off the throne at the end of the war is unclear. Throughout the conflict, she continued to insist that Luxembourg was officially neutral. Still, despite her claims and the undoubtedly difficult position in which she found herself, Marie-Adélaïde's politeness to the Germans stands in stark contrast to the actions taken by King Albert and Queen Elisabeth of the Belgians – the former fought against the Germans throughout the war, the latter established nursing units on the front line.

On 30 August 1914, the Kaiser arrived in Luxembourg as part of the government's plan to keep the Emperor constantly on the move between the various fronts. The Chancellor, Theobold von

Bethmann-Hollweg, believed that the Kaiser's presence was vital given the Hohenzollern dynasty's long history of support for the military: 'A King of Prussia, a German emperor, who did not stay in the middle of his armies was an idea which would have been unbearable both to the emperor and the troops.'[1] Although she did not offer him or his entourage accommodation in any of her palaces and they had to make do with rooms at the German consulate, the Grand Duchess Marie-Adélaïde did invite the Kaiser to join her for dinner at the Grand Ducal Palace in Luxembourg City.

The Kaiser was still in Luxembourg when he heard news that his youngest son, twenty-four-year-old Joachim, had been wounded in the German advance on Paris. Joachim had borne himself bravely, like a soldier, and a Swedish friend of the Kaiser who was visiting him in Luxembourg said that the Emperor's pride in his youngest son was touchingly visible. But the advance itself was not going well and during the First Battle of the Marne, the Germans had to accept that the Schlieffen Plan had failed. Paris would not fall as it had in 1871. The German army had to dig in and hold its position in the trenches against the British, the French and the Belgians.

Shortly after the failure in France, the Crown Prince came to Luxembourg to visit his father. Relations between the two men were still strained – in 1910, he had ordered his son to be temporarily kept away from any official duties after he failed to participate in the ceremonies to mark the centenary of the death of Queen Louise of Prussia, the Hohenzollern family's most celebrated matriarch who had helped unite the country against attacks by Napoleon. Four years later and the Kaiser expressed to him none of the affection he usually showed for the five younger brothers; the reunion did not improve the dynamic. Young Wilhelm began his visit by expressing his contempt for his father's advisers and insisting that von Bethmann-Hollweg should be replaced as Chancellor by someone more agreeable to the military. He also wanted General Paul von Hindenburg to become Chief of the General Staff, in effect, the man in charge of directing the war. The failure of the Schlieffen Plan had utterly crushed the spirits of the previous incumbent, Field Marshal von Moltke, and Wilhelm was considering replacing him with Erich von Falkenhayn, a

Prussian aristocrat who had previously served with the German army corps in China and as Prussia's Minister of War since June 1913. The Crown Prince thought von Falkenhayn was the wrong man for the job and that the esteemed von Hindenburg should get it instead, at the same time von Bethmann-Hollweg should preferably be replaced by Admiral von Tirpitz, thus creating, in effect, a military government. From Berlin, the Empress added her voice to the Crown Prince's, warmly expressing her admiration for von Hindenburg.

Father and son argued and the Kaiser refused to dismiss von Bethmann-Hollweg. He was also irritated by his wife and eldest son's support for von Hindenburg, a sixty-six-year-old *grand seigneur* of the Prussian aristocracy who could count among his ancestors Martin Luther, the first great leader of the Protestant Reformation. Von Hindenburg had a distinguished military career, including service in the wars against Austria and France that had facilitated the unification of Germany. He had been present as a victorious soldier at the ceremonies that declared the birth of the Second Reich in 1871 and he was so old, so venerable, that he had already retired by the time the war began in 1914. Such was his reputation that the army had begged him to come out of retirement, something which did nothing to dampen von Hindenburg's colossal sense of his own brilliance. Elderly and rotund, he had a statesman-like air that convinced people like the Empress and the Crown Prince that here was a man who could be trusted in both army and cabinet. He was given the command of the armies in the Eastern Front, which moved much more quickly than the stagnant trench-trapped forces in the West, with the result that throughout the war von Hindenburg looked like a man who was getting things done.

The Crown Prince left Luxembourg without getting what he wanted and convinced that his father was already failing in his duty as Supreme Warlord. This was a view widely shared by many of the younger Wilhelm's allies. Wilhelm II's continued reluctance to approve the harshest wartime measures, his visits to talk with French and British prisoners of war, his insistence on sending telegrams of condolence to relatives in Britain in the case of any bereavements and above all his behaviour, from manic energy to depressed malaise, all gave the impression to his advisers at various points of the war that 'His Majesty has no understanding of the seriousness of the situation' facing his people.[2] By the time the Kaiser left Luxembourg and took up temporary residence in the French town of Charleville, accompanied by his faithful dachshund Senta, his doctors had prescribed him sleeping pills.[3] He was not eating enough, contrary to the anti-monarchist propaganda at the end of the war that claimed he gorged himself, although the over-protective Empress did not help with that when she secretly circumvented her husband's orders that he should live on the same rations as the rest of the population; he was suffering anxiety attacks and even by his own standards he was behaving unusually. Albert Ballin had an audience with him during one of his short trips back to Berlin: 'I have seen the Emperor, whom I found full of confidence in the future, though also full of wrath against England, and in this the Empress encourages him. So that personal rancours and dislikes seem to play a considerable part in policy, and that appears to me very dangerous.'[4]

Augusta Victoria's Anglophobia was in step with public opinion as the war progressed. By 1915, the British navy's blockade of Germany was beginning to severely affect living standards. In retaliation, Admiral von Tirpitz wanted to unleash a policy of unlimited submarine warfare against any ship sailing into Britain. Chancellor von Bethmann-Hollweg opposed the move, claiming that it would play badly internationally as a violation of the traditional rules of warfare. Ordinarily, a warning would have to be given so that the passengers and crew would have time to evacuate. Von Tirpitz argued that the British had already changed the rules by counting foodstuffs as contrabands of war and in doing so they had declared *de facto* war on the German civilian population. The Kaiser sided with his Chancellor, to the admiral's fury – the admiral wrote of 'more than a hundred torpedo boats, rusting at anchor while Germany is engaged in a struggle for its existence'.[5] The Empress and the Crown Prince leant their support to von Tirpitz and urged Wilhelm to listen to reason. Initially, he held out by arguing that unrestricted submarine warfare in the waters around the British Isles would lead to the deaths of many innocent civilians and might therefore bring the United States into the war on Britain's side. 'As Chief Warlord,' he wrote later, 'I had absolutely to prevent this.' However, when supporters of lifting restrictions on the U-boats' activities were able to furnish the Kaiser with proof that American companies were providing the British with munitions, which were being brought into the United Kingdom on passenger and cargo ships, Wilhelm finally gave in and on 4 February 1915 one of von Tirpitz's subordinates, Admiral Hugo von Pohl, announced in the German press that unrestricted submarine attacks would now take place in British waters. During a visit to his dentist, an American practising in Berlin called Dr Arthur Davis, the Kaiser launched into an anti-American tirade, 'Why is it that your country is so unfair to Germany? Why do you persist in supplying munitions and money to the Allies? Why doesn't your president treat the European warring nations the same as he treated Mexico, by putting an embargo on munitions and letting us fight this thing out ourselves? You do not ship munitions to us. Why do you ship them to the other side?' Believing that he was answering his own question, Wilhelm said, 'Dollars! Dollars! Dollars!', hitting his left arm with his right each time he said the word.[6]

On 7 May, the U-boat policy claimed its most famous and most damaging victim. The 32,000-ton *Lusitania* had once been the pride of the British mercantile fleet. Built in 1907 as a response to Germany's recent spate of four-funnelled super-ships, all named after members of Wilhelm II's family, the *Lusitania* was nearly twice the size of her largest German rival and she retook the coveted Blue Riband, the award given to the fastest commercial crossing of the North Atlantic. In the years since her maiden voyage, she had been eclipsed in speed by her own sister ship, the *Mauretania*, and in size first by the *Mauretania,* then by the rival White Star Line's *Olympic*, then by the *Titanic*, then by Germany's *Imperator* and finally by the *Imperator*'s larger sister, the patriotically named *Vaterland*, which entered service only a few weeks before the outbreak of the war. She was still, however, a splendid ship and her two-storey first-class dining saloon with its Rococo dome was generally considered one of the finest rooms afloat. By the spring of 1915 she was also the only major luxury liner still in regular transatlantic service. Her two sisters, the *Mauretania* and *Aquitania*, had been called up to serve in the British war effort as troop transports and hospital ships, as had the rival White Star Line's *Olympic* and the recently completed *Britannic*.[7]

Controversy lasts to the present day about the British government's role in what happened to the *Lusitania*. For years, there have been claims that they deliberately let the *Lusitania* sail into harm's way because they knew that such a high-profile casualty would decisively turn American public opinion against Germany. Some in the government, including Winston Churchill, were confidently awaiting the day when the U-boats would attack a ship like the *Lusitania*, but that was because they understood the nature of total war at sea, not because of any deliberate planting of the liner in the sightline of a submarine. Far more damaging were allegations that the *Lusitania*'s hold was filled with explosives meant for the British war effort. The German embassy had placed advertisements in the American newspapers warning US citizens not to travel on British ships because of the new submarine policy, but very few listened. The U-20, a submarine commanded by Captain Lieutenant Walter Schweiger, spotted the *Lusitania* just off the south-eastern coast of Ireland, sailing home from New York, and fired a torpedo at her starboard side. In his diary, he recorded, 'An unusually strong explosion took place ... The explosion of the torpedo must have been accompanied by a second one (boiler or coal or powder?). The superstructure right about the point of impact and the bridge are torn asunder, fire breaks out and envelops the high bridge.'[8] The U-boat's pilot, a young man called Lanz with a fascination for British luxury liners, took a look through the periscope and gasped, 'My God, it's the *Lusitania*!'[9]

It was that 'unusually strong explosion' that prompted the most furious debate in the months and years to come. The British claimed, and many of them quite seriously seemed to believe, that the Germans had carried viciousness to new heights by firing two torpedoes into the side of the ship. The Germans insisted that it must have been the *Lusitania*'s illicit stock of contraband munitions that exploded on impact with the U-20's torpedo. Later German depictions of the sinking showed the Cunard Line ticket offices being staffed by the figure of Death as the ship set sail with the appearance of a well-stocked dreadnought. The debate over the second explosion was particularly significant because at the time it was believed to be the reason why the *Lusitania* sank in less than twenty minutes.[10] As she tipped over on her side to the point that Schweiger thought she was about to capsize, on-board fires made the water crashing over her decks so hot they scalded the people trying to escape, half the lifeboats could not be lowered because of the angle the ship was tilting at, some collapsed out of their davits crushing packed boats that were being lowered beneath them, there were horrible scenes of first-class passengers, en route to or from luncheon when the torpedo struck, trapped and screaming as they drowned in the ship's gilded elevator, the bodies of children washed ashore in the villages on the nearby Irish coast. There was just under 2,000 people on board the *Lusitania* when she sank; about 1,200 of them lost their lives, including 128 Americans.

It is difficult now to fully appreciate the damage that the sinking of the *Lusitania* caused to Imperial Germany's reputation in the United States. American goodwill towards Germany had already suffered when the latter's army torched the Belgian town of Louvain, dousing its fifteenth-century university library's 200,000 books with petrol and then setting those treasured repositories of centuries of scholarship alight. Later, they had turned their guns on Reims Cathedral in France, a medieval wonder that had once hosted the coronations of most of France's pre-revolutionary kings. One German professor later remarked, 'Today we may say that the three names Louvain, Rheims, *Lusitania*, in almost equal measure have wiped out sympathy with Germany in America.'[11]

Wilhelm, en route to inspect his troops on the Eastern Front in Galicia, initially refused to meet with the US ambassador in Berlin because he was still so angry at claims that American-supplied weapons were part of the ship's cargo. His conversations from this time reveal the depth of his anti-American sentiments and it was October, five months after the sinking, before he finally granted the American ambassador an audience. The Kaiser was back in Berlin briefly to celebrate the Empress's birthday and the ambassador, James Gerard, a New York lawyer rumoured to be sympathetic to the British, was invited to join the Kaiser briefly at the New Palace, a Baroque residence near Potsdam built by Friedrich the Great to commemorate Prussia's victory in the Seven Years' War. It was one of Wilhelm's favourite homes and the ambassador found him there, pouring over his maps. Wilhelm had not completely mellowed in his antipathy towards Gerard's homeland, but when the *Lusitania* was finally brought up Wilhelm appeared upset and said, 'No gentleman would kill so many women and children.'[12]

The extent of international outrage over what happened to the *Lusitania* seems to have sincerely surprised the German government. President Woodrow Wilson told Berlin that if there were another incident like it then the United States would have no choice but to declare war. A meeting of the Crown Council was held on 31 May, three weeks after the attack, at which, in light of recent events, the Chancellor argued for a suspension of unrestricted warfare by the U-boats. A day later, Wilhelm issued an order stating that if in doubt, U-boat captains should run the risk of letting enemy ships through rather than sink a vessel flying a neutral flag. Von Tirpitz was so angry at the decision that he offered his resignation. 'No!' Wilhelm answered. 'The gentlemen have to obey and to remain.' When von Bethmann-Hollweg secured further restrictions on the U-boats' activities in August, von Tirpitz again threatened to resign and Wilhelm again refused to let him. The Crown Prince blamed von Bethmann-Hollweg, a tacit reproach of his father because the Chancellor's support of restrictions was undoubtedly in line with the Kaiser's own views. He had been bounced into making the decision to allow unrestricted warfare in the first place and it had never been something that sat easily with his conscience. Unlike von Tirpitz or the Crown Prince, the Kaiser believed 'that to torpedo huge passenger ships full of women and children was a barbarous brutality without parallel, with which we will bring upon us the hatred and the poisonous rage of the entire world'.[13]

In the middle of 1915, Wilhelm II had briefly reasserted himself to support moderates in the cabinet and to repeal a highly damaging war policy. However, as conditions deteriorated at home, the German populace looked more and more to the army's leaders, like General von Hindenburg, as men who understood that harsh measures were required to help them. Several of Wilhelm's biographers have pointed out that his views on unrestricted submarine warfare were astute, as was his belief that everything should be done to keep America out of the war, but in 1915–16 the

Kaiser looked increasingly out of touch with the public mood and as his battle with depression, his mood swings, his unhealthy eating habits and his insomnia continued, he was not sufficiently strong, confident or stable to hold fast against the wishes of his family, his generals or public opinion.

6

The Death of Franz Josef and the Accession of Karl

'May God bless Your Majesty'

Courtiers reported that the Hapsburg family's sole empress regnant, the eighteenth-century Empress Maria Teresa, took the business of ruling so seriously that even during her contractions she liked to keep reading government papers. It was only during the labour itself that she would set them to one side.[1] The same spirit lived in her descendant Franz Josef. As he approached death in the autumn of 1916, the Emperor stuck to his daily routine, filling in pardons for condemned criminals, receiving well-wishes from the Pope and pouring over documents that concerned recruitment for the army. The bronchitis that had left him so weak in 1914 came back, this time supplemented by an attack of pneumonia. Romania had recently entered the war on the side of Austria-Hungary's enemies, despite its seemingly genuine commiseration on Franz Ferdinand's death in 1914 and the accession of a Hohenzollern king, Ferdinand I; news of the German and Austro-Hungarian armies' approach on Bucharest temporarily lifted the Emperor's spirits.

The Archduke Karl was back from the front for a few days and he and Zita called in to see Franz Josef on the morning of 20 November. When Franz Josef heard that Zita was accompanying Karl, he sent a servant to ask them to wait outside for a few minutes because, fastidious to the last, he would never dream of receiving a lady in casual attire. Knowing how weak he was, the Archduchess asked him to dispense with the protocol for the time being and he reluctantly agreed. The couple were shown in and they found him with a temperature of 102 degrees still doggedly examining the recruitment proposals. Zita remembered that 'the Emperor still made a normal impression and talked quite normally, despite his fever and weakness. He told us how happy he was to have received the blessing of the Pope and also what joy our victories in Romania had brought him.'[2]

That night, Karl and Zita were fetched by members of the Emperor's household who told them that His Imperial Majesty was losing consciousness. By the time they rushed into his apartments, in Zita's words, 'He was already in the last deep sleep from which he never awoke.' Franz Josef's sixty-eight year reign, the longest reign of a sovereign in European history since Louis XIV, ended a few minutes before nine o'clock in the evening on 22 November 1916 at the Schönbrunn Palace. When the doctors confirmed that the Emperor was dead, Karl and Zita walked out into a small anteroom next to his bedchamber, accompanied by a few members of his and their household staffs. For a few minutes, they all stood in silence. Then Karl's long-serving chamberlain, Prince Lobkowitz, a Czech aristocrat descended from one of the great patrons of Beethoven, walked over to the couple with tears in his eyes and made the sign of the cross. As he did so, he said, 'May God bless Your Majesty.' Zita, at twenty-four now Empress of Austria and Queen of Hungary, wrote later, 'It was the first time we had heard the imperial title used to us.'[3]

Throughout the empire, the death of the seemingly immortal Emperor who had sat upon the throne for longer than most of his subjects had been alive caused shock despite his advanced age; the monarchy's supporters and critics both thought that his death in the middle of the war would destabilise the throne. As a result, Karl's succession was greeted without the usual celebrations that mark the accession of a young and enthusiastic monarch with an even younger and pretty wife. The first sight that most Austrians had of the couple as Emperor and Empress came at Franz Josef's funeral on a freezing and overcast afternoon, eight days after his death. The Emperor wore a general's uniform, accompanied by his son, the Crown Prince Otto, a cherubic four-year-old in a white sailor's outfit, and the Empress, swathed from head to toe in the deepest of mourning and a veil so dark the crowds could barely see her face.

The body was conducted to the imperial vault at the Capuchin monastery, where the procession found its way barred by the monks. The court's Master of Ceremonies approached the door and knocked on it three times with his staff of office. From the other side of the closed door, the prior of the monastery asked who sought to enter the church. The Master of Ceremonies replied that the man seeking burial in the church had been His Imperial and Royal Apostolic Majesty, Franz Josef I, by the Grace of God Emperor of Austria; Apostolic King of Hungary, King of Bohemia, Dalmatia, Croatia, Slavonia, Galicia, Lodomeria, Illyria; King of Jerusalem, *et cetera.*; Archduke of Austria; Grand Duke of Tuscany, Crakow; Duke of Lorraine, Salzburg, Styria, Carinthia, Carniola, the Bukovina; Grand Prince of Transylvania; Margrave of Moravia; Duke of the Upper and Lower Silesia, Modena, Parma, Piacenza, Guastalla, Oswiecin, Zator, Cieszyn, Friuli, Ragusa, Zara; Princely Count of Hapsburg, Tyrol, Kyburg, Gorizia, Gradisca; Prince of Trent, Brixen; Margrave of the Upper and Lower Lusatia, in Istria; Count of Hohenems, Feldkirch, Bregenz, Sonnenberg, *et cetera*; Lord of Trieste, Kotor, the Wendish March; Grand Voivode of the Voivodship of Serbia *et cetera*, *et cetera*. All these titles conjured up seven centuries of empire-building and a throne that stretched back to the Crusades, Lepanto and the Siege of Vienna.

The prior replied, 'We do not know him.' As the mourners waited in the chilly air, the question was repeated and this time the Master of Ceremonies answered that it was the Emperor. Again the answer came, 'We do not know him.' Finally, on the third try, the Master of Ceremonies replied, 'Franz Josef, a mortal and sinful man.' It was a grand piece of religious and political theatre, a staple of imperial funerals for centuries, intended to showcase the Hapsburgs' devotion to the Catholic faith's teaching that all are humbled before the throne of Almighty God, a reminder of the old Catholic dictum: '*Meménto, homo, quia pulvis es, et in púlverem revertéris*' – 'Remember, man, that thou art dust, and to dust thou shalt return.' The prior said, 'Then let him enter,' and the doors at last swung open.[4] The brethren of the monastery stepped out into the square with lit tapers in their hands to flank the coffin as it was brought inside so that Franz Josef could be taken down into the vault to rest between the sarcophagi of his wife and son.

Rumours were already circulating that the new reign would see something of a break from the traditions that had ossified under Franz Josef. The fact that Zita walked behind the old Emperor's coffin upset some of the courtiers, who pointed out that tradition proscribed that at funerals the Empress should appear in procession after the other male members of the imperial family at funerals. Karl overruled them by regally declaring, 'It is I who decide on ceremony.'[5] His determination to command etiquette rather than let it command him struck a very different note to the attitude taken by his predecessor and there were those who believed, rightly, that he might prove equally revolutionary in a political sense.

Karl was a young man of nineteen when his father, Franz Ferdinand's handsome and promiscuous younger brother, succumbed to syphilis at the age of forty-one. An unending tidal wave of speculative nonsense has accused so many royal and political figures of suffering from syphilis that it would be easy to dismiss all such stories as scurrilous idiocy based on the laws of probability, however every now and then, as in the case of Karl I's father, the rumour was true and undeniable, particularly in an era when there was no possibility of hiding the disease's devastating progression.[6] Initially, stories of the 'gorgeous Archduke' and his many lovers seemed to amuse rather than horrify, such as the story in which he was caught one evening preparing to enter a young lady's bedroom wearing nothing but his ornamental sword and a big smile. In the end, however, his bed-hopping became so compulsive that even his uncle the Emperor, who was very fond of him and defended 'handsome Otto' at every turn, began to distance himself. His wife, Maria Josepha of Saxony, tried to shield their children from their father's terrible example and she largely succeeded. Otto contracted the disease sometime around 1900, by which point he and Maria Josepha were essentially leading separate lives. He died in 1906 and the final few years of the disease had been excruciating as well as disfiguring, forcing him to retire almost completely from public life.

The paternal void left by Otto's illness and then by his death was filled by Franz Ferdinand, who took a protective interest in his two young nephews, particularly once the conditions laid upon his own marriage to Sophie Chotek meant that Karl was now second in line to the throne. Karl's closeness to his uncle caused many in the Hungarian parliament to worry that he might share some of Franz Ferdinand's prejudices, most worryingly, from their point of view, the plan to replace the Dual Monarchy with a federal system under which the Magyars would be forced to share parity of esteem not just with the Austrians, but also with the Slavs and Croats. They were right to be worried and so were the Germans: the new Emperor was largely an unknown quantity and despite his service on the front line, there was no guarantee that he would be as committed to maintaining the war for honour's sake as his great-uncle had been. On top of that, there were his close pre-war friendships with his brothers-in-law, two of whom were now serving in the Allied armies.

German distrust of their ally hardened with the publication of Karl's accession manifesto on 22 November. It began by praising Franz Josef's 'wisdom, insight and fatherly care' for the peoples of the empire and promising to continue his legacy, it then moved on to cover equally conventional topics: Karl's trust in the army, his respect for the institution of monarchy, faith in Christianity, a promise to maintain law, order and the execution of justice. A far more unconventional paragraph was the one in which Karl vowed to 'do everything to banish, in the shortest possible time, the horrors and sacrifices of war and to win back for my peoples the sorely-missed blessings of peace'.[7] The wording was as important as it was deliberate. It did not mention the word 'victory', it did not vow to carry the war to the last extremity, instead the Emperor promised to 'do everything' to end the war 'in the shortest possible time'.

Within twenty-four hours of his accession Karl was articulating the antithesis of the justification for unrestricted U-boat activity; he did not want victory at any price. What he wanted was to 'win back for my peoples the sorely-missed blessings of peace'. In doing so, he attracted the dangerous enmity of men like Paul von Hindenburg and his right-hand man, General Erich Ludendorff, a middle-class tactical genius with an impeccable work ethic and decidedly unsavoury racial views, even by the undemanding standards of an age with confidence in Social Darwinism. A virulent nationalist of the kind that had featured in the late Franz Josef's political nightmares, he was no respecter of the old class system if he felt it was being used to shore up wishy-washy ideas of international co-operation. He was a firm believer in the idea of *Lebensraum*, a belief that Germany had a right to expand its territory to the east and expel the communities already living there to create a living space for her own rapidly expanding population. He was also a key proponent of the theory of total war and in the years after Germany's defeat he wrote a book on the subject as well as becoming one of the earliest supporters of Adolf Hitler.

Ludendorff regarded the new Austrian Emperor as more of a target than an ally. With his blessing, a steady stream of propaganda undermining the imperial family's prestige was leaked into the Austro-Hungarian Empire. In 1915, Italy had reneged on her peacetime alliance with Germany and Austria-Hungary and declared war on them in the hope of expanding her territory if the Hapsburg Empire were defeated. This development made it much easier to criticise the new Empress: Zita of Bourbon-Parma had been born in Italy on 9 May 1892, the fourteenth surviving child of Roberto I, Duke of Parma. She was a descendant of King Charles X, the last Bourbon King of France who had been driven into exile during the revolution of 1830. She and her sister Francesca had been educated at a Catholic girls' boarding school on the Isle of Wight and two of her brothers, Sixtus and Xavier, had joined the Belgian army. Austria-Hungary was fighting a war against, among others, Italy, France, the British Empire and Belgium, but it had an empress who had been born in Italy to a French family, educated in England and with relatives in the Belgian military. Like many European princesses, Zita had an international upbringing – she was fluent in German, French, Italian, Spanish, Portuguese (her mother's native language) and English. But in the fevered environment of the First World War, all of this was a liability rather than a strength.

Karl and Zita's marriage was a love match. They had known each other when they were young and became reacquainted in adulthood. Everyone who met her commented that she was charming and Karl was so smitten that when he heard a rumour that the Duke of Madrid had proposed, he left his regiment to pay a hurried visit to Zita's aunt to ask if it were true. She replied that as far as she knew Zita was still unattached, to which Karl replied, 'Well, I had better hurry in that case or she will get engaged to someone else.'[8] Like many young officers, Karl had enjoyed a few youthful flings and the pious Zita was devastated to discover that he had not been a virgin on their wedding night. She rather unfairly blamed his uncle Franz Ferdinand for not keeping him away from immoral women, since the equally religious Archduke had done everything in his power to warn Karl of the dangers of casual sex.

Awkward confessions on their wedding night notwithstanding, the couple shared a commitment to the Catholic faith that bonded them closer together as husband and wife. She was very clever and perhaps more cynical than her husband when it came to politics and especially politicians, having been brought up in a family that had never quite released the ghosts of 1789 or 1830. It was this émigré legacy which sometimes caused Zita to make errors in political judgement and which explained her predilection for slightly absurd conspiracy theories. She felt such a revulsion towards the French republic that she apparently believed its agents had somehow been involved in the murder of the Crown Prince Rudolf back in 1889, clinging to this belief despite the mountain of evidence that showed the young man had committed suicide and the lack of any real motivation for the French wanting to kill him. She was also markedly less enthusiastic about federalism than her husband, who seems to have been quite prepared to go much further than Franz Ferdinand would ever have contemplated in allowing, if absolutely necessary, some of the smaller regions of the Hapsburg Empire to become semi-autonomous republics if they would agree to regroup into a system that sounds very similar to the commonwealth that was created to ease the dissolution of the British Empire after 1949. It was a radical solution, far more so than anything hitherto contemplated, and Zita, who had been brought up with the attitude that one should fight the legacy of the French Revolution until hell froze over and once that happened take the battle on to the ice, does not seem to have been wildly enthusiastic about any dilution of monarchical authority.

On the very day his manifesto was published, Karl's dreams of far-reaching reform suffered a serious setback. At eleven o'clock in the morning, he received a visit from the Prime Minister of Hungary, Count István Tisza, an Anglophile aristocrat who had studied as an undergraduate in Berlin then gone on to receive his doctorate in political science at Oxford. Tisza possessed that rarest of combinations: great intellect matched with savvy political awareness. He was a monarchist but also a Hungarian patriot who arrived in Vienna determined to prevent his new king from doing anything that might weaken or irrevocably alter the Dual Monarchy established in 1867. The audience was ostensibly to talk about Karl and Zita's coronation as King and Queen in Hungary – the Hungarian monarchy and its constitution still operated with a near-medieval regard for the ritual of the coronation and without the ceremony by which Saint Stephen's Crown was placed upon his head, few Hungarians would regard anyone as their lawful sovereign, even if he had inherited the title without dispute as Karl had. What they did in Austria was their business, but in Hungary they played by their own ancient and unique national rules.

Count Tisza cleverly used discussions about the ceremony in Budapest to outmanoeuvre Karl. By stressing the weakness of Karl's authority in Hungary without a coronation, Tisza was able to propose a crowning at the first available date, 30 December, far too soon for Karl to attempt any significant constitutional changes, and of course at the coronation he would be required to pledge an oath that would compel the King 'not [to] alienate the boundaries of Hungary and her associated countries, nor anything belonging to those countries under any title whatsoever'.[9] Hungary's position within the empire could not be easily changed once Karl was crowned and sworn in, one of the reasons why Franz Ferdinand had vowed to postpone a coronation in Budapest for as long as possible so that he could find a way to implement his changes before he was bound by oath from doing so. With the war raging and Hungarians making up such a large part of the armies while its fields served as grain basket to the empire, Karl had to concede to Tisza's suggestion of a coronation on 30 December. All his advisers, even those strongly supportive of his plans for reform, agreed with him that he had to go to Budapest at the first available opportunity and swear what was asked of him.

That coronation, the last of the old Hapsburg Empire, saw displays of pageantry and hope. One young aristocrat wrote of the splendid procession from Castle Hill in Buda to the Mathias Church: 'Like a dark serpent, the carriages swept up the hill. For fifty years, the Hungarian nobles had longed for their sovereign to give them, and the capital, the glamour of royalty, of court life with its celebrations, of titles and decorations ... Now there was hope that all this would change ... that the peace-loving young King and Queen would have the courage to resist the German Kaiser and stop useless bloodshed.'[10]

Zita's brother-in-law, Tsar Ferdinand of Bulgaria, was one of the few fellow royals who could attend the festivities and he later remarked that they were among the most splendid and beautiful he had ever seen. The coronation lasted for three hours, during which time Karl took the sword of Saint Stephen and slashed it into the air as a symbol of the king's role in defending Hungary from enemies in all directions. He was anointed and crowned by the Cardinal Archbishop of Budapest, who proclaimed him King Carol IV of Hungary. Zita, wearing a gown of white brocade with roses embroidered in gold (she had to avoid the heraldic fleur-de-lys of her French family due to the war), stepped forward to have Saint Stephen's Crown briefly touch her right shoulder before a more modern consort's crown of diamonds and rubies was placed on her head, then Cardinal Archbishop Csernoch escorted her to sit next to her husband. A banquet followed, after which Karl, Zita and their eldest son returned by train to Vienna. Given the war, they had decided that to host the customary balls and dances would be tasteless. The aristocracy did not share their scruples and Budapest society danced the night away, celebrating what they saw as a grand affirmation of Hungarian statehood.

Back in Vienna, Zita began to feel the pressure of the whispering campaign against her. Karl's youth and lack of experience gave him the appearance of a political dilettante, while her composure and confidence seemed more like the mark of a consummate intriguer than a poised queen-empress. Feelings against 'the Italian Schemer' heightened when it was reported that she would often sit in on her husband's audiences with his ministers and his military briefings. She seemed to be doing nothing more innocuous than carrying on with her sewing, but even so political audiences were not traditionally for royal consorts. To keep her informed of the progress of the war, Karl ordered that she could receive her own daily report from military attachés about developments at the front. This in turn led to a rumour that it was Zita, not Karl, who was running the war effort. Germany's wartime ambassador in Vienna, Count Otto Wedel, sent regular reports on the Empress's activity to Berlin, but he did not seem to have many of his compatriots' antipathy towards her; he viewed her with clinical detachment. He told Ludendorff that 'the German style is foreign to [her] and difficult to comprehend ... Despite her personal charm and friendliness, the popularity of the empress is on the wane. People do not entirely trust the Italian and her brood of relatives.'[11]

Zita's actual influence is difficult to gauge because she was both subtle and graceful, usually hiding her opinions more cleverly than her German or Russian counterparts, except in rare moments of high temper. Prior to the Sixtus Affair, there is only one recorded incident of the Empress attempting to influence her husband directly on the issue of managing the war and it was on the treatment of captured enemy prisoners. After she had finished speaking, Karl told her, 'You must leave such things to me, my dear. The truth is that I am the soldier, and you are not.'[12] However, if Zita was not allowed any say in how the war was run, she soon came to have an enormous role in deciding how it should end. Almost from the beginning of her husband's reign, the Empress cultivated the idea that it would be permissible to abandon Germany in order to achieve it. Her objections to the conflict were humanitarian, based on what she had seen in her visits to the hospitals and heard from those who had served at the front; political, because she was concerned about how the supremacy of Germany would be exercised if they won and what the fate of the monarchical system in Austria would be if they lost; and moral, because she believed it was a sin for so many lives to be wasted. What she did in 1917 was nothing short of treason in the eyes of many of her contemporaries. She saw it as her duty to influence her husband to save the Hapsburg monarchy by leaving Germany to face the war alone.

7

The Assassination of Grigori Rasputin

'I cannot and won't believe that he has been killed'

The Grand Duchess Anastasia of Russia turned fifteen in the summer of 1916 and although she and the sister closest to her in age, seventeen-year-old Maria, were still considered too young to work in the Tsarskoe Selo hospital with their elder sisters, the Tsarina encouraged them to visit the soldiers. This arrangement suited the naturally ebullient Anastasia perfectly. She was the most outgoing of Nicholas II's children, with a talent for mimicry, an irrepressible sense of humour and a fascination with other people. Her high spirits and insistence on getting her own way prompted her cousin Nina to hate any playtime spent in her company, but adolescence had brought a new maturity and Anastasia was in her element at the hospital, making the soldiers laugh, playing cards with them and even sneaking outside with some of the nurses she befriended to smoke an illicit cigarette.

The grand duchesses' Irish nanny believed that Maria, the Tsar's third daughter, was 'born good, I often think, with the very smallest trace of original sin possible'.[1] Once, when she miserably confessed to having pinched an extra biscuit from the dinner table, the Tsar laughed and said he was relieved to see some mild naughtiness in her, otherwise she would soon have sprouted wings. Unlike her sisters, particularly Tatiana and Anastasia, who looked far more like their mother's English and German relatives, Maria was the sibling generally considered to have the most typically Russian appearance. Her best features were her eyes, so big that they were often nicknamed 'Maria's saucers'. By 1916, Maria was very conscious of her recent weight gain, which her mother noticed despairingly and her sisters gleefully, without perhaps fully realising how much their teasing might occasionally annoy her. She also struggled with a natural sense of middle-child isolation, for although their mother liked to group the girls into 'the Big Pair' (Olga and Tatiana) and 'the Little Pair' (Maria and Anastasia), in reality Anastasia often seemed closer to their little brother Alexei. Sometimes upset at what she saw as her siblings' closeness to each other rather than to her and without a natural ally in a large family, Maria developed as the most sensitive of the Romanov children and the most prone to tears.

Had the war and her mother's reticence not intervened, Maria should have made her debut into society in 1915. She instead made her first entrance at a dinner held in honour of Romania coming into the war on the Allied side, at which Baroness Buxhoeveden thought she looked 'very pretty in her pale blue dress', which had very much been a last minute job because the evening before Tatiana had realised, to her horror, that Maria did not fit into any of her old ball gowns that she had been planning to borrow.[2] The Grand Duchess's ceremonial entrance was rather spoiled by the servants' overzealous waxing of the parquet floor. She slipped, toppled over and sat on the ground, laughing hysterically at her own embarrassment. Her ability to laugh at herself smoothed over any awkwardness caused by the fall, although Tatiana felt she laughed too hard for too long and should have popped back on to her feet sooner. With the Empress frowning on socialising even more than usual because of the war, Maria spent most of her days at the hospital with Anastasia, where her kindness and goodness won her many friends among the convalescents.

Alexei was gone for much of 1916. Accompanied by their French tutor, the Swiss-born Pierre Gilliard, he left Tsarskoe Selo on the imperial train to join his father to *Stavka*, a move the Empress supported as essential training for his future vocation as Emperor, but the separation wreaked havoc with her nerves. Her surviving letters to Nicholas are full of pieces of advice to stop the excitable boy from running on the train, taking any undue risks with his safety or playing too boisterously. Alexei wrote back happily that he had found a stray cat at military headquarters, named her Zubrovka and planned to bring her back to Tsarskoe Selo on his next trip home. Alexei slept on a camp bed next to his father's and at night after they had said their prayers together the Emperor would read aloud letters from Alexandra and the girls. The Tsarevich was developing into a very handsome young man, which belied his poor health; he had the perfect blend of his parents' respective good looks, and photographs from the time show a growth spurt to a developing build that was thin but athletic, like most of the Romanov men. His growing strength worried his mother, who warned Nicholas 'he is so strong and forgets that he must be careful'.[3] Like Anastasia, youthful spells of bad behaviour, in Alexei's case mostly acts of rebellion against the Tsarina's constant supervision, had evaporated with the onset of adolescence. He began to replicate his father's exquisite manners and the British military attaché to *Stavka*, Major-General Sir John Hanbury-Williams, wrote that the Tsarevich 'had excellent manners and spoke various languages well and clearly'.[4]

One of the greatest misconceptions about Nicholas II was that he was always dominated by his wife. A dynamic that occurs at one stage of a relationship does not necessarily show that it was ever thus. This is especially true in the case of Nicholas and Alexandra. The Tsar's seeming gentleness, his politesse and the lengths he would go to in order to avoid awkward scenes or to avoid embarrassing anybody made him seem like weak putty in the hands of his assertive Anglo-German wife, who was forthright to the point of brazen when attacked. The scandal of Alexandra and Rasputin and the role they both played in the disintegration of the Russian monarchy has given rise to a version of her marriage in which she was always in charge and Nicholas kowtowed to her wishes.

In fact, prior to the First World War, Alexandra had almost no political influence. Nicholas allowed her none and deliberately kept her in ignorance of policies which he felt she either would not understand or would be upset by. Many times before 1915, her ladies-in-waiting were surprised 'to find that she remained in absolute ignorance as to what was taking place'.[5] The collapse of Alexandra's health after her son's diagnosis of haemophilia worried Nicholas, who was prepared to do anything Alexandra wanted in terms of their schedule and daily routine to avoid causing her any more discomfort – hence his own retirement from the Saint Petersburg social scene, despite the fact that as a young man he had enjoyed it immensely, his decision to avoid inviting relatives to Tsarskoe Selo whom he knew aggravated Alexandra, again despite his own sociable nature and previously close relationship to the other Romanovs, and his constant organisation of longer and longer trips on the family's yacht or to the Crimea, where she seemed to be in better spirits.

Domestic concern in a husband for his wife did not, at least until 1915, translate into an Emperor's political dependence on his consort. He had ignored Alexandra's opposition to the October Manifesto in 1905, she had not been consulted in any of the political manoeuvres that took place in 1906 or 1907, he had continued to promote and support Peter Stolypin despite her dislike of him and nowhere was his independence of his wife more apparent than in how he handled the issue of Grigori Rasputin.

Thanks to the reports set on his desk by the Okhrana, the empire's secret police service, Nicholas knew of Rasputin's heavy drinking and sexual shenanigans. After his gruesome murder, Rasputin's libido was transformed by hearsay into one of Zeus-like proportions, but the truth was that he was an essentially a simple man with a weakness for cheap Madeira wine and easy women. The Empress's favour towards a simple *moujik* from Siberia had gone to Rasputin's head and it made him behave unwisely, particularly when he was in his cups. Nicholas shielded Alexandra from the worst of the reports, firstly because he knew how much Rasputin's apparent ability to stop their son's bleeding meant to her and secondly because she did not believe any of it even when he did tell her. On several occasions when Rasputin's behaviour had been particularly poor or his lies outrageous and uttered in public, Nicholas banished him from Saint Petersburg to teach him a lesson, overriding Alexandra's pleas that everything uttered against Rasputin were smutty deceptions from people whose own minds were obviously in the gutter or who were jealous of him. One memorable incident that particularly enraged the Tsar occurred when Rasputin got spectacularly drunk at a racy Moscow night club, clambered on to the table, pulled down his trousers, thrust his penis in the general direction of the other patrons and informed them that he was allowed to appear like that at the palace all the time.

It was Rasputin's drunken bombast that proved to be his undoing, because his reckless behaviour in the city led inevitably to speculation about the nature of his relationship with the Empress, particularly in the absence of any information about Alexei's haemophilia. It was a shame, because tempering the image of him as a lecherous buffoon is the fact that Rasputin's advice to the Romanovs was not uniformly moronic. He was against the war because he knew that the bulk of the burden would fall on the empire's peasants and, unusually for so many Russians at the time, he was also uncomfortable with his country's treatment of its Jewish people; in this his views accorded with Alexandra's, who had grown up with her grandmother's favourite prime minister being a Jewish convert and many of her uncle Edward VII's closest friends being Jewish businessmen or recently ennobled peers. However, for every one piece of good advice, there were at least ten bad, and with Nicholas away at the front and Alexandra assuming a political role for the first time in her husband's reign, more attention turned to Rasputin, her right-hand man, at the very time when he seemed to be drinking more than ever, behaving inappropriately and struggling against the newfound hostile interest in his private life.

Alexandra's letters to Nicholas on the front were published shortly after the Revolution and they confirmed every negative impression of her – she comes across as a harpy, a domineering termagant endlessly nagging her pathetic and henpecked husband. The truth was more complex. Alexandra's appearance of strength was essentially a front. It was a performance she mounted to help her husband at a time when his own behaviour was beginning to worry her. Alexandra was not a well woman by 1916. No matter how invigorating she found it or how much good she was doing by being there, the hospital work was exhausting her as Nicholas feared it would. Her sciatica had returned with a vengeance, her heartbeat and her sleeping patterns were both irregular and she often felt dizzy. Rasputin's soothing words of comfort, his homespun spirituality which seemed to her to be so close to that of the apostles in the New Testament and his assurance that God was watching over her were exactly what she wanted to hear. Rasputin was steadying her so that she could steady Nicholas and she badly needed to do so because by 1916 her husband was showing signs of a full and imminent nervous breakdown.

Initially, Nicholas's presence at *Stavka* and his appointment of General Alekseev as the new Chief of Staff had paid dividend. The year after his arrival was the most successful of the Russian war effort: Kiev was saved from the Germans, supply lines were improved and successful counter-attacks were launched on the German, Bulgarian and Austro-Hungarian armies. However, even at this stage Nicholas complained of chest pains in his letters home, claiming that he had first felt them when he heard the news of the defeat at Tannenburg: 'I am beginning to feel my old heart. The first time it was in August of last year, after the Samsonov catastrophe [a reference to General Alexander Samsonov, the Russians' commanding general at the Battle of Tannenburg, who committed suicide after the shame and scale of the defeat], and again now – it feels so heavy in the left side when I breathe.'[6] The defeats and the slaughter pained him, the fact that there was no viable way out of the war was even worse. Mikhail Rodzianko, an enormous liberal politician who served as the President of the Duma and who had thus earned the uncharitable and unimaginative nickname of 'Fat Rodzianko' in the Tsarina's correspondence, arrived for an audience with the Tsar at *Stavka* and noticed a further deterioration: 'In comparison with last year his tone has changed and he has become less self-confident.'[7] A few months later, another of the Tsar's guests thought he had 'greatly aged and his cheeks were sunken. Sitting almost opposite His Majesty and not taking my eyes from him, I could not but pay attention to his terrible nervousness, which had never existed before. It was evident that the Emperor's spirit was troubled and that it was difficult for him to hide his agitation successfully from his entourage.'[8] His mother was shocked at how quiet he had become and how much he had aged.[9] At times, the Tsar appeared distracted during ministerial meetings, his hands nervously clutching a religious icon, and his lack of focus, noticeable in someone usually so polite, was commented upon by several ministers, including those in charge of agriculture and finance, the former being surprised when Nicholas 'kept on interrupting me with questions that were not related to the business side of my official journey but rather everyday trivia' and the latter unsettled by 'the apathetic attitude of the Emperor'.[10]

Eventually, Nicholas's courtiers tried to step in. Count Paul Benckendorff, the Grand Marshal of the imperial court, wrote a sharply worded letter to Dr Evgeny Botkin, the Tsar's personal physician. 'He can't continue this way much longer. His Majesty is a changed man. It is very wrong of him to attempt the impossible. He is no longer seriously interested in anything. Of late, he has become quite apathetic. He goes through his daily routine like an automaton, paying more attention to the hour set for his meals or his walk in the garden, than to affairs of state. One can't rule an empire and command an army in the field in this manner. If he doesn't realise it in time, something catastrophic is bound to happen.'[11]

Almost all the observers who knew the Tsar agreed with Benckendorff's assessment that Nicholas was 'a changed man'. The Emperor who had been prepared to sanction firm and decisive action to secure the throne in 1906 and 1907 and who had even signed one of the most momentous constitutional documents in Russian history, however unhappily, had been replaced by a man who seemed to be functioning like a robot, even to his closest courtiers and servants. He was trying to hide his mental ill health from them, but it was impossible. In 1905, he told his mother that he was prepared to bite the bullet, to 'cross oneself and give what everyone was asking for', but by 1916 he could barely get through a ministerial briefing without wandering off topic. Exhausted, heartbroken at the casualty figures, sincerely surprised at the depth of his wife's unpopularity and tormented, as he saw it, by squabbling politicians, a disloyal, querulous and unpatriotic parliament and a home front beset by internal divisions, all of which ought to be suppressed in times of war, Nicholas II's preternatural calm and capacity for work gave way to a morose and nervous hysteria, insomnia and a kind of pathological lethargy.

To us, it bears all the hallmarks of the impenetrable haze and misery caused by depression. To his opponents, it was how he was to be remembered, with this depression becoming the alpha and omega of Nicholas II's political reputation. Leon Trotsky gleefully remarked that Nicholas II had not been mentally equipped to run a village post office, let alone an empire.

Another problem which made 1916 different to 1905 was whom Nicholas had access to. For the first decade of his reign, Nicholas had been close to his mother and his four paternal uncles whose advice, while certainly not always perfect by any stretch of the imagination, had at least been honestly given and allowed the Emperor access to a variety of opinions from people he trusted. During that earlier crisis of the monarchy in 1905 and 1906, the advice and steadying presence of the Dowager Empress in particular had proved invaluable. Since then all the years of seclusion at Tsarskoe Selo, the missed parties, the cancelled balls, the declined invitations, the unceasing romanticisation of the rural peasantry as the 'real' Russia and the frigid animosity between the Empress and the denizens of Petersburg society had all combined to produce a profound political isolation.

Alexandra's devotion to Rasputin and her blinkered refusal to tolerate anyone who so much as breathed a whisper of a complaint against him infuriated or distressed many of her in-laws. At Christmas of 1915, Alexandra did not send Christmas presents to her mother-in-law or to any of the other prominent members of the imperial family.[12] The socialite and old friend of the Romanovs, Princess Zenaida Yussopov, was banished from the Empress's presence when she attempted to bring Rasputin up in conversation. When she kept speaking, the Empress rang for a servant and said, 'I hope never to see you again!'[13] The Princess returned home weeping to her son, 'She drove me away like a dog! Poor Nicky, poor Russia!'[14] By 1916, ambassadors in Petrograd heard reports that Nicholas's cousin the Grand Duke Cyril and his mother the Grand Duchess Maria Pavlovna, 'the grandest of the grand duchesses', were openly expressing their hope that Nicholas would abdicate and Alexandra could be banished to internal exile in a convent, like troublesome tsarinas in centuries gone by. A furious row that was never healed erupted between the Empress and her sister Ella when the latter, now living as a nun since the death of her husband, broached the subject of the *moujik*. When Nicholas's youngest and favourite uncle, the Grand Duke Paul, tried to lobby for better relations with the Duma and the dismissal of Rasputin, Nicholas became agitated and Alexandra flew into a rage. When she discovered that her mother-in-law, who openly detested Rasputin, was paying one of her rare visits to *Stavka* to actually spend some time with her son, the Tsarina fired off a letter to Nicholas: 'When you see poor Motherdear, you must rather sharply tell her how pained you are, that she listens to slander and does not stop it, as it makes mischief and others would be delighted, I am sure ...'[15]

The two empresses had never been close – Marie wanted Nicholas to marry the Count of Paris's daughter and she had caused a minor scandal when she tried to hold on to the imperial jewels that should have gone to Alexandra after her wedding. She was also one of the leaders of Petersburg society and believed strongly that only by remaining close to the country's elite and listening to its opinions, often casually and sincerely expressed at social occasions, could a monarch remain connected to the most powerful people in his empire. A strained relationship had eventually given way to one of thinly veiled animosity, limiting Marie's access to her son and reducing her political influence. In private conversations with Nicholas's sister Xenia, Marie expressed a half-sincere belief that Alexandra must have gone mad. She bewailed her daughter-in-law's actions and Rasputin's prominence to anyone who would listen, but nothing changed and in the summer of 1916 she gave up completely and left the capital to set up residence 800 miles away at the Mariyinsky Palace in Kiev.

The result of this isolation from his peers meant that Nicholas's sole source of sustained advice from a person he trusted was Alexandra. Working herself up into a fever of self-righteous anger against what she chose to see as politicians' plots to weaken the monarchy, Alexandra's letters were full of woefully inept advice. Although Nicholas was firm and even irritable when she passed on 'Our Friend's' views on military matters, he was so preoccupied with what was going on at the front that he was content to listen to the Empress's assessment of developments at home. She had no political experience and she was compulsively honest to the point of brutal rudeness with the result that she alienated nearly everyone she came into contact with. Anyone who criticised Rasputin attracted the Regent's ire; very early on, she scored dismissals for four of her high-ranking opponents – a state councillor, the Procurator of the Holy Synod (the ministry for the Orthodox Church) and the ministers of the interior and agriculture. She then secured another damaging coup when she visited Nicholas at the front and persuaded him to fire Sergei Sazonov, the Foreign Minister, after he suggested in cabinet that once the war was over Russia might have to consider granting independence to Poland. Interpreting this as an attempt to dismember the monarchy, Alexandra turned against him. When Nicholas wanted to relieve the Prime Minister, Prince Ivan Goremykin, on account of his wish to retire in his old age, Alexandra suggested Boris Stürmer, a deeply unpopular bureaucrat who had won Rasputin's friendship ('which is a great thing'), and who had, like her, a German-sounding surname, the significance of which Alexandra seemed blithely unaware of.[16] The French ambassador described Stürmer as a 'third-rate intellectual, mean spirit, low character, doubtful honesty, no expertise and no idea of State business.'[17] The Tsar, 1,500 miles away, believed his wife's glowing assessment of Stürmer's character and he became Prime Minister.

The Duma protested vociferously at the appointment, and speeches made on the floor of its meeting place at the Tauride Palace were openly critical of the Tsarina. Their anger had no immediate outcome other than to stiffen Alexandra's resolve to press ahead and spare her husband from the tribulation of having to deal with them. She suggested Alexander Protopopov as the new Minister of the Interior; it was not quite as unpopular a choice as Stürmer. At sixty-four, Protopopov was the Vice President of the Duma, he was more centrist in his political views than Stürmer and he had no clear ties to the court. He also enjoyed a sterling reputation internationally and he was known to be strongly supportive of the Allied war effort. He had represented the Duma in visits to Russia's allies in London, Paris and Rome earlier in the year, where he was described as 'a good orator and conversationalist, and anything but a stupid man ... the King of England expressed his joy that Russia possessed such outstanding people'.[18] Alexandra first met him in the summer of that year and she was immediately taken with him, unusually so for a man who was rumoured to be a liberal and who had served in the Duma for years. She described him as 'a man whom I liked very much' in her letters to Nicholas, who agreed with her take on his personality but seemed reluctant to give him such a prestigious ministerial post. 'He is a good, honest man,' he wrote, 'but he jumps from one idea to another and cannot make up his mind on anything ... it is risky to leave the Ministry of Internal Affairs in the hands of such a man in these times.'[19] Protopovov's colleagues in the cabinet agreed with the Tsar. Peter Bark, the Minister of Finance, conceded that 'One must do him justice as regards one talent – he was extremely eloquent and could talk without end ... It was impossible to get angry with him. He was in the highest degree a well-educated person, attentive, courteous, winning sympathy by his kind treatment of people,' but 'his explanation and judgements were unusually superficial, he enjoyed no authority and seemed a pitiful figure because of his lack of competence or knowledge.'[20] Worn down by Alexandra's persistence and perhaps swayed by the glowing reports of Protopovov's success with the Allies, Nicholas gave in and the Duma was in a ferment. As much as many of them liked the charming Protopopov on a personal level, he was a disastrous choice for the portfolio and they blamed the Tsarina for making it happen.

In the sixteen months of Alexandra's political career, Russia had four different prime ministers, five ministers of the interior, three ministers of war, four ministers for agriculture, two procurators of the Holy Synod and two foreign ministers. Nicholas had to intervene to fire men like Stürmer when he was caught trying to withdraw 5 million roubles from the Treasury without offering an explanation of where it was going. Even monarchist deputies in the Duma who had previously extolled loyalty to the throne unto death felt compelled to speak out against the regency. Insisting that their fealty to the Emperor remained undiluted and anxious lest any of their words be interpreted as a criticism of the dynasty itself, the politicians of the Right focussed mainly on Rasputin – the Empress's malign *éminence grise*, the shadowy power behind the throne who was corrupting the court from within. Rasputin was the tumour in the body politic. Remove him and the empire's health would recover.

One such speech was given at the Tauride on 20 November 1916 by Vladimir Purishkevich, of whom the only thing further to the right was the wall behind him. Purishkevich was one of the more popular monarchist politicians in the Duma, not least because of his extrovert personality and flamboyant speeches. If they had expected the usual paeans of love and devotion to Tsar and Mother Russia, his fellow delegates must have been surprised when for two extraordinary hours Purishkevich launched into a tirade that excoriated the current government for debasing the sacred institution of the monarchy. 'It requires only the recommendation of Rasputin to raise the most abject citizen to high office,' he thundered. Sitting near the French ambassador in the visitors' gallery, Prince Felix Yussopov, a slim and effeminate young man with high cheekbones and an arresting face, watched enraptured as Purishkevich's words spoke straight to his heart. He had already made up his mind to do something for his country and Purishkevich's words convinced him that his intentions were justified. To save the Russian Empire, he would have to murder Grigori Rasputin.

On the surface of things, Felix Yussopov was an unlikely assassin. One acquaintance wrote of how people were usually 'very much taken with both his external appearance, which radiated inexpressible elegance and breeding, and particularly with his inner self-possession'.[21] Heir to a family fortune so vast that it was said to eclipse the Romanovs', the vases in some of his family's many homes were filled with jewels rather than flowers and for his beloved mother's birthday, he bought her favourite mountain. As a teenager, he had experimented with cross-dressing, a field in which he was apparently so convincing that at a party in Paris he caught the eye of the aging King Edward VII, a celebrated bon vivant who thought he had espied an especially beautiful young woman. Felix beat a hasty retreat and soon gave up his fad for ladies' dresses and his mother's jewels. He matriculated to University College at Oxford, where he spent the years between 1909 and 1912 living the life of a student that sounds now to have had more than a touch of *Brideshead Revisited*. He hosted champagne-fuelled parties in his rooms and evaded the college curfew by weaving together a long rope to pull fellow undergraduates up the walls and into his room. Things took rather an awkward turn when he accidentally hoisted up a policeman one night and had to explain his behaviour to the provost, but overall they were happy years for Felix, 'the happiest of my youth,' in his own words, and he developed a talent for polo and cricket.[22] Like Evelyn Waugh, Felix's Oxford days were a chance for youthful exploration and he had numerous affairs with fellow students. All the evidence points to him having been a homosexual, there can be little doubt of that and his most important love affair took place when he came back to Russia after graduation.[23]

Felix's memoirs capture something of his early infatuation with Nicholas II's much younger cousin, the Grand Duke Dmitri. Felix thought he was 'extremely attractive: tall, elegant, well-bred, with deep, thoughtful eyes, he recalled the portraits of his ancestors. He was all impulses and contradictions; he was both romantic and mystical, and his mind was far from shallow. At the same time, he was very gay and always ready for the wildest escapades. His charm won the hearts of all ...'[24] Later in life, Dmitri's sexual partners included Coco Chanel, whose early business ventures he helped to finance, but conversations from Russian émigrés who knew the pair well and comments made in Felix's own letters and memoirs confirm that members of the imperial family and Felix's circle in Saint Petersburg knew that at some point in 1912 and possibly in 1913, Felix and the Grand Duke were romantically involved with one another. In letters to her husband, Alexandra, who was fond of Dmitri and felt protective over him after his mother's death in childbed in 1891, noted archly that when he was in Saint Petersburg with his regiment he 'did not go out in the ladies' companies – but out of sight, [he] gets into other hands.'[25] Rumours increasingly seemed to link Dmitri to Felix, whom Alexandra already distrusted because of his reputation for extravagance in all areas of his life. 'The Tsar and Tsarina, who were aware of the scandalous rumours concerning my mode of living, disapproved of our friendship,' Felix wrote later. 'They ended up forbidding the Grand Duke to see me, and I myself became the object of the most unpleasant supervision.'[26] Felix's modern biographer Greg King has suggested that the affair actually continued for quite some time after that and it may indeed only have ended at Felix's instigation, rather than Dmitri's.[27]

In 1914, Felix's elder brother was killed in a duel and the tragedy of his death made Felix the heir to one of the oldest and most prestigious names in the Russian aristocracy. Pressure mounted on him to find a wife and Felix apparently decided to put his homosexuality behind him, ending the affair with Dmitri. He seemed to have acquired a predilection for Romanovs and transferred his affections to the Tsar's only niece, the beautiful and innocent Princess Irina. He was out riding one afternoon when he saw her sitting next to her mother, the Grand Duchess Xenia, in their carriage. He spoke to the women briefly and later claimed to be smitten. With his ancestry and wealth, Xenia thought he was a very attractive candidate for her daughter's hand and Irina seemed entranced by Felix's obsessive interest in her. However, somebody, perhaps the Tsar himself, tipped off Irina's father, the Grand Duke Alexander, about Felix's love life. At the same time, Dmitri suddenly suggested that he wanted to marry Irina himself. At the time, Dmitri's interest in Irina surprised many people, but whether it was because he wanted to stop the wedding for Irina or for Felix is impossible to say.

Alexander called on Felix with a few friends to discuss, man to man, the rumours about his private life. Felix was perfectly candid. He admitted that he had been a homosexual but claimed he had given it up because he wanted to marry Irina. Alexander, perhaps unsurprisingly, was not entirely convinced that this was enough of a surety for either his daughter's future happiness or Felix's. But Felix and his mother had a trump card in her friendship with the Romanov matriarch the Dowager Empress Marie, who invited the couple to join her for lunch while she was holidaying in Copenhagen. The prospective bridegroom behaved wonderfully and the Dowager Empress was thoroughly charmed. Although she too had heard some whispers about Felix's romantic escapades, she believed him when he said he had fallen in love with her granddaughter. After lunch, she turned her radiant smile on him and said, 'I will do what I can for your happiness.'[28] On 22 February 1914, the couple were married at the Dowager Empress's residence in Saint Petersburg. Irina wore a white satin gown with a long train and an exquisite lace veil, said to have belonged to Marie Antoinette. Then it was off on their honeymoon to meet with trouble in Berlin before they were rescued by the entreaties of the Crown Princess Cecilia and the Spanish embassy.

The appearance of Marie Antoinette's veil at his wedding would have pleased Felix greatly. Today, photographs of Audrey Hepburn or Marilyn Monroe are ubiquitous in many bedrooms across Europe, Britain and America. These roles, for better or worse, as chosen icons of modern femininity were filled in the nineteenth and early twentieth centuries by the spectral figures of Lady Jane Grey, very much as Delaroche imagined her, Mary, Queen of Scots, and Marie Antoinette. A small industry lionising Marie Antoinette as the most sublime symbol of wronged womanhood, who had maintained her ladylike demeanour even as she was harried so cruelly to her death, touched Victorian sensibilities. A large portrait of the unhappy Queen hung over Alexandra's desk at Tsarskoe Selo and in the Moika Palace, one of several homes owned by the Yussopovs in the capital, there was another portrait of her, joined by a matching rendering of her husband, King Louis XVI. They were there at the command of Felix and every day he would arrange fresh bouquets of flowers beneath their images to commemorate their martyrdom during the French Revolution.

This veneration of the fallen King and Queen of pre-revolutionary France hinted at another side of Felix, for he was a fascinating mixture of contradictions, more so even than most people. The acclaimed ballerina Anna Pavlova, who was a close friend, believed that Felix always had 'God in one eye and the Devil in the other'.[29] He was a sincere, even a fanatical, monarchist who believed completely in monarchy as the only civilised and unifying force of government. His political beliefs were matched by his religious fervour – he had a particular devotion to veneration of the Virgin Mary and at one point, during a period of religious ecstasy brought on after visits to the poorest slums in Moscow and Saint Petersburg, his family had to talk him out of giving most of their money away to charity. Even the altruistic Tsarina thought he was behaving immoderately and pointed out that he would do more good by distributing money wisely and in smaller packages to the right charities, rather than just firing it out indiscriminately.

It was in 1916 that this side of Felix, that of the Christian and monarchist zealot, became the dominant force in his life. The

1. (*Previous page*) Emperor Franz Josef, who ruled over the Hapsburg Empire from 1848 to 1916, with Karl and Zita's son, the future Crown Prince Otto.

2. (*This page*) 'Almost inhumanly slender': Franz Josef's wife, Elisabeth of Bavaria. Considered one of the great beauties of the nineteenth century in her youth, the Empress's murder by an Italian anarchist in 1898 was one of many bereavements to befall the Emperor in old age.

3. The Schönbrunn Palace in Vienna, where the Austrian monarchy was signed out of existence in November 1918.

4. The Archduke Franz Ferdinand and Sophie, Duchess of Hohenburg with their three children, Sophie, Maximilian and Ernest.

5. (*Left*) The Emperor attends the wedding of his grand-nephew, the Archduke Karl, to Princess Zita of Bourbon-Parma in 1911.

6. (*Below left*) 'By no means a fool, and ready to face his end as bravely as his ancestress, Marie Antoinette': Franz Josef's successor, the Emperor Karl, who acceded to the throne at the age of twenty-nine.

7. (*Below right*) 'One of the three great royal women of the war': Karl's wife, the Empress Zita, was a devout Catholic who caused a crisis with her attempts to secretly end the war.

8. (*Right*) The Emperor arrives at the front to visit troops during the war.

9. (*Below left*) The 'greatness of ancient times lay far beyond him': Karl I's Foreign Minister, Count Ottokar von Czernin, who resigned in 1918.

10. (*Below right*) 'The parvenu across the Sea.' The American President Woodrow Wilson, whose insistence that Europe would be better off without the monarchies helped seal the fate of the Austrian and German empires.

16. General Paul von Hindenburg (left) and General Erich Ludendorff (right) discuss strategy with the Kaiser. The photo was staged; throughout the war, the two generals lobbied to make the army the most powerful force in German politics, even at the Kaiser's expense.

17. 'To torpedo huge passenger ships full of women and children was a barbarous brutality without parallel, with which we will bring upon us the hatred and the poisonous rage of the entire world.' The sinking of the British passenger ship *Lusitania* by a German submarine in 1915 prompted Wilhelm to make one of his last successful interventions in government.

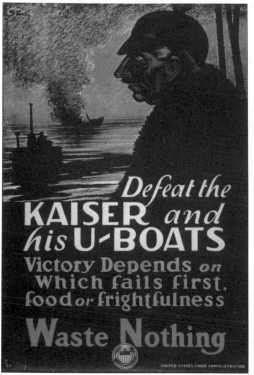

18. (*Above left*) After the *Lusitania*, Wilhelm II regularly featured in British and American propaganda as the malignant 'Kaiser Bill'.

19. (*Above right*) Wilhelm and Augusta Victoria's youngest son, Prince Joachim, who committed suicide in 1920.

20. (*Below right*) The elderly Kaiser in exile in Holland, where he spent the last twenty-three years of his life. He is accompanied by one of his beloved dachshunds.

21. (*Top left*) Nicholas II, Emperor and Autocrat of all the Russias from 1894 to 1917.

22. (*Top right*) Nicholas's most brilliant adviser, Peter Stolypin, Russia's Prime Minister from 1906 until his assassination by an anti-monarchist radical in 1911. The Dowager Empress described his murder as 'horrible and scandalous'.

23. (*Above*) The imperial family's private yacht, the *Standart*. Nicholas II was on board when he heard the news of Franz Ferdinand's death in Sarajevo.

24. (*Right*) Nicholas II's controversial but devoted wife, the Empress Alexandra, with their haemophiliac son, the Tsarevich Alexei. Caring for and worrying about Alexei destroyed Alexandra's health.

25. (*Below*) The Russian imperial family – standing, from left to right, the grand duchesses Olga and Tatiana. Seated, from left to right, the Grand Duchess Maria, the Empress Alexandra, the Tsarevich Alexei, Tsar Nicholas II and the Grand Duchess Anastasia.

26. (*Left*) The Tsar's cousin Grand Duke Nikolai, who commanded the Russian armies for the first year of the war.

27. (*Below*) An early photo opportunity for the Allies in which the Tsar is shown sampling the food given to his soldiers. In reality, Nicholas's presence at the front was a political catastrophe that inflamed tensions between the court and the politicians.

28. The eldest, cleverest and most socially aware of Nicholas II's children, the Grand Duchess Olga.

29. The elegant Grand Duchess Tatiana in her uniform as a Red Cross nurse during the war.

30. (*Previous page*) The Tsar's third daughter, the Grand Duchess Maria, as an infant. Her Belfast-born nanny thought the girl was so kind that she must have been born 'with the very smallest trace of original sin possible'.

31. (*Above*) 'May the Lord God Help Russia.' The town of Pskov, where the imperial train was diverted during the Revolution.

32. (*Right*) The Empress Alexandra under house arrest in 1917. Lifelong problems with her back and heart had caught up with her and she spent much of her final year confined to a wheelchair.

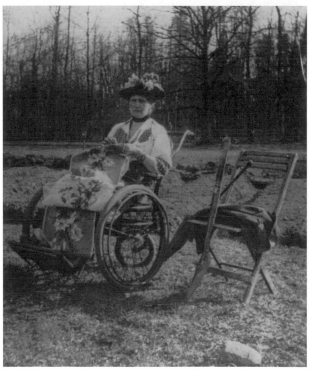

33. (*Next page*) 'Goodbye. Don't forget me.' The Grand Duchess Anastasia, the youngest and most famous of Nicholas II's children. The legend that she had survived the massacre that killed the rest of her family helped keep her name alive for decades.

imperial government had enacted a law that exempted only sons from being sent to serve on the front. Felix was an only (surviving) son and although he did not volunteer, he still seems to have felt that people were judging him. If he felt that way, he was correct. Nicholas and Alexandra's eldest daughter Olga was spending more time in Saint Petersburg chairing various charitable committees and she decided to call on her cousin Irina for tea. Felix was there, as Olga informed her father in a letter later that night. 'I went to see Irina ... Felix is "downright civilian", dressed all in brown, talked to and fro about the room, searching in some bookcases with magazines and virtually doing nothing; an utterly unpleasant impression he makes – a man idling in such times.'[30]

But Felix was not exactly idling. A slew of pornographic pamphlets depicting the Tsar as a cuckold and Rasputin in bed with the Empress were circulating in the capital and making their way to soldiers on the front. Alexandra was referred to on the streets as *Niemetzkaia bliad*, 'the German whore'. He and Irina talked at length about her family's fears about Rasputin's influence and the Tsarina's refusal to listen to any of them. When Felix tried to voice similar concerns to one of the Empress's friends, she responded, 'Nobody has the right to criticise the actions of the Emperor and the Empress. What they do concerns no one. They stand by themselves, above all public opinion.'[31] Praying about it night after night, he became convinced that the only way to save the Tsar from the Tsarina and the Tsarina from herself was to murder Rasputin. 'All my doubts and hesitations vanished,' he claimed afterwards. 'I felt a calm resolution, and gave myself over to the set purpose of destroying Rasputin.'[32]

As he formulated his plans, he reached out again to Dmitri. In his numerous interviews and three sets of subsequent memoirs written in exile, Felix was always very vague about why he felt the need to include the Grand Duke in the plot. It may have been because he missed him and wished to recapture something of their former closeness with a shared enterprise. It may have been, as cynics suggested, that he knew a Romanov could not be condemned in an ordinary law court – a member of the imperial family, and their co-conspirators, were subject to the direct judgement of the Tsar himself. Perhaps Felix was counting on that and his family's close

ties to Nicholas's if the murder caused a backlash. Or it may have
been because, as he acknowledged in his memoirs, Dmitri was
adventurous, brave and 'always ready for the wildest escapades'.

Whatever the reason, Dmitri shared his other relatives' hatred
of Rasputin and despite his former closeness to the Empress, he
agreed to help. Felix then paid a visit to Vladimir Purishkevich's
apartment and asked him if he would like to turn the fiery words of
his speech to the Duma on 20 November into reality. Purishkevich
was enthusiastic, as well as captivated by Felix's glamour and steely
certainty. They recruited an army sergeant, Dr Stanislas Lazovert,
who was charged with the task of poisoning the victim after they
decided that would be the best way to get rid of him. Felix initially
wanted to turn up and shoot him in his own apartment, but
given the police protection that surrounded him at the Tsarina's
insistence that was impractical. Felix was very uncomfortable
when the others argued that the only logical place to do it was at
the Moika Palace, which would mean inviting a man to partake of
his hospitality and then murdering him. Eventually conceding that
they were right, Felix contacted Rasputin, claiming that he had a
problem he needed to have cured. Rasputin's daughter Maria said
later that her father told her it was because he wanted to cure his
homosexuality. The suggestion, made by some historians, that
Felix and Rasputin were themselves sexually involved is stretching
credulity beyond breaking point.[33]

Having submitted himself to several sessions with Rasputin,
Felix felt he had established a friendly enough rapport to invite the
moujik to visit him at home. It is often stated that Felix dangled the
possibility of Rasputin having a romantic *rendezvous* with Irina as
bait to lure him to the Moika Palace, but that is to misread Felix's
personality utterly. He revered his wife as a princess of the blood
and he would never have wanted anyone to think that she had been
added to Rasputin's list of conquests. Where Irina's honour was
concerned, Felix was tenacious in defending it. He did however
promise Rasputin a supper with her and a few friends. Given the
rest of the imperial family's detestation for him, it is possible that
Rasputin was excited at the prospect of one of them granting
him a sign of their favour. Maybe he had heard of Felix's lavish
hospitality. Either way, he went to the Moika on the evening of 16

December, the soonest date the conspirators could pick because of Grand Duke Dmitri's busy social calendar. Invitations in the capital were often sent out weeks or months in advance, to have cancelled any engagement at the last minute might therefore have raised suspicions and so the sixteenth, a day which dawned with 'wee pink clouds' streaking the sky according to an early morning letter from the Tsarina to her husband, was Rasputin's last.[34]

The exact details of how they killed him have changed many times in the telling, not least in the numerous slightly conflicting accounts left by Felix himself and the other conspirators. With the exception of the Grand Duke Dmitri, who never liked to talk about that night but who may have been the one to fire the final fatal shot, all involved left accounts of the killing. Felix, with his tendency towards the dramatic, may have exaggerated his version of events, which had Rasputin repeatedly surviving the numerous glasses of poisoned Madeira wine and cakes given to him, but equally he could have been telling the truth. When the poison did not work, Felix fired the first shot and over the course of the evening, Rasputin was hounded through the palace like a dying animal, choked, beaten, shot, stabbed and finally chased into the snow-covered courtyard screaming that he would tell the Empress. There, possibly after a shot fired by Dmitri, he collapsed. They wrapped him in a curtain, dragged the body out on the ice of the frozen River Neva, cut a hole and shoved the body through it.

That evening, Anna Vyrubova mentioned casually to the Empress that Rasputin was going to the Moika Palace to attend a dinner party given by the Princess Irina and Prince Felix. As she had at the outbreak of the war, Alexandra looked confused by what her lady-in-waiting was telling her. She must be mistaken, Grigori could not have gone to see Irina because Irina was on holiday in the Crimea with her mother. The next morning, Alexander Protopopov told her that a police report mentioned that there had been disturbances at the Moika in the small hours and Rasputin's teenage daughter telephoned Anna to tell her that her father had gone out but not come home. For a few days, the Empress remained calm, on the surface at least. As investigations continued, she wrote to her husband at the front, 'I shall still trust in God's mercy that one has only driven him off somewhere ... I cannot and won't believe that he has been killed. God have mercy, such utter anguish (am calm and can't believe it).'[35]

A few days after the killing, divers recovered the body from beneath the ice. Alexandra was devastated and as news of who had killed him leaked out, crowds surged forward in Saint Petersburg's Cathedral of Our Lady of Kazan to pointedly light candles beneath icons of Saint Dmitri. Nicholas was disgusted at the assassination. 'I am filled with shame that the hands of my kinsmen are stained with the blood of a simple peasant. A murder is always a murder.'[36] Olga and Tatiana both chose to sleep in their mother's room that night as she dosed herself heavily with veronal, a popular barbiturate used to combat insomnia. Olga wrote in her diary, 'Confirmation that Father Grigori has been murdered, most probably by Dmitri, and thrown from the Krestovsky bridge. They found him in the water. So awful and can't bear to write it.'[37]

But while Tatiana truly believed, as her mother did, in Rasputin's saintliness, Olga's attitude to the deceased favourite was more ambivalent. A few weeks later, when she was back working at the hospital, Olga brought the matter up with a fellow nurse called Valentina Chebotareva, with whom she and Tatiana had developed a firm friendship. In the course of their conversation, Olga remarked quietly, 'Maybe it was necessary to kill him, but not in such a terrible way.'[38] Of all the children, she had seen and understood the most of the outside world. She travelled into the capital regularly to chair charity committees aimed at combating poverty and the impact of the war. Olga may not have known that the more extreme elements of anti-monarchist propaganda were printing lewd drawings in which she and her pubescent younger sisters were handed over to Rasputin to be used as his harem with their mother's connivance, but she was astute enough to realise that whatever Rasputin's presence at her parents' side had done to their family's position, it had not been positive. General Alexander Spiridovich, a hero of the Russo–Japanese war who had also helped suppress the Bolsheviks in the 1905 revolution, now worked as commander of the Tsar's private guard and he admired his master's eldest daughter very much. He claimed that as she grew into adulthood, Olga had 'instinctively sensed there was something bad in Rasputin'.[39]

Felix's gamble paid off – he and Dmitri were merely banished to the empire's edges, a move which saved their lives when the revolution came. Even Purishkevich and Lazovert, described as heroes in the press, were left relatively alone. In the face of public adulation, there was little that Nicholas II could do to punish a crime that appalled him. The murder seemed to inflict far more damage on a revolted Nicholas, who was particularly aghast when members of his wider family petitioned him to show clemency to the assassins, than it did on Alexandra. Despite what her many critics had hoped, she was not broken by Rasputin's death. Instead, after mourning him, she seemed to continue on as normal, although it is hard to tell how long that would have lasted because the monarchy now had so little time left.

The killing of Rasputin was a desperate act, carried out by men loyal to the Romanov throne who believed that their terrible crime would free the dynasty from his baleful influence. It was a reflection of how much damage Alexandra had done in sixteen months that this attack was carried out by monarchists. Yet what Felix Yussopov and Vladimir Purishkevich intended as a sign of strength was in reality a display of pitiful weakness. The legitimacy and popularity of the government had almost evaporated, one of the coldest winters on record was lashing the streets of Petrograd and Moscow, the railway lines were buckling in the cold, the food supplies could not reach the city and the proper channels of political protest had reached such a nadir of effectiveness that the empire's elite had felt the only way to get things done was to trick a semi-literate peasant, then poison him, shoot him, stab him, bludgeon him and shove him beneath the ice. Killing Rasputin did not remove the rot; it simply advertised it.

Years later, Nicholas II's youngest sister, the Grand Duchess Olga Alexandrovna, wrote from her exile in Toronto, 'There was nothing heroic about Rasputin's murder ... Just think of the two names most closely associated with it even to this day – a Grand Duke, one of the grandsons of the Tsar-Liberator [Alexander II], and then a scion of one of our greatest houses whose wife was a Grand Duke's daughter. They proved how low we had fallen.'[40]

8

The February Revolution and the Fall of the Russian Monarchy

'May the Lord God help Russia'

Nicholas II remained at Tsarskoe Selo for two months following Rasputin's funeral. Those who hoped that he would use that time to rectify the problems in the government were destined for disappointment. Nicholas did nothing but sink further into his malaise. The participation of his cousin and his niece's husband in the murder of his wife's spiritual adviser was a terrible blow to his already beleaguered pride. His own family had mounted a kind of rebellion against him when they killed Rasputin, conveying to the entire empire that this was the only way in which Nicholas could be trusted to seek the right advice. Some 3 million Russians had lost their lives as a result of the war, the terrible winter temperatures had heightened the problems of distributing food in the empire's major cities and as a result bread queues snaked through streets battered by ice and freezing winds.[1] Despite how often it is stated and glibly assumed to be true, there was no starvation. Tsuyoshi Hasegawa has convincingly demonstrated that 'the tsarist government's over-all performance in handling this enormous task of food supply was not as bad as is often argued ... no one in the cities starved. The collapse of the mechanism for supplying food actually came after the February Revolution.'[2] Still, there were shortages and the rationing of supplies intensified significantly when peasant farmers, worried by inflation, refused to sell their crops to the government. Moving the resources that were available became more difficult because of the damage the weather had inflicted on the railways.

For two years, the monarchy had ignored the Duma. Nicholas had vetoed any kind of deal with its Progressive Bloc and Alexandra's hostility towards it, as well as her total disregard for its opinions, had been well-advertised by her games of ministerial leapfrog. Nicholas's brother-in-law, the Grand Duke Alexander, Felix Yussopov's unhappy father-in-law, went to the Alexander Palace to speak to the imperial couple. Alone of the Romanovs, he had always been friendly towards Alexandra and he and Nicholas had been close friends since childhood. He was shown into their private apartments where Alexandra had been forced to lie down because of her bad back, while Nicholas sat and smoked nearby. The Grand Duke began by telling Alexandra bluntly that although her intentions had been pure, her involvement in affairs of state had harmed her husband rather than helped him. Then he said that although he had always been uneasy at the idea of a constitutional monarchy, he had come to accept that the only way for the Crown to continue to function was to appoint a government that was acceptable to the Duma. In doing so, it would buy back the support of the political class and remove Nicholas from having to accept sole blame for all of the country's problems.

Alexandra was angered by his change of heart. She told him that he was being ridiculous and that Nicholas was an autocrat who could not be expected to share his powers with a parliament. Alexander pointed out, or later claimed that he did, that Nicholas had not been an autocrat since 17 October 1905. Nicholas remained silent, Alexandra attempted to argue her point and Alexander began to shout, 'Remember, Alix, I remained silent for thirty months! For thirty months I never said as much as a word to you about the disgraceful goings-on in our government, better to say *your* government. I realise that you are willing to perish and that your husband feels the same way, but what about us? Must we all suffer for your blind stubbornness?'

'I refuse to continue this dispute,' Alexandra declared. Alexander had no choice but to get up, kiss her hand, bow to the Emperor and leave. Alexandra would not give him the customary farewell kiss for a relative and Alexander never saw her again.[3]

The Tsar's alienation from the aristocracy and members of his extended family was complete. When his former Prime Minister Count Vladimir Kokovstov arrived for an audience at Tsarskoe Selo, he found the Emperor gazing over some military maps with no idea of what day it was. The stalemate between the monarchy and the Duma meant that initiative had fallen away for moderates and liberals to support the regime in a crisis, as they had in 1905 and 1906. Some of them still believed that it was in their shared best interests to find a workable political solution, thereby preventing a revolution or a coup, but more and more speeches with a distinctly republican hue were being delivered on the floor of the Tauride. The Duma's president, Mikhail Rodzianko, returned to the palace to see the Tsar. Despite his animosity towards the court and the Tsarina's less-than-flattering nickname for him, in happier times Rodzianko had come to Tsarskoe Selo in a jocular spirit – when the Tsar first presented him to the Tsarevich Alexei, Rodzianko cheerfully introduced himself as the fattest man in the Russian Empire.

In January 1917 he came in a different mood. According to his own, no doubt slightly self-aggrandising, memoirs, he dared to harangue the Tsar and spoke to him in the bluntest language possible in the hope that it would stir Nicholas from his apathy and force him to grant a cabinet of ministers that was approved by the Duma and not hand-selected by the Empress.

> Chaos reigns everywhere. There is no Government, no system … At every turn one is confronted by abuses and confusion. The nation realises that you have banished all those in the Duma and the people trusted and replaced them with untrustworthy and incompetent men. … It is an open secret that the Empress issues orders without your knowledge … and that by her wish those whom she views with disfavour lose their jobs … Your Majesty, do not compel the people to choose between you and the good of the country.

At the end of Rodzianko's speech, Nicholas allegedly sat at his desk with his head cradled in his hands. 'Is it possible that for twenty-two

years I have tried to act for the best and it has all been a mistake?'
Rodzianko nodded. 'Yes, Your Majesty, for twenty-two years you
have followed a wrong course.'[4] At the end of the audience, and it
is the previous exchange which rings as the least probable part of
Rodzianko's story, Nicholas bade Rodzianko a fond farewell and
the President of the Duma was relieved and touched that there had
been no sign of anger or personal animosity from the Emperor.

Rodzianko's dire warnings, however exaggerated they might
have been when it came to writing his memoirs, were backed
up by Prince Nicholas Golitsyn, the second prime minister since
Boris Stürmer. He used his friendship and long years of service
to implore the Emperor to listen to Rodzianko's advice and go to
the Duma in person to promise a cabinet of ministers agreeable to
them. The old magic of a royal appearance, the Tsar in communion
with his people once again, might just work and quieten the
naysayers. It would inject a fresh vigour into the politicians and
more importantly than that it would provide the country with a
more stable and more popular government. Nicholas agreed to
his suggestion. Had he stuck by that decision, it is highly possible
that the Romanov monarchy could have weathered the storms of
1917. As it was, an hour after the audience was over Golitsyn was
summoned back to the Alexander Palace. There has always been
a heavy suspicion that Nicholas went to Alexandra to discuss the
plans with her and she persuaded him not to act so hastily, but that
is conjecture and her private letters to Nicholas seem to contradict
it.[5] It is also possible that because the army's luck at the front had
started to turn Nicholas felt he needed to get back in time for the
anticipated victories. All we know for certain is that when Golitsyn
was brought back into the Tsar's study, Nicholas told him that he
was going to go back to *Stavka*.

'How is that, Your Majesty?' the Prime Minister asked. 'What
about a responsible Ministry? You intended to go to the Duma
tomorrow.'

'I have changed my mind. I am leaving for headquarters tonight.'[6]

*

As the imperial train pulled away from the Tsarskoe Selo station,
Nicholas found a letter already waiting for him in his compartment

from Alexandra. 'My own beloved Sunny,' he wrote, 'Loving thanks for your precious letter – you left in my compartment – I read it greedily before going to bed. It did me good, in my solitude, after two months being together, if not to hear your sweet voice, at least to be comforted by those lines of tender love!'[7] By the time he reached *Stavka*, a telegram was waiting for him, again from his wife, in which she informed him that Olga and Alexei had come down with the measles. Nicholas wrote back that the disease was sweeping two cadet corps at *Stavka* and that Alexandra should not meet too many people if she was nursing their children lest she pass the disease on.[8]

Back in Petrograd, the weather had begun to turn and milder temperatures brought more people out on to the street to protest against the terrible winter they had endured, the unaccountable incompetence of the government, the damage inflicted by inflation and the seemingly unending slaughter of the war. Prime Minister Golitsyn and Alexander Protopopov braced themselves for the riots and made sensible plans to contain them, hoping that they would only have to use soldiers against the protesters as a last resort. For four days, they held off but by Sunday 11 March, three days after the Tsar returned to the front, the rioting in Petrograd was no longer manageable. Alexandra wrote to her husband:

Precious, beloved Treasure,
8° & gently snowing – so far I sleep very well, but miss my Love more than words can say. – The rows in town and strikes are more than provoking. I send you Kall's [the Empress's nickname for Alexander Protopopov] letter to me, the paper is not worth while, & you will get a more detailed for sure fr. the police chief. It's a hooligan movement, young boys & girls running about & screaming that they have no bread, only to excite – & then the workmen preventing others fr. work – if it were very cold they wld. probably stay in doors. But this will all pass & quieten down – if the Duma wld. only behave itself – one does not print the worst speeches but I find the antidynastic ones ought to be at once very severely punished as it's a time of war, yet more so. – I had the feeling when you go, thing wld. not be good ... Do go to the Virgin & pray there quietly for yr. sweet self to gain strength

for our big & little family ... Am writing by a dark lamp on Olga's sofa. Just placed candles at [church] – tired ... No shooting is required – only order & not let them cross the bridges as they do. – The food question is maddening. Excuse dull letter, but so much worry all around.[9]

In the same letter, Alexandra suggested that the problem of the bread queues could be fixed if Russia adopted rationing cards, like the system operating in Britain. She also passed on the news that Tatiana had caught the measles and been sent to bed, and that she thought Anastasia might be coming down with them as well. So far only the Grand Duchess Maria remained in rude good health, much to her mother's relief, and she and Anastasia were helping her take care of the others.

On the fourth day of the rioting in Petrograd, the cabinet sanctioned, apparently with great reluctance, the use of gunfire to clear the city centre of demonstrators, despite the Tsarina's belief that it was not necessary. The gunfire prompted Rodzianko to cable the Tsar at General Headquarters. The telegram was sent from Petrograd at eight minutes to ten in the evening and received by the Tsar forty-eight minutes later. Even at this juncture 'Fat Rodzianko', the man portrayed by the Empress's faction as a covert republican, indicated how much he and many liberals did not want a revolution, only some sign of strong leadership from the throne.

To His Imperial Majesty, Army in the Field
Headquarters of the Commander in Chief
Your most faithful servant reports to Your Majesty that popular uprisings, having begun in Petrograd, are taking on uncontrollable and threatening dimensions. Their cause is a shortage of baked bread and poor delivery of flour, which is sowing panic, but the main reason is the absolute distrust of the authorities, who are not competent to lead the country out of its difficult situation. Because of this, events will certainly unfold that can be temporarily held at bay at the expense of innocent citizens' spilled blood but that will be impossible to contain in the event of a repetition. Outbreaks could spread to the railways, and then the life of the country will come to a standstill at the worst

possible moment. Factories working for the military in Petrograd are shutting down for lack of fuel and raw materials, the workers are left with nothing to do, and the hungry, unemployed throng is starting down the path of elemental and uncontrollable anarchy. In all of Russia, railway communications are in total disorder. Out of 63 blast furnaces in the south, only 28 are working because of the lack of fuel deliveries and necessary raw materials. Out of 92 blast furnaces in the Urals, 44 are at a standstill and the production of pig iron is shrinking from day to day, which threatens a major reduction in the production of shells. Fearing the inept orders of the authorities, the people do not take their grain products to market, bringing the mills to a stop and threatening the army and the rest of the population with the full force of flour shortages. State authority is totally paralysed and utterly unable to impose order. Your Majesty, save Russia; she is threatened with humiliation and disgrace. In these circumstances, the war cannot be brought to a victorious conclusion because the ferment has already spread to the army and threatens to grow if a decisive end cannot be put to anarchy and governmental disorder. Your Majesty, urgently summon a person in whom the whole country can have faith and entrust him with the formation of a government that all the people can trust. Having been re-inspired by faith in themselves and their leaders, all of Russia will heed such a government. In this terrible hour, unprecedented in its ghastly consequences, there is no other way out and to delay is impossible.

Chairman of the State Duma,
Mikhail Rodzianko[10]

The next day, the Petrograd garrison mutinied and vowed that they would never again open fire on the protestors. The men who might have obeyed the government's orders, who would have died in the last ditch defending the monarchy, had long ago perished at the front – cut down in the cavalry charge at Tannenburg or killed in the campaigns to defend the Ukraine. These soldiers were usually new recruits with little or no loyalty to the Tsar and his adulteress German spy wife and they would not fire on people whose views they shared. The mutiny of the garrison meant that the imperial government had lost control of its own capital; one general in the admiralty went so far as to write that they were in a state of siege. Nicholas at last decided to come home. Orders were dispatched for General Nikolai Ivanov to take some front line troops back to Petrograd and crush the insurrection before it got any worse. The director of the Hermitage Art Museum at the Winter Palace wrote, 'The city reverberates to the most terrifying noises: broken glass, screams, and gunshots.'[11] Statues of the Romanov emperors were torn from their plinths, the smashed plaster face of Alexander II, the Tsar who had ended serfdom, was kicked around in the streets like a football. On street fronts and government buildings, the double-headed eagles of the dynasty were torn down and hurled into the gutter. The crowds freed nearly 8,000 prisoners, most of them petty criminals who had every reason to encourage the next phase of the riots – the ransacking of the Palace of Justice, the court buildings, the prisons and the offices of both the ordinary and secret police. All those institutions' records conveniently went up in flames. Middle-class homes were broken into, their inhabitants frequently robbed and assaulted by the thieves and rapists who had been liberated from the city's gaols. In only a few days, 1,500 people lost their lives and nearly 6,000 were injured in the capital alone as a result of mob violence. At the same time, the Prime Minister was told that the Tsar wanted to temporarily disband the Duma and rule with the military until the unrest subsided. When this order was brought to the Tauride Palace, the deputies tossed it to one side. Vasily Shulgin, a monarchist, turned to Rodzianko and said sadly, 'Take the power. The position is plain; if you don't, others will.'[12] The empire's former ministers were all arrested, partly to save them from being lynched by the mob, but also to give the impression that the Duma was doing something to remedy the situation. In another wing of the Tauride, the socialist movement had, at long last, attempted to control the situation to their own advantage – the Petrograd Soviet of Workers' and Soldiers' Deputies set up residence. The two Russias seeking change, Liberal and Left, were separated by a corridor. Like Juan Perón thirty years later, when the Left-leaning Alexander Kerensky went from the Duma to make speeches to the Soviet, he took off his coat and removed his collar to make himself look more like a member of the working classes.

As the Tsar's train sped towards Tsarskoe Selo, it found its path blocked by soldiers sympathetic to the revolution. It had to divert and seek shelter at the nearby town of Pskov, where those on board tried to decide on the best way to proceed. The Tsar sent a telegram to Petrograd promising a new cabinet and a prime minister with vastly increased powers who would be acceptable to the Duma. But it was like trying to change the course of a ship that had already hit an iceberg. Rodzianko cabled back to one of the generals, 'His Majesty and yourself apparently are unable to realise what is happening in the capital. A terrible revolution has broken out. Hatred of the Empress has reached fever pitch. To prevent bloodshed I have been forced to arrest all the ministers ... I am hanging by a thread myself. Power is slipping from my hands. The measures you propose are too late. The time for them is gone. There is no return.'[13]

The next morning, at breakfast, General Ruzsky presented the Tsar with telegrams from those from whom he had belatedly sought advice – monarchists, liberals, generals and admirals. His Chief of Staff, General Alekseev, wrote of 'the constantly growing danger of anarchy spreading to the whole country, the continued disintegration of the army, and the impossibility of continuing the war in the present situation ... In light of this I vigorously beg Your Imperial Majesty to deign to immediately publish from Headquarters the following manifesto ...' The former Commander-in-Chief, Grand Duke Nikolai, telegrammed saying that the current crisis 'calls for the adoption of extraordinary measures. According to the duty and spirit of my oath as a loyal subject, I think it is necessary to beg Your Imperial Majesty upon bended knee to save Russia and your heir, knowing your feeling of holy love for Russia and for him. Having made the sign of the cross over yourself, transfer to him your legacy. There is no other way out.' The acclaimed military tactician General Alexei Brusilov, responsible for some of the army's most impressive victories against Austria-Hungary, had written that 'based on my loyalty and love for the motherland and the tsar's throne ... at this moment the only way to save the situation and create the possibility of continuing to fight the external enemy, without which Russia will perish, is to abdicate in favour of His Majesty's heir [the] Tsarevich with Grand

Duke Mikhail Alexandrovich as Regent. There is no other way out.' General Alexei Evert wrote that the army would no longer follow Nicholas and that 'it is necessary to come to an immediate decision'. Admiral Nepenin of the Baltic Fleet said he could no longer control his troops or crews. All of them were unanimous.[14] The only way to save the empire was for Nicholas II to abdicate.

Reading these telegrams, Nicholas drained of all colour, rose from the table and walked over to the other end of the dining car, where he lit a cigarette and stared out the window. The betrayal, as he saw it, of the army hurt him the most and the Romanov family's centuries-long veneration of the military meant that he knew he could not rule without it. Politicians and generals were at last apparently in agreement – Nicholas must go for Russia's sake. After a few moments of thunderously loud silence, he turned back to his entourage. 'I have decided that I will give up the throne for my son.'[15]

The news was cabled to Petrograd and two politicians from the Duma, the monarchist Vasily Shulgin, he who had advised Rodzianko to seize power before the Soviet did, and the right-of-centre Alexander Guchkov, the former Minister for Trade and Commerce, left immediately. They would come to Pskov to witness the act of abdication and carry the document back to Petrograd so that the Duma could make arrangements to proclaim the accession of Alexei II.

As the delegates travelled to Pskov, Nicholas began to have second thoughts. He summoned Doctor Federov, part of his on-board entourage and one of the few physicians who knew the truth about Alexei's medical history. Nicholas asked bluntly if Alexei would be physically capable of becoming Emperor at such a young age, given his haemophilia. Federov answered, 'Science teaches us, Sire, that it is an incurable disease. Yet those who are afflicted with it sometimes reach an advanced old age. Still Alexei Nicolaevich is at the mercy of an accident.'[16] Federov then pointed out that if the abdication went ahead as planned, Nicholas, Alexandra and their daughters would probably be sent to live abroad. Even if they were allowed to stay in Russia, and given Alexandra's unpopularity that was as unlikely as it was ill-advised, there was very little chance that they would be allowed regular access to Alexei. One way or the other, the child would almost certainly be removed from his mother's care.

By the time Shulgin and Guchkov boarded the stationery train at nine o'clock that evening and were shown into its salon car, Nicholas had changed his mind. He invited them to sit down and explained that now he intended to abdicate in his own name and in Alexei's. 'I have decided to renounce my throne. Until three o'clock today I thought I would abdicate in favour of my son Alexei, but now I have changed my decision in favour of my brother Mikhail. I trust you will understand the feelings of a father.'[17] It was a catastrophic decision, but an understandable one. To have separated Alexei from Alexandra might very well have caused her to suffer a heart attack and it would put the boy's life in great danger if he fell again and Alexandra was not there to take care of him. His elevation to the throne would also have meant advertising his condition to the host of men and courtiers who would now be charged with serving and protecting the new Tsar. Even so, Nicholas technically had no legal right to abdicate for Alexei. Monarchists in the years to come were to weep and storm over the double abdication, arguing that it had thrown away a well-thought-through plan to save the monarchy. Sergei Sazonov, Nicholas's former Foreign Minister, expressed the bitterness of many of them when he told a friend, 'I needn't tell you of my love for the Emperor and with what devotion I have served him. But as long as I live, I shall never forgive him for abdicating for his son. He had no shadow of a right to do so. Is there a body of law in the world which allows the rights of a minor to be abandoned? And what's to be said when those rights are the most sacred and august on earth? Fancy destroying a three-hundred-year-old dynasty, and that stupendous work of Peter the Great, Catherine II, and Alexander I. What a tragedy! What a disaster!'[18] At Pskov, Shulgin and Guchkov were unsettled by the change in plan. 'We had counted on the figure of little Alexei Nikolaevich having a softening effect on the transfer of power,' Guchkov said.

'His Majesty is worried that if the throne is transferred to his successor then His Majesty will be separated from him,' explained one of the generals. Shulgin admitted, 'I cannot give a categorical answer to that.' Guchkov insisted that their priority was to save the monarchy, not to guarantee the imperial family's future happiness:

'We are afraid that if a republic is announced, there will be civil strife.' But before long they were beginning to waiver. Shulgin spoke of the Soviet occupying a wing of the Tauride: 'It's hell at the Duma, a madhouse. We are going to have to begin a decisive battle with leftist elements, and we need some sort of basis to do this. Concerning your plan, let us think about this for a quarter of an hour. This plan has the advantage of containing no thought of separation and, on the other hand, can contribute to furthering calm if your brother, Grand Duke Mikhail Alexandrovich, as full monarch, swears to the constitution while simultaneously assuming the throne.' Nicholas actually offered them longer to think it over, but Guchkov ultimately waived the offer aside, 'Your Majesty, the human feeling of a father spoke in you, and politics has no place there, so we can make no objection to your proposal.'[19] Shulgin, Guchkov, the doctor and the generals' support, after some initial hesitancy, at least absolves Nicholas II of the charge that he signed the double abdication in the face of monarchist advice to the contrary.

To the chief of staff:

In these days of great struggle with an external enemy who has tried to enslave our country for nearly three years, the Lord God saw fit to send down upon Russia a harsh new ordeal. The developing internal popular disturbances threaten to have a catastrophic effect upon the future conduct of the relentless war. The fate of Russia, the honour of our heroic army, the good of the people, the whole future of our dear fatherland demand that the war be brought to a victorious end no matter what. A cruel enemy is summoning his last strength, and the hour is near when our valiant army, together with our renowned allies, can completely smash the enemy.

During these decisive days for the life of Russia, We considered it a duty of conscience to facilitate Our people's close unity and the rallying of all popular forces in order to achieve victory as quickly as possible, and, in agreement with the State Duma, We consider it to be for the good to abdicate from the Throne of the Russian State and to surrender supreme power.

Not wishing to part from Our beloved son, We name as Our

successor Our Brother Grand Duke Mikhail Alexandrovich, and bless his assumption to the Throne of the Russian State. We entrust Our brother to conduct state affairs in complete and unshakeable unity with the representatives of the people in the legislative institutions according to principles they will determine, and on this to take an inviolable oath.

In the name of our deeply beloved homeland, we call all faithful sons of the fatherland to fulfil their holy duty to this land in obedience to the Tsar in this difficult moment of national trials and to help Him, together with the representatives of the people, to lead the Russian State along the path of victory, prosperity and glory.

May the Lord God help Russia.

Nicholas

As Nicholas signed, the usually reserved Shulgin burst into tears. 'Oh, Your Majesty,' he wept, 'if you had done all this sooner, even as late as the summoning of the last Duma perhaps all that ...' He broke off, unable to finish and continued crying. Nicholas looked at him in a curiously unaffected way and asked, 'Do you think it might have been avoided?'[20] There are few questions in the study of history to which the answer can be more resoundingly and more certainly, yes. It was 2 March 1917 in Russia, 15 March, the Ides of March, in the West.

In the Duma, republican politicians like Alexander Kerensky greeted the news of the abdication with relief but argued that the Grand Duke Mikhail would have to go as well. Crowds outside the Tauride jeered Mikhail's name and cried, 'Long live the republic!', while other politicians argued that the monarchy needed to be maintained because it was the sole force holding the empire together. Without its ancient laws and prerogatives, Russia would have to release countries like Finland, the Baltic States and maybe even the fertile plains of the Ukraine. No such moves could be contemplated at a time of war.

Outside the Duma, others were stunned by Nicholas's decision, including many members of his extended family. His brother-in-law Alexander, who had shouted at Alexandra only a few weeks earlier, thought that, 'Nicky must have lost his mind. Since when does a sovereign abdicate because of a shortage of bread and partial disorders in the capital?'²¹ In Kiev, the Dowager Empress called it 'the greatest humiliation of her life'.²² She insisted on dashing north to see her son, who had been allowed to go back to *Stavka* briefly to collect his things, gather his servants and bid farewell to the troops. 'To think that I should live to witness such horror,' she lamented and when she swept across the snow-dusted platform to board her son's train at *Stavka*, she nearly fainted at his feet. When a lady-in-waiting suggested a family photograph to mark their reunion, Marie could not bring herself to have him captioned as the ex-Tsar and waved the camera away. When she asked him how he could have given up the throne, Nicholas replied, 'What could I do when Nikolasha [the family's nickname for the Grand Duke Nikolai] and General Alekseev asked me to resign for the country's sake?'²³

Nicholas's remark to his mother raises one seldom-discussed aspect of the abdication. The telegrams that General Ruzsky placed on the Tsar's desk at Pskov were united in agreement that only his abdication could save the empire. Those telegrams had in turn been collected and passed on to Ruzsky by General Alekseev, the army's Chief of Staff, who had been in discussions for days with Rodzianko. Both men agreed that Nicholas must abdicate if the war was to be won and Rodzianko was privately convinced that monarchism may have run its course in Russia, because it had been forever tainted by Nicholas and Alexandra's poor decisions. In order to persuade Nicholas to jump, they had carefully controlled the information he had access to. Why, if telegrams could reach the Grand Duke Nikolai, the admirals and the generals, were efforts not also made to reach other members of the imperial family? Why did nobody make any attempt to contact the Dowager Empress, Nicholas's uncle the Grand Duke Paul, who was in regular contact with the Duma about proposals to safeguard the monarchy's future, or the Grand Duke Alexander? That they could all have been reached quickly and even brought to his side was shown by the speed with which the Dowager was able to join him at *Stavka* within days of the abdication. Those who believed, for perfectly valid reasons, that Nicholas II needed to abdicate deliberately manipulated the flow of information in that crucial thirty-six-hour period at Pskov and they denied him access to the views of those who believed, with equal sincerity, that Nicholas could still salvage the situation and that any change in monarch under the present circumstances would prove fatal to the empire's survival.

At Tsarskoe Selo, the Empress was still fussing around the sickrooms of her children. She had been right to fear that Anastasia was sickening with measles like her brother and eldest sisters. She too was now in bed. Maria, sensing something was wrong with the world outside, was running around helping her mother and her puppy-fat weight was rapidly dropping off. Late one night, Alexandra, Maria and one of the Empress's ladies-in-waiting went out to speak to the guards, with a fur coat draped over Alexandra's white uniform. She thanked them for their loyalty to her family and sent tea out to them as they assumed their positions, preparing to defend the palace if it was attacked in the dead of night. The next morning two palace servants arrived clutching pamphlets from the capital that proclaimed the Emperor's abdication. Alexandra dismissed it as a republican lie until Nicholas's uncle Paul, the father of Rasputin's assassin Dmitri, made his way out to Tsarskoe Selo to tell her the truth. She was preparing to go to the hospital and was dressed in her nurse's uniform when he was shown in. As soon as he broke the news, tears began rolling down her face. To his surprise, there was no anger, only great sadness. She wept over the agony Nicholas must have endured over the last few days – 'If Nicky has done this, it is because he had to do so ...' She accepted her brother-in-law's position as the new Tsar and made plans to move her family south to their summer palace in the Crimea.[24] Alexandra emerged from their meeting with her eyes bloodshot and her face distorted by shock. Her lady-in-waiting Lili Dehn thought she was walking strangely. She 'rushed forward and supported her until she reached the writing table between the windows. She leaned heavily against it, and taking my hand in hers said brokenly: "*Abdiqué*".'[25] The Empress went in search of Maria and a lady-in-waiting later discovered mother and daughter in the corner of Maria's bedroom, hugging one another, weeping pitifully. The next day, Viktor Zborovsky, one of the palace guards who had known the grand duchesses for years, wrote that Maria's former naïveté had vanished and in its place 'a serious, sensible young woman, who was responding in a deep and thoughtful way to what was going on'.[26]

The news of the abdication had been brought to the Grand Duke Mikhail, who subsequently attended a meeting at Millonnaya Street in Petrograd at which Rodzianko informed him that Nicholas's decision to abdicate in favour of Mikhail rather than Alexei had not gone down well. A provisional government had been declared in the interim to resolve the crisis and they unfortunately could not control what informal powers the Soviet had already accrued for itself or how the garrison would react to news of another fully grown Romanov on the throne. The displays of anti-monarchist violence and the desecration of the monarchy's symbols throughout the capital told their own story. The fact that the Soviet knew of Mikhail's nomination to the throne and were already calling for his arrest and possible execution frightened the others. A fire roared in the drawing room's grate as Rodzianko, Kerensky and other assembled politicians informed Mikhail of the dire situation facing all of them, and him in particular. Shulgin and Guchkov were present and they were surprised that what had seemed so reasonable aboard the imperial train at Pskov was judged impossible in Petrograd. Once again, the information being fed to the head of the House of Romanov was being very tightly controlled. Prince George Lvov, a left-of-centre aristocrat, said, 'I cannot answer for Your Highness's life.'[27] It was a revealing statement, not least because Lvov had referred to Mikhail by his grand ducal 'Highness' rather than the sovereign's 'Majesty'. The meeting dragged on for two hours, in which hypothetical scenarios of civil war between the Duma and the Soviet were trotted out and the unrest on the streets was discussed at length.

Mikhail, ten years younger than Nicholas II, was a tall and thin gentleman with a wry sense of humour who had already proven himself to be competent and brave in his service on the Eastern Front.[28] Despite his previous popularity with his relatives, he had been estranged from many of them for over a decade when he caused a scandal by entering into a morganatic marriage with Natalia Brasova, a socialite divorcée, the daughter of a lawyer from Moscow. The family feud over Natalia had resulted in yet another blood relative's inability to pass on advice to Nicholas II in the years preceding the Revolution. Now Mikhail was called upon to assume the throne of his ancestors with little or no forewarning from his brother. For some monarchists, there was something poetic about his nomination because the first Romanov tsar, who had also rescued the country from the scourge of foreign invasion on its Western borders and restored law and order, had also been called Mikhail. It is not true, as Rodzianko later claimed, that Mikhail was afraid for his own safety or that he had no interest in becoming Tsar. On his way to the meeting, Mikhail had told one of his cousins, 'I shall leave as Tsar from the same house where I was received as Grand Duke.'[29] However, he had always been more sympathetic to the idea of constitutionalism than his brother (the British consul to Petrograd thought he was 'a prince who would make an excellent constitutional monarch'), and in the meeting at Millonnaya Street he listened to the advice being given to him by the Provisional Government.[30] The compromise reached was for the new regime to be given time to stabilise itself. Once that was done, they would formally offer Mikhail the crown, which would remove any suggestion that it was the successor to the detested court politics of the last two years. There were still those in the room, like Paul Milyukov, the leader of the Constitutional Democratic Party, who thought that the monarchy could and should be saved, but he was in the minority. Under great pressure, Mikhail agreed to temporarily abjure his brother's nomination and he issued the following statement:

> By my brother's will, a heavy burden was placed upon me when I was assigned the All-Russian Imperial Throne during a time of unprecedented war and popular unrest.
>
> Inspired, in common with the whole people, by the belief that the welfare of our country must be set above everything else, I have taken the firm decision to assume the supreme power only if and when our great people, having elected by universal suffrage a Constituent Assembly to determine the form of government and lay down the fundamental law of the new Russian State, invest me with such power.
>
> Calling upon them the blessing of God, I therefore request all the citizens of the Russian Empire to submit to the Provisional

Government, established and invested with full authority by the Duma, until such time as the Constituent Assembly, elected within the shortest possible time by universal, direct, equal and secret suffrage, shall manifest the will of the people by deciding upon the new form of government.[31]

It was unintentionally the document that signed Imperial Russia out of existence. Mikhail was eventually placed under house arrest and he was the first Romanov to die under the Revolution, when he and his English secretary Nicholas Johnson were marched into the woods around Perm and shot by the Bolsheviks in June 1918. Mikhail, wounded before he was killed, crawled over to his secretary and said to the guards, 'Let me say goodbye to my friend.' Their bodies have never been recovered.[32]

Unable to bring herself to tell Alexei of what his father had done, Alexandra asked his tutor to do it for her. Gilliard went to sit by the young man's sickbed, where he found Alexei, as his mother had said, sporting 'one rash, covered like a leopard' thanks to the measles.[33] He began by telling him that Nicholas was coming home and that this time there would be no return to *Stavka*. When he told him it was because Nicholas did not want to be Tsar anymore, Alexei 'looked at me in astonishment, trying to read in my face what had happened. "What! Why?"'

Gilliard answered, 'He is very tired and has had a lot of trouble lately.' Alexei nodded, 'Oh yes! Mother told me that they had stopped his train when he wanted to come here. But won't Papa be Tsar again afterwards?' Gilliard explained the double abdication and his uncle Mikhail's decision to renounce the throne for the time being. 'But who's going to be Tsar, then?' Alexei asked.

'I don't know,' the tutor answered. 'Perhaps nobody now ...'[34]

It took a week for Nicholas to make it back to Tsarskoe Selo after his farewell trip to *Stavka*. Over those few days, Alexandra finally seemed to succumb to the ill health and bad nerves that she had been struggling against for so long. Even those who knew her well were stunned by her body's reaction to the monarchy's implosion. Elisabeth Naryshkina, her Mistress of the Robes who had served at court since the reign of Alexander II, was frightened at the way Alexandra was speaking. Her speech was disjointed and rambling;

she did not make much sense. Watching her at close quarters, the family's physician, Dr Evgeny Botkin, was angry that he had not noticed sooner how much damage had been done to her by stress. Elisabeth wrote, 'He now feels as I do when seeing the state the Empress is in and berates himself for not have realised it sooner.'[35]

On 22 March, Nicholas arrived home. At the train station, delegates from the Provisional Government formally handed him over to the new palace guard, with the information that the ex-Emperor and his household were under house arrest at the Alexander Palace. He was driven under guard from the train station to his home, where Alexandra was waiting with the children and Alexei kept nervously checking his watch to see if his father had been detained. The palace gates were padlocked when the car pulled up and the presiding sentry pretended not to know who was inside so that he and his comrade could go through the process of introducing him as 'Nicholas Romanov'. Some of the remaining courtiers saw the whole thing from the palace windows; in his memoirs, the outraged Grand Marshal described the incident as 'an offensive comedy'.[36]

The Grand Marshal descended quickly to greet Nicholas and made a point of bowing in front of the guards. Nicholas politely shook his hand and gave no sign of intimidation as he and one of his more loyal aides, Prince Vasily Dolgoruky, made their way through the entrance hall and antechambers that were now full of hostile soldiers sympathetic to republicanism. As he reached the entrance to the imperial family's private apartments, a servant chose to ignore the threat of retaliation and swung open the doors with the booming announcement of, 'His Majesty the Emperor!' Alexandra lurched to her feet and ran over to her husband. She threw herself into his arms and Nicholas, at last, broke down weeping.[37]

9

The Triumph of Military Government in Imperial Germany

'The Military Dictatorship hardly veiled any more'

Crown Princess Cecilia gave birth to her fifth child and first daughter in the spring of 1915 at the Marble Palace in Potsdam, an elegant structure built during the reign of King Friedrich Wilhelm II, a monarch with 'deep and wide-ranging cultural interests' who ruled Prussia between 1786 and 1797.[1] The child was christened Alexandrine in honour of Cecilia's elder sister, the then Queen Consort of Denmark.[2] The new princess had Down's Syndrome and as a result she was seldom seen in public. However, it is not true that she was hidden away completely. She was occasionally shown on commemorative postcards like all the Kaiser's other grandchildren and private family photographs show Alexandrine, in defiance of the era's usual standards that often extolled institutionalisation, happily posing on her parents' estate arm in arm with her brothers Wilhelm, Louis Ferdinand, Hubertus and Friedrich, and her younger sister Cecilia, who was born two years later.[3]

Between the two princesses' births, the political situation in their grandfather's empire changed significantly. In June 1916, the British and German navies finally came to blows at the Battle of Jutland in the North Sea. Although the British actually lost more gross tonnage, there was no question that it constituted 'an unambiguous defeat' for the Second Reich.[4] On the basis of that technicality, Wilhelm initially claimed it had been a victory for Germany and in a speech delivered at the port of Wilhelmshaven four days after its conclusion he claimed it eclipsed the British victory at Trafalgar in 1805.[5] (He admitted that it had been a defeat years later.) The year 1916 also saw greater setbacks on the Western Front. The Battles of Verdun and the Somme achieved almost nothing. As a result of the latter, the Allies acquired six miles of territory in a battle that cost a combined total of just over 1 million lives. Both sides threw nearly everything they had into these battles in an attempt to break the stalemate. Tanks, aeroplanes and poisoned gas made their presence significantly felt for the first time. Yet still nothing seemed to have changed in the bloody fields of Flanders where only the poppies now grew and the air was thick with smoke and the smell of blood.

On May Day 1916 Karl Liebknecht, the leader of Far Left Spartacus League, was arrested at an anti-war demonstration in Berlin. Dissent was also coming from the Right with Bavarian royalists urging their court to lead Bavaria's secession from the Reich and re-establish its pre-1871 independence. Given all this and their own frequent liaising with rebels in enemy nations, the German government may have counted themselves fortunate that armed insurrection did not break out as it did in the United Kingdom, when the Irish Republican Brotherhood attempted to start a nationalist revolution on the streets of Dublin. The so-called Easter Rising was defeated with more force than many in Ireland, even its critics, felt was necessary, but the capture of a German trawler in Tralee Bay with 20,000 rifles intended for the rebels allowed the government and their unionist supporters to paint the uprising as one that had the backing of a hostile foreign power.[6] There were even rumours that some of the Irish nationalists wanted to offer an independent Irish throne to Prince Joachim, Wilhelm's youngest son. The idea of a Hohenzollern king of Ireland is certainly an arresting hypothetical, but it is a particularly tenuous one even as a flight of counter-actual fantasy. It was only in 1917, the year after the uprising, that Irish separatists definitively rejected any of their movement's previous interest in monarchism, but even before that most of its leaders were republicans in their hearts and it is difficult to imagine how a Protestant prince like Joachim could possibly have been accepted as king in a predominantly Catholic country like Ireland, particularly since many nationalists were already planning to grant special status to Catholicism after independence.[7] Nor would Joachim's parents ever have countenanced a religious change even for the sake of a crown, if their reaction to his aunt's conversion to Greek Orthodoxy were anything to go by.

A far more serious proposal of a Hohenzollern throne abroad came from Finland at the end of 1917, when the country declared independence after the Russian Revolution. At the same time, feelers were being put out from a newly independent Georgia, again about the possibility of offering a crown to Joachim, while the Finnish parliament elected to offer their crown to Wilhelm's brother-in-law, Prince Friedrich Karl of Hesse, who was married to Wilhelm's younger sister Margaret.[8] A design for the new Finnish crown was even drawn up, but events soon overtook the plans for new monarchies of the countries liberated from the ruins of the Russian Empire and by the time of the Armistice in 1918 the Allies, particularly France and the United States, would never have allowed a German prince to assume the throne of Finland.[9]

Dreams of future monarchies in states planning on independence from Russia or Britain proliferated, with even the Hapsburgs promoting the not totally unfeasible idea of giving the crown of an independent Ukraine to Karl's distant and fantastically charismatic cousin the Archduke Wilhelm, but the reality for existing crowns was far from promising. In the spring of 1916, Chancellor von Bethmann-Hollweg tried to appease his liberal base and the vocal elements of socialism by promising significant reforms to the electoral system after the war, in a move that was bitterly denounced by the Crown Prince. At the same time the popularity of von Hindenburg and General Ludendorff on the Right seemed unstoppable. Despite von Hindenburg's public deference towards the Kaiser, he was still more than prepared to undermine him when he felt it was necessary. As their power and prestige grew, Wilhelm's diminished. A significant quarrel between them arose over the future of Erich von Falkenhayn as Chief of Staff – von Hindenburg's clique wanted him to go, the Kaiser wanted him to stay. Von Hindenburg obviously thought the war effort's priority should lie in breaking the Eastern Front, while von Falkenhayn thought it was more important to break through the British and French trenches in Flanders. The fact that the two were often seen as oppositional agendas shows the divisive effect of von Hindenburg and Ludendorff's egos. As usual, the Empress and the Crown Prince lobbied for von Hindenburg, and Wilhelm, who had resisted them in 1914, caved in 1916. He wept as von Falkenhayn left military headquarters and squirmed when von Hindenburg replaced him as Chief of Staff, accompanied, as ever, by Ludendorff.

Rather than confine himself solely to military matters, von Hindenburg used his newfound position to pursue a political agenda as well. He and Ludendorff picked a fight with the Chancellor, whom they and most of von Hindenburg's fellow Junkers had distrusted for a very long time. In March 1917, the two generals secured the reimplementation of unrestricted submarine warfare in the North Sea and the Atlantic waters around the British Isles. This was something directly contrary to the Kaiser's wishes. In the spring of the previous year, he had increased restrictions on when the U-boats could attack to the point that their activity was effectively cancelled for a time in the Atlantic and the English Channel.[10] In doing so, the Kaiser showed that he had a keen eye on the international arena and above all on keeping America out of the war, where memories of the *Lusitania* were still fresh, but he was flying more than ever in the face of a German populace who were suffering greatly because of the British blockade. At the same time, a Reichstag revolt led by the Social Democrats in protest at the unchecked power of the military in the government meant that von Bethmann-Hollweg no longer had any significant force in German society that supported him. Only the Emperor could save him and it was a testament to Wilhelm's diminished political importance that he did not. The final quarrel took place over von Bethmann-Hollweg's plans for electoral reform, when both Ludendorff and von Hindenburg threatened to resign if the Kaiser continued to support his Chancellor.

As the Crown Prince rather unnecessarily pointed out, Wilhelm could not possibly hope to pit von Bethmann-Hollweg against von Hindenburg in the public's estimation and expect the former to win out. What was actually at stake was the Kaiser's popularity, for a chancellor exercised power solely at the monarch's discretion. Von Bethmann-Hollweg's strength was thus a reflection of his imperial master's. The Crown Prince was right – nothing could trump von Hindenburg when it came to the public's confidence and affection. Sensing that the Crown Prince was about to mount a campaign of character assassination, hoping to save the Emperor from further embarrassment and exhausted by frustration at the state of German politics, the Chancellor tendered his resignation. The Crown Prince and the two generals arrived at the palace prepared for an almighty row, whereupon the weary Kaiser informed them that they had already won: von Bethmann-Hollweg was gone. They persuaded Wilhelm to replace him with Georg Michaelis, a political nonentity who worked in the department responsible for the wartime distribution of wheat and corn in Prussia. Like Ludendorff, he was a commoner and Wilhelm tried to halt his promotion to the chancellorship on those grounds. Once again, he was thwarted. The high command liked the reliably quiescent Michaelis, so he got the job. He was appointed on Bastille Day, and the Kaiser seems to have regarded this as another day when unwanted commoners came pouring over the parapets. The Empress told him not to worry. She knew Michaelis through his support for one of her Protestant charities.

In July 1917, Wilhelm received news that his English cousins had changed their family name from Saxe-Coburg-Gotha to Windsor. Ever since the sinking of the *Lusitania*, Wilhelm had featured prominently in the torrent of anti-German propaganda flooding Britain and America, much of which cast him as a near-demonic warlord. He could hardly begin to fathom how deeply he was detested in his mother's homeland. The figure of 'Kaiser Bill' was one axiomatic with evil and the rising tide of xenophobia in Britain with its hatred of all things Germanic was beginning to shake the foundations of the British throne. Although King George was the son of a Danish princess and his own wife had been born in England, every British sovereign from George I, who succeeded to the throne in 1714, to Queen Victoria, who died in 1901, had married a German. As a result, the British royal house had numerous German relatives, a

German dynastic name and a host of Teutonic connections that they needed to jettison.

The month before the name change, German Zeppelins had commenced air raids on London and the U-boats were once again unchecked on the high seas. In an article for *The Times*, H. G. Wells referred to George V's family as 'an imported dynasty'. He argued that the 'European dynastic system, based on the intermarriage of a group of mainly German royal families, is dead today. It is freshly dead, but it is as dead as the rule of the Incas. The British Empire is now very near the limit of its endurance with a kingly caste of Germans. The choice of British royalty between its peoples and its cousins cannot be definitely [*sic*] delayed. Were it made now, publicly and boldly, there can be no doubt that the decision would mean a renascence of monarchy and a tremendous outbreak of royalist enthusiasm in the empire.'[11] When Wells suggested that their court was alien and uninspiring, George V snapped to a courtier, 'I may be uninspiring, but I'll be damned if I'm an alien.'[12]

'Publicly and boldly' was exactly how the British royal family proceeded. All German connections were ditched, those relatives who had sided with Britain had to rebrand themselves from the Battenbergs into the Mountbattens and the dynastic name itself was changed by public proclamation to Windsor, in homage to the castle first built by King William the Conqueror and associated with England's monarchy for the best part of 900 years. When Wilhelm heard the news he wryly asked if anyone wanted to go to the theatre to see a performance of *The Merry Wives of Saxe-Coburg-Gotha*. (The German connections of the British royal house today are even more slender, with the subsequent marriages of the future King George VI to the Scottish aristocrat Lady Elizabeth Bowes-Lyon in 1923, Prince Charles to the English Lady Diana Spencer in 1981 and Prince William to Catherine Middleton in 2011. Despite the curious persistence of the xenophobic quip that the House of Windsor are essentially German, the last time a member of the immediate royal family married a German counterpart was when Princess Beatrice married Prince Henry of Battenberg in 1885.)

George V had taken a step that Wilhelm II seemed incapable of; he was doing everything in his power to keep the British monarchy in step with its empire's volatile mood and if that meant making difficult or even occasionally embarrassing decisions, then so be it. In contrast to George V, Wilhelm's leadership was seen by many people to be completely out of sync with the army, navy and Reichstag, a difficult task given that those three were also often at odds with one another. Kurt Riezler, secretary to the former Chancellor von Bethmann-Hollweg, noted in his diary, 'The Emperor is quite terrifyingly unpopular among the upper classes, conservative and liberal.'[13] As with Nicholas II, Wilhelm's constant visits to the front and absence from Berlin removed him from public visibility and since everybody knew that it was Ludendorff and von Hindenburg who were in charge of the actual operations, Wilhelm appeared like a spoiled and slightly ridiculous dilettante who was contributing nothing to the army but the expense of his entourage. Von Bethmann-Hollweg's earlier belief that keeping the Hohenzollern king away from his soldiers would dent his popularity no longer carried weight as the war dragged on and opinions about it within Germany became further divided. If Wilhelm had spent more time in Berlin, he might have given the impression that von Hindenburg and Ludendorff's dominance of the high command was a deliberate policy with the generals commanding one field because the sovereign needed to remain in the capital to oversee the whole government. As it was, Wilhelm gave the impression of a dog chasing at von Hindenburg's heels and hoping for the scraps of glory that fell from his table.

The year 1917 saw the triumph of the 'Silent Dictatorship' in the Second Reich with a government dominated by the high command, who had flexed their muscles by changing policy and ministers, and who now possessed a practical power far greater than anything enjoyed by the two institutions specifically recognised by the constitution, the monarchy and the Reichstag. Ludendorff's new nickname was 'General What-do-you-say', because everyone deferred so readily to his commands. Talking of the future, General What-do-you-say promoted the idea that there were only two options for Germany, either total victory or going under. So intense and fanatical was his dogged determination to face ruin, and inflict it on millions of his compatriots if they could not win, that even the Crown Prince began to regard Ludendorff with horror. In the end, Ludendorff was to cave and then blame everybody else for the defeat, but no one could be sure in 1917 that he would not use his influence to drag the war out to the last drop of available blood. The Crown Prince's fears were especially lively when the reintroduction of total war at sea brought about the nightmare long feared by his father – the United States entered the First World War on the side of side of Britain and her allies. Thousands of fresh recruits would come pouring over the Atlantic to supplement the Allied troops and hurl themselves across the trenches at the beleaguered German soldiers in Flanders.

In Vienna, the news convinced the Empress Zita that the time had come to jump and leave Germany to face defeat alone. Members of the German high command were watching her closely and suspected where her allegiances lay, but as of yet they could prove nothing. At an official luncheon given for guests of the German embassy in Vienna, Admiral Henning von Holtzendorff, a member of the German delegation and a strong supporter of unrestricted U-boat activity, did nothing to dispel Zita's low opinion of her allies' manners when he challenged her from across the table, 'I know you are against the U-boat war, just as you are against the war in general.'

'I am against war, as is any woman who would rather see people happy than suffering,' the Empress replied smoothly.

Then, echoing the beliefs of his friend Ludendorff, von Holtzendorff laughed derisively. 'Suffering – what does it matter? I work best of all when I have an empty stomach; then it's a case of tightening the belt and holding out.'

Zita responded by glancing meaningfully at the admiral's prodigious belly and declaring, 'I do not like hearing talk of "holding out" when one is sitting at a fully laden table.'[14] The Empress then lapsed into a decorous silence. Five days earlier, she and her husband had made contact with her brothers in the Belgian army for the first time since the beginning of the war.

10

The Sixtus Affair and the Attempts to End the War

'It seems to me that we would gladly conclude peace with you'

Count Ottokar von Czernin, the Austro-Hungarian Foreign Minister between 1916 and 1918, was the first major political appointment the Emperor Karl made after his accession. Von Czernin had previous experience as an ambassador abroad, serving at the embassies in Paris, The Hague and Bucharest; he was urbane if somewhat emotional and very clever. The scion of an ancient aristocratic house, he had been a great favourite of the Archduke Franz Ferdinand because he shared the Archduke's stalwart monarchism as well as his hostility towards Hungarian nationalism. Within weeks of his appointment as Foreign Minister, the count was reluctantly grappling with Germany's decision to reintroduce unrestricted submarine activity on the high seas. Both he and Karl were strongly against the policy in principle, but felt powerless to stop it in practice: 'I found with the emperor the same opposition to this new found method of fighting, and the same concern about its effects. But we knew that Germany was already firmly resolved to engage on an intensified, U-boat war, come what may, and that all our arguments had, therefore, no practical weight.'[1]

Two conferences were held between the Austro-Hungarians and the Germans about the U-boat issue and in the words of

Zita's biographer Gordon Brook-Shepherd, on both occasions 'the frightened called out to the deaf'.[2] Morally, the Emperor and Empress's Catholicism was offended by the idea of civilians, especially those from neutral countries, losing their lives because of the strategy. On a more pragmatic level, like the Kaiser, they believed its reintroduction would bring the United States into the war against them. With this in mind, Zita used her considerable charm to set about befriending Frederic Courtland Penfield, the US ambassador to Vienna, and his wife, Anne. Educated at private schools in England and Germany as a young man, Penfield was a popular choice as ambassador and his wife was the daughter of the late manufacturing tycoon William Weightman I, who had been responsible for the introduction of quinine to the United States. Mrs Penfield was thus an enormously wealthy woman, today her father would have been a billionaire several times over, and she could afford to entertain in the world of the Viennese beau monde. She was also – unusually for American diplomats and their wives, who were nearly always drawn from the East Coast or the old Protestant families of the South – a devout Catholic who had recently bequeathed her father's celebrated Pennsylvanian mansion to the Religious of the Assumption, a teaching order of nuns.

If Zita hoped that her friendship with the Penfields might help subtly convey the message that Austria-Hungary still valued amicable relations with the Great Republic, it was a fool's errand in the sense that while her husband was never detested in the same way Wilhelm II was, there was ultimately nothing that she, or anyone, could do to stop America entering the war once the U-boats began firing into the Atlantic again. Admiral von Holtzendorff's jaw-dropping rudeness to her over lunch and his disregard for palace etiquette was indicative of a much wider problem facing Austria by 1917. Their empire and their military were now viewed as Germany's junior partner and the perception had solidified the reality. Von Hindenburg's control over the Eastern Front was so complete that he was able to dominate the other Central Powers' armies in the same way he did Germany's. A central component of von Czernin's strategy as Foreign Minister was the policy that Austria-Hungary must not attempt to seek a separate peace or abandon her alliance with Germany, because to do so would court disaster. When Karl and von Czernin visited the Kaiser in January 1917 to reluctantly agree that they would stand by unrestricted submarine warfare it was because neither could see any way of getting out of the war without bringing the full wrath of von Hindenburg and Ludendorff down upon their heads.

The Empress did not share the Foreign Minister's views. She knew that their other two allies, Bulgaria and the Ottoman Empire, were useless – Bulgaria because it was too small and economically backward, the Ottoman Empire because it was falling apart internally and had been for years. She feared American intervention, distrusted the Germans and abhorred the use of the U-boats. She was also astute enough to realise that the empire could not go through another winter like 1916 and that its many ethnic and nationalist rivalries were making it impossible to co-ordinate a military strategy for much longer. Her brother Sixtus, now serving in the Belgian army, shared her views and in 1915 he had even spoken to Pope Benedict XV about his belief that peace could be achieved if Austria-Hungary could only be freed from Germany's orbit. The Holy Father, apparently, was not discouraging. The next step was to approach one of the Entente powers who might be receptive to a Hapsburg peace offer.

The cachet of Sixtus's Bourbon ancestry still carried a great weight in a country like France, where many people remained strongly sympathetic to royalism for most of the late nineteenth and early twentieth centuries. His sister's position as the wife of the future Emperor also made him worthy of interest to several French politicians who were intrigued by rumours that Austria-Hungary might bow out of the war early, helpfully leaving Germany to make the final stand on her own. One such man was Charles de Freycinet, France's former Prime Minister, who invited Sixtus to meet with him in Paris during his leave from the Belgian army in the autumn of 1916, shortly before Franz Josef's death. A subsequent interview with the current Prime Minister, Aristide Briand, gave Sixtus the hope that some kind of negotiation between Paris and Vienna was possible now that Karl had inherited the throne. On 21 January 1917, five days before the mortifying lunch at which the Empress was insulted by Admiral von Holtzendorff, Karl contacted his military attaché in Switzerland and asked him, in greatest secrecy, to make contact with Sixtus. Eight days later, Zita's mother, Maria Antonia of Portugal, Dowager Duchess of Parma, boarded a train for Neuchâtel in Switzerland, carrying a private letter from Zita formally inviting Sixtus and their younger brother Xavier to come to Vienna incognito and in contravention of the conditions on which Franz Josef had allowed them to leave the empire when the war began.

There were many reasons why the siblings were prepared to take such grave risks to be reunited. The first and most important reason was that they both genuinely wanted the war to end. What Zita had said to von Holtzendorff was true. She opposed anything that brought suffering to so many people. The second was their closeness to Karl – Zita as his much-loved wife and Sixtus as one of his closest friends. They both knew that, despite the assurances he was giving to Berlin, Karl wanted out. Thirdly, there was the future of the Hapsburg monarchy to consider, which Zita rightly believed grew less certain with each new slaughter on the battlefield. Furthermore, it was not just the Austrian monarchy which prompted the siblings to embark upon their putative peace mission. They were also considering the future of their natal house, the Bourbons.

It has already been mentioned that Sixtus, Zita and Xavier were members of a very large family. Their father, Duke Roberto I, married twice. Firstly to Princess Maria Pia of the Two Sicilies, with whom he had twelve children, three of whom died in infancy. After his first wife's death giving birth to their twelfth child in 1882, Roberto married Zita's mother, Maria Antonia, a daughter of the late King of Portugal. They had another twelve children together – when the family moved between their various homes, which included the magnificent Château de Chambord in France, they needed over a dozen railway cars to transport them and their servants. Of the twelve children born to Roberto and Maria Antonia, all grew into adulthood. In the Bourbon-Parma household, the values of faith and family were inculcated into the children – the twin glories of their family's rule in Ancien Régime France and the sublime mysteries of Catholicism were constantly emphasised. None of the siblings ever forget those lessons; four of Zita's sisters – Maria delle Neve Adelaide, Francesca, Maria Antonia and Isabella – became nuns, and as a young girl she had considered a similar vocation herself. The possibility that both Sixtus and Zita hoped that a successfully negotiated peace between Austria-Hungary and France would revive the Bourbon line's fortunes in the latter cannot be discounted.

It was not such a far-fetched idea in 1917. After being deposed in 1792, the family had been restored to the French throne three times over the course of the nineteenth century and in 1871 they had come tantalisingly close to a fourth. Tensions between royalists and republicans had been an ongoing feature of French political life for most of the Third Republic's existence.[3] Royalists could and did still occupy prominent positions in the armed forces and the government. Zita's celebrated ancestor King Henri IV had become the first Bourbon King of France in 1589 because he was able to bring to an end the French Wars of Religion. If Sixtus could play a leading role in freeing the country from an even more bloody conflict in the twentieth century, it might revive the royalist movement's fortunes in France or at the very least pave the way for the repeal of some of the legislation preventing princes of the old royal line from participating in French public affairs.

Via her mother and brothers' meeting at Neuchâtel, Zita learned of the French conditions for a separate peace. The first was that the provinces of Alsace-Lorraine should be returned to France, undoing Germany's annexation of them in 1871. The second was the full restoration of Belgian independence and her colonies in the Congo. The third was an Austrian guarantee to respect the independence of Serbia and the fourth was that the Ottoman city of Constantinople (now Istanbul) was to be given to Russia, fulfilling centuries of Romanov ambition to retake the ancient citadel of the Orthodox faith. She took this proposal to her husband and they worked on his response together.

A week later, Karl and Zita asked Count Tamás Erdödy, a Hungarian aristocrat who had been Karl's childhood playmate, subsequent lifelong friend and a man with almost no political ambitions, to join them for a private meeting. It was not his interest in government that the imperial couple needed. It was his devotion and his discretion. Zita gave him a small map of Neuchâtel and told him to meet her brothers at Rue du Pommier 7, a house a few streets back from the waterfront. He was not to get involved in any discussion with either of the two men, simply hand over a package containing several documents and, despite her affection for her brothers, Zita also warned Erdödy not to breathe a word about the deteriorating situation in Vienna, lest it weaken the empire's negotiating position with the French. According to Erdödy, at this audience it was Zita who gave most of the instructions and the Emperor finally spoke at the end when he begged his friend not to betray their trust in him. The only people who knew of this apart from him were Karl, Zita and Count von Czernin. If peace was to be achieved, Germany must not find out; secrecy was paramount.

Count Erdödy made it to Neuchâtel on the day before the Feast of Saint Valentine and handed the documents over, in which Karl agreed to all of the French conditions bar the clause about Serbia. While he conceded Serbia's right to exist, he would commit himself to nothing that might allow it to expand, either in Bosnia-Herzegovina or, as the French seemed to be proposing, into Albania. Erdödy's package also contained a letter from Zita again asking Sixtus and Xavier to come to Vienna in person, despite the risks, because, as von Czernin said, 'half an hour of talk is better than a dozen journeys'.[4] Von Czernin was by this stage having regular meetings with Zita to discuss the peace proposals, but the Emperor and Empress were playing their cards very close to their chests. Although it is unclear how much everyone involved actually knew, it seems as if von Czernin was kept deliberately in the dark about some of the details of the French conditions. He was still anxious not to anger Germany and since his preference for a peace negotiated between all the warring countries was public knowledge, he seems to have believed that at this stage nothing more substantial than the opening of diplomatic channels was being discussed. Once they were on a firmer footing, they could take the offer of peace talks to the Germans, who might be more inclined to agree if the plans were slightly more concrete. He apparently had no idea that Karl had already committed himself to supporting the French reconquest of Alsace-Lorraine and he would have been horrified if he had known. Von Czernin would not even sign any document that contained a phrase as innocuous as 'if Germany wishes to give up Alsace-Lorraine, then Austria-Hungary would naturally not stand in the way', despite Karl's repeated suggestion that he do so.[5] When he was with von Czernin, Karl still paid lip service to the theory of the alliance with Germany, but in private he had already told his wife, 'We will support France and will use all the means in our power to bring pressure to bear on Germany.'[6] Unlike von Czernin, the Empress took Ludendorff at his word and she was therefore sceptical about the German high command's receptiveness to peace in any guise.

More information was smuggled back to Neuchâtel with Count Erdödy on 21 February, with some of von Czernin's thoughts on the matter and memoranda personally annotated by the Emperor. Sixtus was explicitly told to burn everything after he read it, but he felt he needed a copy to show the French as proof of the Hapsburgs' commitment to ending the war, so he translated some of his brother-in-law's letters and von Czernin's papers into French before torching the originals. The translations were handed over to President Poincaré at the Élysée Palace on 5 March. Seeing that Karl himself had left personal comments on the proposals, Poincaré was convinced that this was something significant. He advised Sixtus and Xavier to accept their sister's invitation to Vienna and to keep the government informed of their discussions.

The brothers were disguised and taken through Austria dressed as civilians to stay at Count Erdödy's town house in Vienna. It was unseasonably cold and despite it being the last week of March, snow was falling when they were driven over to Laxenburg Castle, one of the imperial family's homes on the outskirts of the city. It was eight o'clock in the evening by the time they arrived and the light was already failing as they were let in through a small side door that led to Zita's apartments. The Empress was overjoyed to see them after two years apart and for the next ninety minutes she and her husband caught up on family news. At half past nine, Count von Czernin arrived and Zita decorously withdrew. Even she could not stay at a political conference between the representatives of a foreign power, her Emperor and his country's Foreign Minister.

Karl, von Czernin and Sixtus never wrote down what happened that night at the Laxenburg, but Xavier, twenty-nine at the time of the mission, did. In light of the Tsar's abdication eight days earlier, the proposal that Constantinople be given to the Russians was dropped. The retaking of the Byzantine heartlands and the reconsecration of Hagia Sophia had always been a Romanov obsession. Now that they were gone, Karl and von Czernin saw no reason why Constantinople should feature as a condition in any peace talks. The points about Belgium and Serbia, with Karl's aforementioned caveats, were accepted but when the French demands for Alsace-Lorraine were brought up, von Czernin balked. Austria could not possibly be expected to promise away areas of land that were not hers. It was not only dishonourable but lunatic. Possession of Alsace-Lorraine was the burning issue between French and German nationalists long before 1914 and so even to contemplate getting involved, let alone to side with France, would provoke fury in Berlin. The talks thus ended inconclusively, sinking on the issue of Alsace-Lorraine. Sixtus and Xavier went back to their safe house under the cover of darkness, where they discussed how to win Count von Czernin over. They managed to arrange a meeting with him at Erdödy's on the following evening, 24 March, at which he promised to obey his sovereign's commands, whatever they might be, but kept talking about the 'might of Germany' and the harm it could inflict on Austria-Hungary if these negotiations went wrong.[7]

Back at the castle, Karl decided to proceed without his Foreign Minister's full complicity. All of 25 March, the Feast of the Annunciation, was spent drafting a firm and written commitment to the conditions of peace that Sixtus could carry back to Paris, including a promise to stand by a French re-annexation of Alsace-Lorraine. The Empress was present for much of the document's composition, as were her two brothers. The fact that Zita, Sixtus and Xavier's first language was French made the task of writing the document a lot easier and Sixtus left with it, catching the evening train back to Switzerland and making his way back to Paris from there. As the letter was being written, telephone calls were occasionally placed to von Czernin at the Empress's suggestion, ostensibly to go over some of the finer points of diplomatic language. Those telephone calls prove that von Czernin knew a document was being drawn up at the Laxenburg Castle on 25 March 1917 and that it contained at least some of the points that had been discussed there two nights earlier. He may even have known, or suspected, that Austria-Hungary's commitment to resolving the issue of Alsace-Lorraine was being included despite his concerns. His conversation with the two brothers at Count Erdödy's house the night before, in which he promised to follow Karl's lead on the issue, all but confirms that he knew Alsace-Lorraine would have to be mentioned in any correspondence with France, who placed the reclaiming of 'the Lost Provinces' high on their list of war aims.

What Count von Czernin did not know, however, was that a central part of France's conditions was that there would be no negotiation that included a possible peace for Germany. The deal being offered was only for Austria-Hungary. Von Czernin's insistence that they could not decide the issue of Alsace-Lorraine without Germany's involvement had arisen because he believed that Sixtus was bringing a message that correlated with his own views on how best to end the war, a series of compromises between all the powers. To the best of his knowledge, this was an opinion shared by the Emperor and Karl deliberately encouraged him in that belief. Had von Czernin realised that what they were actually planning was to abandon Germany at the first available opportunity, he would never have been party to any of the meetings. As a semi-constitutional monarch, Karl needed to act with the approval of at least some of his cabinet ministers; von Czernin was therefore tricked by only being fed half the relevant information and Karl's repeated requests to get his signature on some of the documents suggest that he saw his Foreign Minister's role as nothing more than a constitutional requirement which could later be used to legitimise the Emperor's covert actions in negotiating with an enemy power. That at no point in discussions at the Laxenburg or later at Count Erdödy's house was the fairly crucial issue of the separate peace raised suggests strongly that Zita, Sixtus and Xavier were also in on the plot, or as they would have seen it the necessity, of hoodwinking von Czernin. There can also be little doubt that Karl knew exactly what he was doing and pursued his strategy with von Czernin deliberately. Earlier on in negotiations, Sixtus had written to his brother-in-law:

It seems to me that we would gladly conclude peace with you on the proposed basis but at the same time the whole of France is firmly resolved to pursue the war with the utmost energy against

Germany, until she is finally and decisively defeated. It is my duty to draw your attention to this most important point. Nobody is ready to treat with Germany before she is beaten.[8]

Although Karl would later deny it, 'this most important point' had been made clear to him from the very beginning: peace with the Allies would come at the price of cutting all ties with Germany. His full understanding of the issue is made clear in the letter he sent back with Sixtus after their meeting at the Laxenburg:

I ask you to pass to the President of the French Republic, M. Poincaré, the secret and unofficial message that I will use all means and all my personal influence to support France's justified return of Alsace-Lorraine. Belgium must be restored as an independent state, keeping all its African territories quite apart from the compensation for the losses she has suffered. The sovereignty of Serbia will be restored and, in order to demonstrate our goodwill, we are willing to guarantee her an appropriate natural access to the Atlantic Sea as well as economic concessions ...[9]

A few weeks after he wrote this, America entered the war, only adding to the Emperor's sense of urgency and frustration. The Hapsburg plans hit a snag when the government of Prime Minister Briand fell in France and was replaced by Alexandre Ribot, who was less keen on negotiating with the Austrians for a separate peace, but when Karl's letter was shown to his British counterpart, Lloyd George, on 11 April 1917, he was enthusiastic but worried about how the Italians would react at losing their chance to carve up bits of the southern Hapsburg Empire. Sixtus was smuggled back to Vienna on 8 May for more talks, while the flailing failure of Russia's new government on the Eastern Front made the German high command confident that the end was now in sight. If the Provisional Government in Russia collapsed, it would leave the Central Powers free to turn most of their combined strength to the West and if that happened Austria's non-involvement would obviously be of huge advantage to the Entente. Lloyd George was interested in the Emperor's offer; Sixtus was brought over to meet with him at 10 Downing Street and then granted an audience at

Buckingham Palace. Karl kept trying and praying for peace, but for months nothing happened as the Allies debated among themselves whether this was an offer worth considering. After all, might it not simply be better to pursue victory over Austria-Hungary as well as Germany?

That autumn, George Clemenceau became the new French Prime Minister. He was a fire-breathing nationalist, nicknamed 'Le Tigre' for his animosity towards his country's enemies, and he wanted total victory no less than Ludendorff did in Germany. In the spring of 1918, von Czernin made the mistake of publicly criticising Clemenceau when he labelled his policies as the major obstacle to the quest for peace in recent months. Clemenceau responded to the insult by vindictively handing over all of Karl's letters to the press, who published them in the journalistic coup of the decade.

The reaction in Germany can only be described as hysterical. Karl and 'the Italian Schemer' were denounced left, right and centre. In political terms, quite literally. Von Czernin dashed to the palace for a frenzied audience with the Emperor in which the Foreign Minister demanded Karl sign a document denying that any of the letters to Sixtus had been issued in an official capacity and that at no point in any discussion had Belgium or Alsace-Lorraine even been mentioned. Why Karl signed this patently false denial is still astonishing. It may have been, as Zita's biographer Gordon Brook-Shepherd believed, that blackmail had been brought to bear on the couple about the safety of her brothers or, far more probably, that they were frightened into lying by the possibility of a German-backed retaliatory coup in Vienna.[10] Others believed that von Czernin's reaction was so unhinged that Karl had no choice but to sign the dishonest pledge in the hope of quietening him, or that von Czernin persuaded Karl that Ludendorff would press for the German occupation of Austria without a full rebuttal of the claims being made in the French press. Then again, perhaps Karl simply lied because that was the easiest thing to do in a very difficult set of circumstances.

Whatever his motivation, it was a mistake. After his denial, more documents from the correspondence were published, proving how much he had known and approved of. Angry at being hoodwinked over the clause that based the whole negotiation on the premise of a separate peace and frightened by the situation they now all found themselves in because of it, Count von Czernin asked to resign and Karl accepted. But before handing his own resignation in, von Czernin broke every precept of aristocratic etiquette when he tried to persuade Karl to do the same. The Empress wrote in her diary of a 'dreadful scene with Czernin. He again tries to persuade the Emperor to back down and when that doesn't succeed, he has a nervous breakdown, weeps, and suddenly offers his resignation, which H.M. [His Majesty] accepts.'[11] Karl and Zita's Lord High Chamberlain, the wonderfully charming Count Leopold von Berchtold, noted wryly that in times gone by aristocrats were raised to sacrifice themselves to protect the stability of the monarch's reign, but alas, with von Czernin 'such greatness of ancient times lay far beyond him'.[12]

The main result of the Sixtus Affair was a further weakening in Austria's position in the war. To prevent any retaliation from their allies north of the border, Austria-Hungary had to tie herself even more closely to Germany. The great gamble of the Sixtus Affair had failed and now all that was left for the Hapsburgs to do was to perish or triumph with the Second Reich.

11

The Murder of the Romanovs

'Our souls are at peace'

Most of Russia's leaders in 1917 were haunted by the fear that their revolution would follow the pattern set by the French in 1789 and Alexander Kerensky, the brilliant orator who became the Provisional Government's Prime Minister a few months after the February Revolution, was no exception. Kerensky was a republican, but he did not want any violence to befall the deposed imperial family. With the old censorship laws removed under the new regime, it was open season on the Romanovs in the Russian press and all the old lies about 'Nicholas the Bloody' and his wife were given a fresh breath of life. Many people, particularly in the Petrograd Soviet, wanted them to be punished or executed for treason. The Soviet's chairman, Irakli Tsereteli, made a speech at the Tauride in which he argued, 'The Republic must be safeguarded against the Romanovs returning to the historical arena. That means that the dangerous persons must be directly in the hands of the Petrograd Soviet.'[1] Kerensky refused to make any move against them and repeatedly insisted that he did not want to be this revolution's Jean-Paul Marat.[2]

To put pay to the Soviet's claims that orgies were taking place at the Alexander Palace or that the Romanovs were still spying for the Germans, Kerensky travelled out to Tsarskoe Selo, where he met the family for the first time in their drawing room. He instinctively felt the family's 'fear at finding itself alone with a revolutionary whose objects in bursting in on it were unknown. With an answering smile I hurriedly walked over to the Emperor, shook hands and sharply said, "Kerensky" as I always do by way of introduction ... Nicholas II gave my hand a firm grasp ... and smiling once again, led me to his family.'[3]

Kerensky soon warmed to most of the family, whose kindness and vulnerability touched him in equal measure, but he took much longer to find much affection for the Empress. 'The Tsar and Tsarina presented a complete contrast in every trifling detail,' he recalled, 'in bearing, in small mannerisms, in their attitude to people; in word, still more in thought ... The Tsar spoke [to me]; but it was the meaning of the Tsarina's silence that was more clearly apparent to me. By the side of a pleasant, somewhat awkward Colonel of the Guards, very ordinary except for a pair of wonderful blue eyes, stood a born Empress, proud, unbending, fully conscious of her right to rule.'[4] It was only when Kerensky questioned them to ascertain if there was any truth in the accusations of treason or espionage that he grew to admire Alexandra for the 'clarity, the energy and the frankness of her words'.[5] Count Benckendorff, who sat in on Alexandra's interrogation, recalled later that when pressed by Kerensky about her unpopular involvement in government, 'Her Majesty answered that the Emperor and herself were the most united of couples, whose whole joy and pleasure was in their family life, and that they had no secrets from each other; that they discussed everything, and that it was not astonishing that in the last years which had been so troubled, that they had often discussed politics.'[6] Alexandra, for her part, remarked afterwards to Benckendorff that she had been pleasantly surprised by Kerensky's good manners and tactfulness. As he left the palace, Kerensky took the time to tell Nicholas how impressed he was with the Tsarina: 'Your wife does not lie.'[7] Nicholas touched him too due to his 'natural, quite artless simplicity that gave the Emperor that peculiar fascination, that charm which was further increased by his wonderful eyes, deep and sorrowful ... the former Emperor never once lost his equilibrium, never failed to act as a courteous man of the world.'[8] On his return to Petrograd, he informed his government colleagues that the newspapers' and Soviet's campaign against the Romanovs was a tissue of lies.

Even Kerensky's newfound sympathy for the imperial family could not save them from the difficult situation they found themselves in. Fifteen-year-old Anastasia was much more reticent about what she put in her letters, even to close friends, because she believed that their mail was being opened.[9] The children had recovered from the measles, but the girls had all had their heads shaved so that their hair would grow back in a uniform way and they were still very weak. Maria too had since come down with the disease and she was the last to recover. Olga developed post-measles rheumatic fever, Anastasia had pleurisy that aggravated her ears and Maria caught pneumonia, leaving her so weak that for a few days Alexandra thought she was going to die. The Empress herself now had to spend much of her time in a wheelchair as her health collapsed completely, and by spring only Tatiana and Anastasia were strong enough for regular walks in the grounds or to attend the Easter Communion services. When the family were allowed out in the palace gardens for some fresh air, a crowd gathered at the railings to hoot and jeer at them, most having bribed the guards for the privilege of getting so close to the imperial family. Had any of these spectators wanted to murder one of the Romanovs, they would have been completely defenceless. The guards increasingly became a problem. One night, they burst in to the family's drawing room shouting that signals had been made to facilitate a monarchist escape plot – it turned out that the Grand Duchess Anastasia had been sewing while her father read aloud to them when she bent over to pick up fabric her body had covered and then uncovered a table lamp, which the guards mistook for a code to imagined monarchists hiding in the estate.[10] When the Empress or any of her daughters appeared at the palace windows, some of the sentries below would turn to make obscene sexual gestures at them. Alexei's pet goat was murdered and so were the swans on the palace's artificial lake. Some of the soldiers defecated in the children's rowing boat and carved pornographic sketches on to it.[11]

To add to the family's distress, the Provisional Government felt that there were still too many courtiers in residence at Tsarskoe Selo, some of whom had been named in the press as being part of the Tsarina's fictitious German spy ring. Two of Alexandra's favourite ladies-in-waiting, Lili Dehn and Anna Vyrubova, were among those who were arrested and taken from Tsarskoe Selo to imprisonment in Petrograd. Vyrubova, still weak from the train crash that had nearly killed her in 1915 and also recovering from the same sickness as the grand duchesses, had to be removed from her sickbed to hobble out to the waiting car on crutches. Tatiana was particularly upset at the separation and she gave the two women a family photograph album as a parting gift. Dehn, who was used to the Grand Duchess's unflappable composure, was surprised and touched by the weeping that Tatiana gave way to as they were taken from the palace.

Kerensky tried to remedy the situation by appointing a new Captain of the Guard in the form of Colonel Evgeny Kobylinksy, a thirty-nine-year-old veteran and a monarchist. Captivity improved for the prisoners and Nicholas later referred to Kobylinksy as 'my last friend'.[12] Some of the crueller tactics that had been tried on the Romanovs in the weeks immediately after the abdication, like segregating them from each other between meal times and limiting their opportunities to talk to one another, were dropped. A plan to separate the Tsarina from her children was shelved when her Mistress of the Robes pointed out that a separation might kill Alexandra: 'It would mean death to her. Her children are her life.'[13]

Kerensky wanted the family out of Russia as soon as possible. It would guarantee their safety at the same time as removing a large problem for the Provisional Government. Their continued presence riled both monarchists and their most extreme opponents, for obviously very different reasons. In April, Vladimir Lenin had been smuggled back into Russia with German assistance, in the hope that a successful communist revolution would pull Russia out of the war and failing that, that he would at least manage to disrupt the political situation enough to weaken Russia's still-failing performance on the Eastern Front. Despite the role the war had played in destroying the monarchy, the republic incredibly chose to continue fighting it in the hope of holding on to Anglo–French goodwill and investments, and because they could not see any way out of the war which would not leave Germany free to impose a punitive peace settlement on them. Bolshevik pressure was mounting with the death tolls at the front and Kerensky was under no illusions about what would happen to Nicholas's family if the Far Left became more powerful. Plans were made to send them abroad, something which Alexandra was initially uncomfortable with because she did not want to flutter around the Continent from one fashionable location to another being photographed for the world's society pages like so many deposed royals had been happy to do in the past and would do in the future. Such an existence would be anathema to her. However, concerns for her children won her over and she apparently raised the possibility of them moving to Norway, which was a beautiful country, neutral in the war and had a climate which she felt would be beneficial for Alexei. France, Spain, Italy and Switzerland were all briefly mentioned as possible places of sanctuary for the Romanovs, but increasingly the obvious choice seemed to be Britain.

At Tsarskoe Selo, Nicholas brought the subject up several times with his children's English tutor Sydney Gibbes, the son of a bank manager from Rotherham who had been hired years earlier when Alexandra's uncle Edward VII told her that her children were picking up unattractive regional twangs from their then-teacher, a Mr Epps.[14] The Kaiser, anxious to help, irked his generals when he promised that any train or ship carrying the Romanovs abroad would be guaranteed safe passage by Germany. The family began to pack in preparation for the move and then quite unexpectedly a mortified Sir George Buchanan, the British ambassador in Petrograd, told Kerensky, apparently with tears in his eyes, that his country was no longer willing to take in the deposed Tsar and his family. They would have to go somewhere else.

The British refusal to grant the Romanovs asylum in 1917 is notorious and for many years blame was fixed upon the country's Left-leaning Prime Minister, David Lloyd George, whose political scruples allegedly prevented him from offering help to a deposed autocrat. This fiction was maintained even by some of the Romanovs' and the Windsors' closest mutual relatives like Lord Louis Mountbatten, who may have known the truth, and Edward VIII, who apparently genuinely believed that 'just before the Bolsheviks seized the Tsar, my father had personally planned to rescue him, but in some way the plan was blocked. In any case, it hurt my father that Britain had not raised a hand to save his cousin Nicky. "Those politicians," he used to say. "If it had been one of their kind, they would have acted fast enough. But merely because the poor man was an emperor – "'[15]

But Lloyd George had in fact supported welcoming the ex-Tsar to England in order to help the Provisional Government and because he could not conceive of any way in which he could refuse Nicholas, who was George's first cousin on his mother's side, and Alexandra, a granddaughter of the revered Queen Victoria. The Prime Minister's view that the Romanovs could not sensibly be turned away was not shared by everyone. The British ambassador in Paris, Lord Bertie, said the Allies should avoid helping the imperial family because 'the Empress is not only a Boche [a pejorative term for a German] by birth but in sentiment. She did all she could to bring about an understanding with Germany. She is regarded as a criminal or a criminal lunatic and the ex-Emperor as a criminal from his weakness and submission to her promptings.'[16] Left-wing demonstrations at the Albert Hall in London, the entry of the United States into a war that was now presented as one of democracy against the last vestiges of absolutism, and the British crown's recent spate of public relations difficulties thanks to its numerous foreign relatives made the King worry about the political implications of asylum and he sought the advice of his private secretary, Lord Stamfordham. His considered opinion was that the granting of asylum to the Romanovs would associate Britain's constitutional monarchy with an oppressive foreign autocracy and incite 'all the people who are at present clamouring for a republic in England'.[17] In the second week of April, His Majesty's Foreign Office in London curtly informed the Provisional Government in Petrograd that 'His Majesty's Government does not insist on its former offer of hospitality to the Imperial Family.'[18]

The British withdrawal of help meant that Kerensky had to find a way to move the Romanovs somewhere else beyond the reach of the Petrograd Soviet. They would have been safe in Sweden or Norway, as the Empress had hoped, but getting them over those borders required putting them on a train that would run through or near Petrograd. What if somebody informed the Soviet that the Romanovs were being moved and the Petrograd garrison helped them intercept the train? The integrity of the family's guards could not be relied upon. The possibility that they would all be lynched could not be ruled out.

It was in these circumstances that Alexander Kerensky considered moving the family to a place of temporary internal exile, far away from the capital. The Tsar suggested the Crimea, where they could be housed at their old summer home of Livadia, a family favourite. Kerensky conceded that the idea had merits. The Crimean population was still predominantly sympathetic to the imperial family, and other members of the Romanov clan, including the Dowager Empress and both of Nicholas's sisters, were already making their way there. If the situation deteriorated further and civil war struck, as many feared it might, the Crimea was easily accessible by sea and the Romanovs could quickly be moved abroad. The possibility of sending them to one of the country manor houses owned by Nicholas's brother Mikhail was also toyed with, but in both scenarios it would require moving the imperial family through areas of Russia that were in the grips of revolutionary violence and lawlessness.

In his memoirs, Kerensky justified the final decision taken in August 1917 to move the family to the town of Tobolsk in Siberia, although it is still not clear whether, even without the benefit of hindsight, Livadia would have been a more sensible choice. By the time he wrote his memoirs in 1935, the eventual terrible fate that befell the family weighed heavily on Kerensky's mind; he was keen to exculpate himself from the charge that he had not done enough to save them and had in fact accidentally sent them to their deaths. 'I chose Tobolsk because it was an out-and-out backwater ... [with] no industrial proletariat, and a population which was prosperous and contented, not to say old-fashioned ... the climate was excellent and the town could boast a very passable Governor's residence where the Imperial Family could live with some measure of comfort.' He was embarrassed when he arrived at Tsarskoe Selo to tell Nicholas that they were going to Siberia rather than the Crimea, but the Tsar put him at his ease. 'I have no fear. We trust you. If you say we must move, it must be. We trust you.'[19]

Their life at Tsarskoe Selo was packed up. The day before they left was Alexei's thirteenth birthday and an icon of Our Lady of Znamenie was brought to the palace at Alexandra's request to mark the occasion. As the priests processed it back through the grounds, the Romanovs stood on the balcony to watch it go. Several wept and Count Benckendorff, watching with them, thought 'It was as if the past were taking leave, never to come back.'[20]

On the evening of their departure, Kerensky arranged for the Grand Duke Mikhail to come and say goodbye. The brothers hugged and chatted quietly. Kerensky, who for some reason felt he had to supervise the meeting, noticed that both brothers seemed so overwhelmed at the potential finality of the situation that they did not know how to express themselves. Years later, Kerensky was moved at the memory of how they kept 'getting hold of one another's arm or coat button'.[21] Mikhail left in tears and kissed Alexei, who was wandering from room to room with his spaniel, Joy, trotting along at his heels. Alexandra was in her mauve boudoir, weeping, and Kerensky assured a group of courtiers that after the elections in November the political situation would stabilise and the Romanovs could leave Tobolsk, either for a life abroad or for the Crimea. He also took time to address the soldiers who were being sent to Tobolsk with the family: 'You have guarded the Imperial Family here; now you must guard it at Tobolsk where it is being transferred by order of the Provisional Government. Remember: no hitting a man when he is down. Behave like gentlemen, not like cads. Remember that he is a former Emperor and that neither he nor his family must suffer any hardships.'[22]

The cars arrived just before six o'clock in the morning. The sun was rising – a beautiful dawn, Nicholas noted later – as Kerensky gave the order for the convoy to set off for the station. Those left behind in the palace came out to say goodbye and waved silently as the Romanovs and the entourage allowed to go with them pulled away. They were put in railway carriages disguised as belonging to the Red Cross and told that the town they were moving to was called Tobolsk. The Empress's back gave out as she was hauled on board. As the train picked up speed, the Grand Duchess Anastasia wrote a note to her English tutor that ended with the words, 'Goodbye. Don't forget me.'[23]

The journey to Siberia was long and uncomfortable. To the grand duchesses' amazement, their small group was being watched over by 336 soldiers.[24] Security was tight. Despite the summer heat, the curtains had to be drawn and the windows closed whenever the train passed through a town or village. One evening, the train stopped near a small isolated house and, since there was no station, the travellers were allowed to bend the rules and stretch their legs. Anastasia was leaning out the window to catch some air when a young boy ran out of the house to greet the train. Anastasia's hair had still not fully grown back since it had been shaved off following her brush with measles and the little boy mistook her for a man. 'Uncle,' he asked, perhaps anxious for news of what was going on with the Revolution, 'please give me, if you have got [it], a newspaper.' For a moment, Anastasia could not understand why she was being addressed as a man before remembering her shorn tresses. 'I am not an uncle but an aunty and have no newspaper,' she replied. As the boy trotted back to his house, Anastasia and some of the convoy's soldiers burst out laughing at the misunderstanding which, as Anastasia ruefully admitted, had been perfectly reasonable given her current appearance.[25]

They were on the train for four days until they reached the station at Tyumen, where they disembarked to take the ferry to Tobolsk, which had no railway station. The voyage took a few days; as far as Kerensky was concerned, the town's sheer remoteness would be their best safety if the winter was a difficult one politically for the new republic, because it could not be accessed at all once summer was over. One of the family's maids, Anna Demidova, was disgusted by the accommodation on the ferry, but even more so when they reached Tobolsk, when she was sent ahead to inspect the house they were all to live in. The former governor's mansion had been seized by a local soviet at the time of the Revolution; they had rechristened it 'Freedom House' and stripped it of all its furniture. They had only been moved out a few days before the Romanovs' arrival and the house was in a disgusting condition. It took the best part of a week to make it inhabitable, during which time the Tsar and his family remained on board the ferry.

Despite its unpromising start, life in Tobolsk was bearable for the Romanovs. Even almost pleasant, at times. Their remaining courtiers and servants were allowed to live with them in the mansion or were allocated perfectly adequate accommodation in a house on the opposite side of the street. The Romanov-sympathising Colonel Kobylinsky arranged for the family to attend services at the nearby church, where they were often cheered or blessed by the crowd. When the autumn chill and winter snows arrived, Anastasia began to organise rehearsals indoors after which she and her sisters would act out scenes from different plays in French, Russian and English, designed to lighten everybody's mood in the evenings. The theatrics fast became a household activity: their tutors took on the task of directing, the Tsar and Tsarina wrote out programmes for the small audience, the family physician played a part in one drama and Nicholas himself finally took up the challenge of playing the role of Smirnov, a middle-aged landowner, in Chekov's one-act comedy *The Bear*. One night, Anastasia, who seemed determined to keep everyone's spirits up, sashayed in to the parlour after dinner wearing her father's Jaeger long johns and began prancing around the room in a spectacle so unexpected and hilarious that even Alexandra was convulsed with laughter, a sight that had been rare for quite some time.[26] During the day, Alexandra oversaw her children's lessons and arranged some of her own when she realised, to her surprise, that she had nearly forgotten how to speak German, the language of her early childhood. Gifts of clothes, food and small luxuries were sent to the house by people in Tobolsk, nuns at the local convent baked them cakes and many of the guards had now developed a rapport with their prisoners. They even began allowing them access to letters from their far-flung friends and family, who were desperate for news of them.

Alexandra took the opportunity to write to Anna Vyrubova, now released from captivity in Petrograd but still under surveillance.

Up at noon for religious lessons with Tatiana, Maria, Anastasia, and Alexei. I have a German lesson three times a week with Tatiana and once with Maria ... Also I sew, embroider and paint, with spectacles on because my eyes have become too weak to do without them. I read 'good books' a great deal, love the Bible, and from time to time read novels ... He [the Tsar] is simply marvellous ... The others are all good and brave and uncomplaining, and Alexei is an angel ... One by one all earthly things slip away, houses and possessions ruined, friends vanished ... I feel old, oh, so old, but I am still the mother of this country, and I suffer its pains as my own child's pains and I love it in spite of all its sins and horrors. No one can tear a child from its mother's heart and neither can you tear away one's country, although Russia's black ingratitude to the Emperor breaks my heart. Not that it is the whole country though. God have mercy and save Russia.

A few days later, she wrote again with more news on the family. 'I have grown quite grey. Anastasia, to her despair is now very fat, as Maria was, round and fat to the waist, with short legs. I do hope she will grow. Olga and Tatiana are both thin.'[27]

Even as Alexandra was writing of Russia's 'sins and horrors', the worst was yet to come when the Provisional Government was overthrown in a second revolution that brought Lenin and the Bolsheviks to power. Civil war was now inevitable as monarchists, nationalists, liberals and even many left-wing groups banded together under the logic of my enemy's enemy is my friend. Communism was, by its very nature, a system that required a dictatorship and the sheer brutality of the regime, even in its earliest months, made it many enemies.

It was not long before the triumph of the Soviet in Petrograd made its influence felt in Tobolsk. Some of the guards formed their own Soviet and voted that all officers should now be banned from wearing epaulets in order to promote a spirit of egalitarianism. Nicholas was jolted out of his usual quiescence by this and point-blank refused to remove the epaulets he had received from his late father, Alexander III. It took the pleas of Alexandra and a distraught Colonel Kobylinsky for him to back down and even then he continued to wear the epaulets in private and simply threw a coat over his shoulders when he went outside. The news of the Bolshevik seizure of power made Nicholas angry and despondent. His abdication had been for nothing. It had not brought peace and stability as promised, but instead chaos and the nightmare of a Bolshevik-led government. Pierre Gilliard noted in his diary at this time, 'Their Majesties still cherish the hope that among their loyal friends some may be found to attempt their release. Never was the situation more favourable for escape, for there is as yet no representative of the Bolshevik government at Tobolsk. With the complicity of Colonel Kobylinsky, already on our side, it would be easy to trick the insolent but careless vigilance of the guards.'[28]

Bolshevik presence in Tobolsk was soon stepped up with the result that security was tightened around the family. Soldiers touted on colleagues who were said to be sympathetic to their former rulers. Those named were dismissed and those who risked going to Nicholas to take their leave of him after their dismissal usually faced arrest and imprisonment for counter-revolutionary activity. The remaining guards went back to the old game of taunting the imperial family, particularly the four grand duchesses. One day, Alexei ran in to tell his father that some dirty words had been carved into the swings in the garden. In a rage, Nicholas stormed out, tore the seats off the swing rope and tossed them away before his daughters could see them.

In Moscow, now declared capital in Petrograd's place, Leon Trotsky dreamed of a grand public show trial of the ex-Tsar 'that would unfold a picture of the entire reign ... proceedings would be broadcast to the nation by radio'.[29] It would be a wonderful opportunity for Trotsky to show off his undoubted skills as a speaker, as well as harkening back to the trials of Charles I and Louis XVI. But not everyone saw the wisdom in Trotsky's plan. The trial could give Nicholas a public platform to exonerate himself or generate sympathy for the old regime. There was a precedent for that, too. Charles I's dignity at his trial in 1649 had turned even some of the most ardent parliamentarians in his favour, while Robespierre had smashed plates in fury at how badly the trial of Marie Antoinette had been handled in 1793, because he felt it had given her 'the triumph of exciting the sympathy of the public in her last moments'.[30] There was also the problem that a trial, even a show trial with the verdict decided in advance, at least suggested the possibility of innocence. Nicholas had been Tsar, therefore there was no question of his guilt.

On 27 April 1918, eight months after their arrival, Commissar Vasili Yakovlev, a thirty-two-year-old member of the Petrograd Soviet who had spent years in exile in Canada after being hunted by the Tsarist secret police, came to Tobolsk to tell Nicholas that he was being moved at four o'clock that morning. When Yakovlev would not tell him where he was being taken, Nicholas refused to comply. Alexandra interrupted their conversation, aghast at what she heard. Alexei had recently fallen and been taken to bed. 'What are you doing with him!' she shouted. 'You want to tear him away from his family. How can you? He has an ill son. No, he can't go, he must stay with us!' Yakovlev told her that he would be leaving at four o'clock in the morning and that Nicholas had no choice in the matter. As he left the room, Alexandra called after him, 'This is too cruel; I don't believe that you'll do this!'[31] Colonel Kobylinsky knew better and he told the couple that Yakovlev would move the ex-Tsar with or without his co-operation.

For hours the Romanovs debated their few options. While it was impossible to move Alexei given his recent injury, Alexandra had never quite forgiven herself for abandoning Nicholas when he was faced with the abdication and she refused to leave him now that there was a possibility of an even greater dénouement. It was a testament to how much she loved her husband and her determination to stay with him to the end that she decided to leave Alexei in Tobolsk in the care of his sisters and go with Nicholas, wherever they were taking him. Yakovlev and Kobylinsky both thought she was leaving because she was afraid that 'left alone he may do something stupid', an oblique reference to what had happened with the abdication. It was, to those who knew her, astonishing that she would consider parting from Alexei when he was unwell, but at four o'clock in the morning Alexandra was at Nicholas's side as they left their home in Tobolsk for a five-day journey in springless carriages to the railway line at Tyumen, with Alexandra in agony almost from the moment they set out. They had decided to take the Grand Duchess Maria with them to look after her mother on the journey, along with a few servants, including Dr Botkin and Anna Demidova, the family's self-possessed maid whom Yakovlev mistook for a lady-in-waiting. Olga, Tatiana, Anastasia, Alexei and most of the remaining household stayed behind in Tobolsk, but even with this large retinue to look after them, Alexandra's decision to separate from them without knowing what the future held must have been a painful one. Whether it was the right choice, or if there even was a right choice to be made in such circumstances, is unknowable.

On the train from Tyumen, with her back agonised and her body beginning to cry out in withdrawal as the medication she was used to was no longer supplied, the Tsarina stayed in her compartment and Maria kept her company. Yakovlev thought she was 'wily and proud' and that she went out of her way to avoid the soldiers, apparently 'if she saw a sentry in the corridor upon exiting the bathroom, she would go back and lock herself in until the sentry left the corridor'.[32] Nicholas and Yakovlev talked as they travelled; the commissar noticed how Nicholas crossed himself every time they passed an Orthodox church. They spoke of innocuous things, family, weather and food. 'He really does love his family,' Yakovlev told a newspaper that spring, 'and cares about them very much.'[33]

After a few days' travel, the train came to a halt at a junction near the town of Omsk, a split in the Trans-Siberian railway. There, it waited for hours while Yakovlev was involved in a telegram exchange with Moscow. The idea of a state trial had lost its appeal and the nearby Ural Soviet wanted to take possession of the family. The Ural Mountains, a vast range generally held to be the dividing line between European and Asian Russia, was a notoriously anti-monarchist region that had once stood at the heart of the Tsarist exile system. On board the train from Tyumen, Nicholas remarked, 'I would go anywhere at all, only not to the Urals.'[34] There is some evidence to suggest that there were those in Moscow, including Lenin, who had always planned for them to end up in custody in the Urals. A telegram sent from the Ural Regional Soviet on 28 April referred to a letter, either from Lenin or from Yakov Sverdlov, the chairman of the All-Russian Central Executive Committee in Moscow, written on 9 April, before the Romanovs had even left Tobolsk, that indicated Nicholas should be taken to the Ural town of Yekaterinburg.[35] Now, the Ural Soviet were threatening to arrest both Nicholas and Commissar Yakovlev if the ex-Emperor was not handed over to them. Sverdlov wired back referring to the Romanovs as 'the baggage' – that and 'the medicine' were their code names in Bolshevik correspondence – assuring them that 'everything being done by Yakovlev ... is in direct fulfilment of an order I have given. I will inform of the details by special courier. Issue no orders concerning Yakovlev ... Yakovlev is to be trusted completely.'[36]

From their halted train at Omsk, Yakovlev continued to message Sverdlov in Moscow. His telegrams confirm that the possibility they would be left in the Urals had been considered before he went to

Tobolsk. The delay in Omsk was caused by divisions within the Executive Committee over what to do with the Romanovs, which had led to multiple outcomes being planned for. The code for depositing them in Yekaterinburg was 'the first route'. Even now, Yakovlev was prepared to face down the wrath of the Ural Soviet if that was what the government in Moscow wanted. If they chose the second route, away from the Urals, 'then you can always transport the baggage to Moscow or wherever you want. If the baggage was taken by the first route, then I doubt you will be able to drag it out of there. None of us … doubt this; nor do we doubt that the baggage will be in utter danger at all times. Thus, we warn you one last time and free ourselves from any moral responsibility for the future consequences.'[37] Moscow's response does not survive, but Yakovlev's side of the correspondence makes it clear. He concluded the final telegram in the exchange with the words, 'So then, I am going by the first route. I'll hand over the baggage. I'll go for the other part of it.'[38]

The train was diverted to Yekaterinburg and the three Romanovs were disembarked into an empty goods' siding in the early afternoon. Greeted by representatives of the local Bolshevik party and commanders of the regional branch of the Cheka, the Bolshevik regime's new secret police service and the progenitor of the KGB, they were driven through the streets of the eerily quiet town, cleared of all spectators until the prisoners were behind the enormous wooden stockade recently erected around the Ipatiev House, Number 49 Voznesensky Street, the former home of a well-to-do local railway engineer who had his home requisitioned by the local Soviet when they wanted to use it as the Romanovs' prison because it was so near to the local Cheka headquarters. It was a big house, but most of the accommodation was given over to those who would be guarding them. Dr Evgeny Botkin, Anna Demidova, a young kitchen boy called Leonid Sednev, the Emperor's Latvian manservant Aloise Trupp, a cook called Ivan Kharitonov and two gentlemen servants went into the house with Nicholas, Alexandra and Maria. The other members of their retinue were taken straight from the train to the town gaol.

For three weeks, the family were kept in a single bedroom, while Alexandra worried about her other children in Tobolsk

and Nicholas passed the days by reading aloud from the Bible.
Yakovlev's promise that he would 'go for the other part of it' came
true at the end of May when the rest of what was left of the imperial
household was brought to Yekaterinburg to share the Emperor and
Empress's fate. As they left Tobolsk, one of Alexandra's ladies-
in-waiting, Baroness Sophie Buxhoeveden, was unnerved by how
boisterous the soldiers were and how heavily they were drinking as
the ferry set out for Tyumen. As the journey progressed, all the men
still left in the imperial household were moved around so much that
they did not realise until it was too late that they had been locked
in their cabins. Meanwhile, the Bolshevik guards told the women
to leave their doors open. Hearing this, the terrified baroness and
all the other women decided to leave their clothes on and sit up the
whole night rather than risk going to bed.

Trapped in his cabin, one of the Romanovs' tutors heard
screams echoing through the ship later that night. Years later, he
told his son, 'It was dreadful, what they did.'[39] The possibility,
almost too horrible to contemplate, that one or more of the Tsar's
daughters was sexually assaulted on the journey from Tobolsk to
Yekaterinburg cannot be ruled out. Baroness Buxhoeveden's story
of how they had all tried to keep their clothes on that night and
the deliberate detaining of the male members of the Romanov
entourage suggest that an attack on the ladies was planned,
while Sydney Gibbes' recollections to his son years later seems to
confirm that something truly terrible did happen on the voyage.
In 1989, Gibbes' son George told the historian Greg King that
what happened on the ferry to Tyumen had been his father's worst
memory of the Russian Revolution, 'more so than learning that the
family had been martyred'.[40] When Olga reached Yekaterinburg,
those close to her were quick to notice that she 'had changed the
lovely, bright girl of twenty-two into a faded and sad middle-aged
woman'.[41]

Against this heartbreaking version of events is the fact that
several of those on board made no subsequent mention of any
attack actually taking place, neither the baroness herself, who
mentioned the circumstances leading up to it, nor Pierre Gilliard,
who was locked in his room. In their study of the Romanovs'
final year, Greg King and Penny Wilson have suggested that the

'near veil of silence surrounding the events of that night ... is not difficult to understand, given the exalted position of the grand duchesses; the horrific murders at Ekaterinburg; the determination by those intimately connected with the Romanovs to present them as paragons of all moral virtue; and the tenor of the times'.[42] In a society with limited understanding of sexual crimes, even a rape could not be reported for the shame it might bring upon the grand duchesses. Yet there is also the fact that there was no noticeable change after the voyage in Tatiana or Anastasia, and the observations about Olga's physical and emotional decline had actually started before she got on the ferry, when she was left alone to look after a rapidly sickening Alexei, who had lost so much weight thanks to the new restrictions in Tobolsk that he looked emaciated and his knee had seized up, temporarily preventing him from walking. That they were harassed but not assaulted seems to be the assessment taken by the grand duchesses' most recent biographer, Helen Rappaport, who wrote in her 2014 biography of them that the journey from Tobolsk saw Alexei locked in his cabin and denied access to the bathroom and the women forced to 'endure the noise of the rowdy guards drinking and making obscene comments outside their open doors'.[43] The mystery of what happened on the voyage from Tobolsk in 1918 is never likely to be solved, but the circumstances the unprotected grand duchesses found themselves in showed how fragile the imperial family's security had become.

Their train reached Yekaterinburg from Tyumen just after midnight on 23 May, where they were told that they were to be separated from all of their servants bar Klementy Nagorny, a burly and devoted sailor from the imperial navy who was assigned to look after Alexei. The family were so used to rules being changed for no reason and enforced temporary separations as displays of the guards' power over them that Tatiana wryly joked, 'We shall all rejoice in each other's company in half an hour's time!' But this time one of the guards leaned over her shoulder and told her, 'Better say "Good-bye", citizenness.'[44]

They were allowed to disembark the train in the morning, by which time a large crowd had gathered to watch them. The three grand duchesses were all wearing dark jackets, with large buttons, and matching skirts. Valentin Speranski, an engineer in the crowd, thought that Olga 'reminded me of a sad young girl in a Turgenev novel', while sixteen-year-old Anastasia 'seemed like a frightened, terrified child, who could, in different circumstances be charming, light-hearted and affectionate'. But it was Tatiana who made the strongest impression on him. Even as her shoes sank in the mud and she struggled with her valise her face did not betray any sign of embarrassment or fear. The engineer thought she carried herself like 'a haughty patrician with an air of pride' even under incredibly trying circumstances. Watching them all struggle unassisted towards the waiting one-horse carts, Speranski 'stared at their lively, young, expressive faces somewhat indiscreetly – and during those two or three minutes I learned something that I will not forget until my dying day. I felt that my eyes met those of the three unfortunate young women just for a moment and that when they did I reached into the depths of their martyred souls, as it were, and I was overwhelmed by pity for them – me, a confirmed revolutionary. Without expecting it, I sensed that we Russian intellectuals, we who claim to be the precursors and the voice of conscience, were responsible for the undignified ridicule to which the grand duchesses were subjected ... We do not have the right to forget, nor to forgive ourselves for our passivity and our failure to do something for them.'[45]

A joyful reunion took place at the Ipatiev House or the 'House of Special Purpose' as it had ominously been renamed by the Soviet, but before long it was back to the familiarities of guards interrupting their meals, limited opportunities for fresh air, soldiers leering as they went to the bathroom to encounter obscene limericks about their father and graphic sketches of imagined sexual scenes between their mother and Rasputin. Or themselves and Rasputin. Civil war swept through Russia, replacing the carnage of the First World War, which the new Soviet government had dropped out of by accepting the humiliating Treaty of Brest-Litovsk, whereby Imperial Germany was given possession of most of Russia's most valuable territories in Eastern Europe and one-third of its total population. The Bolshevik forces, known as the Reds, were pitted against an anti-communist coalition, known as the Whites, who had also achieved some foreign backing, though not nearly as much as they needed. By early summer, the White forces were closing in on Yekaterinburg.

The desire to prevent the liberation of the Romanovs determined the timing of their deaths, but it was not the sole reason for the massacre at the Ipatiev House. From its inception, the Bolshevik leadership had relied upon a policy of terror through class warfare to keep itself in power. This was partly due to necessity because of the political uncertainties facing them – Lenin posed the question to a colleague, 'You certainly don't think we'll survive this as the winners if we don't use the most brutal revolutionary terror?' – and partly from ideology – Trotsky believed, 'We must put an end once and for all to the papist-Quaker babble about the sanctity of human life.'[46] Throughout Russia, terror was being used without discrimination. Felix Dzherzhinsky, the head of the Cheka, justified the policy on the grounds that 'the Cheka must defend the revolution and conquer the enemy even if its sword falls occasionally on the heads of the innocent'.[47] In discussing the Romanovs' eventual fate, Lenin praised a suggestion that every single member of the family should be killed regardless of age, gender or previous political activity as 'simplicity to the point of genius'.[48] Within the Red Army itself, Trotsky advocated mass executions of one in ten randomly selected soldiers for any battalion that had disobeyed orders or attempted desertion.

Inside the House of Special Purpose, some of the younger Bolshevik guards were becoming infatuated with the grand duchesses. 'They were brilliantly pretty,' recalled one of the guards years later, while another called Alexander Strekotin remembered that 'their personalities were fascinating to us. They were the topic of discussion between two or three of us, who passed some sleepless nights speaking of them.'[49] The elder sisters remained more guarded than the younger girls; Olga spent much of her time lost in thought or reading aloud to her mother from the Book of Revelation with its haunting descriptions of an apocalypse followed by the rewards of Paradise, while Valentin Speranski heard that Tatiana was 'pleasant to the guards if she thought they were behaving in an acceptable and decorous manner'.[50] This did not always happen and Tatiana once angrily left the room when one of the soldiers made a blue joke. Maria, who stayed behind, asked, 'Why are you not disgusted with yourselves when you use such shameful words? Do you imagine you can befriend a well-born woman with such witticisms and have her be well disposed towards you? Be polite and decent men and then we can get along.'[51]

It was a rare flash of bad temper from the Grand Duchess Maria, who more often than not was the guards' favourite. In the last week of June, she celebrated her nineteenth birthday and one of the younger guards, a former factory worker called Ivan Skorokhodov, smuggled in a cake for her. He asked to speak to her privately and they were apparently discovered in a compromising position a few minutes later. It was nothing too sordid and certainly not sexual, as his superior's restrained comments on the situation make clear. It may have been a kiss or it may simply have been that they were alone together at all in the first place. Either way, there were grave consequences, far more so for Ivan than Maria.

Those in charge of the House of Special Purpose believed that the smuggling in of the cake proved that security under the current crop of guards had irretrievably broken down. One of them, Peter Ermakov, thought that if the fraternisation was not stopped some of the sentries would 'be helping the prisoners to escape the next thing we knew'.[52] We do not know if the Tsar ever found out about Maria's friendship with Skorokhodov, but her sisters certainly did and Olga in particular was displeased. At his superiors' command Ivan Skorokhodov was removed from duty and carted off to prison, where he subsequently vanished from the records for bringing a small birthday cake to a Romanov. Similar fates had already befallen many of the family's servants, including the sailor Nagorny, who was taken away and shot when he tried to stop one of the Bolsheviks stealing Alexei's collection of religious images, and the Empress's former lady-in-waiting, Countess Anastasia Hendrikova, who was executed that autumn alongside one of the grand duchesses' former tutors, Mademoiselle Schneider.[53]

As the weather outside turned to baking heat, the atmosphere inside the house became unbearable. Alexandra was upset when one of the soldiers was very rude to Ivan Kharitonov, one of their five surviving retainers.[54] A thunderstorm raged on the night of 7 July, but the family's windows had long since been whitewashed, preventing them from having any view of the outside. All they could do was listen to the storm swirling around them. Rumours of the progress of the White Army were whispered alongside complaints at the severity of the house rules under the new commandant, Yakov Yurovsky, who was already attending regular meetings at a local hotel to co-ordinate the family's murder. The Romanovs themselves had not yet given up hope that they might soon be freed by their supporters, but equally an oppressive sense of dread had settled on the family, as they hoped for the best but feared the worst. Everyone knew that their lives in Yekaterinburg were drawing to an end one way or the other – they would be rescued, they would be moved or they would die. During one of the rare religious services they were now allowed access to and which were conducted inside the house to prevent them attracting attention in church, the officiating priest, Father Storozhev, was surprised when the entire family fell to their knees during the prayers for the dead. 'I knew from the way they conducted themselves,' he said later, 'that something fearful and menacing was almost upon the imperial family.'[55] Alexandra and her children prayed together often. 'The atmosphere around us is electric,' she wrote in one of her final letters to Anna Vyrubova. 'We fear that a storm is approaching but we know that God is merciful ... Our souls are at peace.'[56]

On 15 July 1918, Lenin went for a short break to his small summer house near Kuntsevo, a telling indicator that by the time he left the question of the Romanovs had already been settled.[57] Two days earlier, Moscow had confirmed to Yekaterinburg that it had no objection to the murder of the Tsar. A meeting was subsequently held at a Yekaterinburg hotel at which it was decided the deed should be carried out no later than 18 July and that their plan was 'to liquidate the former Tsar Nicholas Romanov and his family and the servants living with them.'[58] Philip Goloshchekin, the Central Executive's man in Yekaterinburg, knew about the decision and although the telegram has never been found, it is nearly inconceivable to believe that at some point over the next three days Goloshchekin did not seek Lenin's permission for the plan to kill them all to go ahead, assuming that this order had not already been given. Given that Moscow had asked to be kept informed, the news of the hotel meeting on the 14th was presumably sent to the capital in time for Lenin to approve the decision and leave for Kuntsevo the next day. At two o'clock in the afternoon of the 17th, Lenin's personal secretary Nikolai Gorbunov received a short telegram from a member of the Yekaterinburg Soviet: 'Inform Sverdlov that the entire family suffered the same fate as its head.'[59]

They had been woken out of bed in the small hours of the morning and told that because of the proximity of the White armies, artillery fire was being exchanged and there was a chance some of it could hit the town. They were asked to get dressed and then taken downstairs just after 2.15 a.m. The Romanovs and their four remaining servants – Dr Evgeny Botkin, Anna Demidova, Aloise Trupp and Ivan Kharitonov – walked out into the courtyard and then through a second door and down a twenty-three step flight of stairs into the cellar with Nicholas carrying Alexei, who was still too weak from his fall in Tobolsk.

In the eighteenth and early nineteenth centuries, Imperial Russia had granted asylum to exiled members of the French royal family. The surviving Bourbons had been forced to flee the Revolution so quickly that they took almost nothing with them and for two decades were passed from one well-wisher to another, incapable of supporting themselves or any of the servants who had risked their lives to join them in exile. Determined not to suffer the same humiliation, Alexandra had decided to smuggle some of her own private jewels out of Russia so that they could sell them, live on the proceeds and avoid becoming a burden their relatives or supporters. Two of those boxes were now hidden inside the pillows carried by Anna Demidova, while the rest of the contraband jewels were sewn into the Tsarina and grand duchesses' corsets. Sixteen years later, Yurovsky would tell a room full of fellow Bolsheviks, 'No one is responsible for their death agonies but themselves, it has to be said ... their greed turned out to be so great.'[60]

When they were all gathered and Alexandra demanded a chair because of her bad back, Yurovsky stepped forward and told the eleven people in the cellar that they were all going to die because of their relatives' 'assault on Soviet Russia', a reference to the British Empire's support for the White armies. Accounts differ of the exact wording used and if he ever got to read on to the point where Nicholas was referred to as 'a crowned executioner' and condemned for 'countless bloody crimes against the people,' a charge rich in irony from the Soviet regime, which was already ankle-deep in its own people's blood within its first nine months. However, all the eyewitness reports agree that Nicholas tried to interrupt him at some point and was shot through the heart.

His blood sprayed over Alexei, who had been set next to his mother. Olga and Alexandra made the sign of the cross before the Empress was hit on the left side of her skull and killed. The eleven men who made up the execution squad began firing at whim, killing Aloise Trupp and Ivan Kharitonov. As the room filled with the stench of the recently dead's emptying bowels, Yurovsky and his men had to step out for a minute. Some of the guards wept and vomited, a sign that some historians have interpreted as signs of compassion or remorse, but we should not get too carried away at an involuntary physical reaction – Himmler vomited when he saw people die as well, it did little to dampen his enthusiasm for Auschwitz or Treblinka; the squad members' years of public speaking in the USSR about what they did that night does not suggest much regret.

They returned with guns and rifle bayonets, killing a wounded Dr Botkin as he crawled across the floor to fulfil an old vow to die at his Emperor's side. Some bullets had ricocheted off the girls' corsets, but Yurovsky was being disingenuous when he claimed that was why it took so long to murder them. He had chosen the location badly and the logistics of the killing even more so. The cellar was too small, the execution gang too large and many of them were either too nervous, too excited or, in some cases, too drunk. Olga and Tatiana were hugging one another in the corner, but Tatiana rose to her feet to take Yurovsky's bullet when he came for her. The others were all finally murdered by being stabbed with the bayonets, beaten with rifle butts and, in Alexei's case, Yurovsky dispassionately confirmed 'I finished him off' with two gunshots to the head.[61] The bodies were then stripped, taken into a nearby forest, doused in sulphuric acid, some of them were burned and then, after various burial sites were tried, they were buried in a forest clearing in the hope that the Whites would never find them. As Yurovsky said later, 'It is easy to see how they would have used this matter to their advantage.'[62]

12

The End of the War and the Fall of the Monarchies

'It was neck and neck to the very end'

A few weeks after the execution of the Romanovs, Empress Augusta Victoria suffered a mild heart attack, adding to the distress of her husband, Wilhelm II, who was already tormented by rumours of his cousin's execution in Yekaterinburg. No matter what Alexandra may have thought of him personally, he had done his best to save the family, and he had counselled against the Treaty of Brest-Litovsk since he knew that once there was no threat of retaliation from Germany, the Soviets could treat the Kaiser's Russian cousins as they liked.

Having triumphed in the East, the German high command now intended to do the same in the West and General Ludendorff had assured the Kaiser and the German people that the Spring Offensive on the Western Front in 1918 would secure the final victory, with the troops going through intensive training over the winter to prepare them for it. But the high command made a serious error in deciding to attack the British lines first rather than those of the French, acting on Ludendorff's low opinion of the British command's capabilities. The British lost nearly 500,000 men, but they defeated the offensive through a mixture of tactical retreat and counteroffensive. The Germans could no longer replace their losses and the men who were being sent to the front were often too old, out of shape or already disheartened by a war that nearly everybody at home believed to be lost. On 8 August, the

Allies launched a counter-attack, buoyed up by a new confidence about their chances of winning and by 10,000 American troops pouring into Europe every day. When Wilhelm heard the news of the Allied victory, he took to his bed and one of his staff officers had to bother the Empress, who was herself still very weak after her heart attack. 'Tell me the truth,' Augusta Victoria asked him, 'is everything really lost? I can't believe that God has forsaken our poor fatherland!' The officer told her that there was little that could be done for the army, but that she still had a role to play in helping the Kaiser face the next few weeks with dignity. 'I will help you,' she said and dragged herself from her own sickbed to tend to her husband.[1]

With the benefit of hindsight, Winston Churchill thought that it could have gone either way up until the Allied counteroffensive in August, 'It was neck and neck to the very end ... The more one knows about the struggle the more one realises on what small, narrow, perilous margins our success turned.'[2] His assessment of the situation was cited by General Ludendorff in his post-war memoirs to give further credence to his own retrospective view that Germany had lost the war because of treachery at home, through a shadowy conspiracy of Catholics, Jews and freemasons who had undermined the empire from within. This idea of a 'stab in the back' causing the Armistice of 1918 was lovingly nurtured by men like Ludendorff and his future cohorts in the Nazi movement, but in 1918 Erich Ludendorff gave the Kaiser very different advice. At the end of September, it was he and General von Hindenburg who informed their Emperor in no uncertain terms that the war could not be won and that they had best make arrangements to surrender in the least humiliating way possible. Wilhelm was stunned at their assessment.

The mood within Germany, palace and populace, was dolorous. Rolling blackouts afflicted everyone as the Reich struggled to produce enough power with so many miners sent off to fight and die in the trenches. Soap was hard to come by and hot water a rarity. Theatres, night clubs, bars and restaurants were closed down to conserve power. There was a clothing shortage in both the army and the civilian market. By the end of 1918, Germans were eating on average between 12 and 20 per cent of the meat,

butter, cheese, eggs and rice that they had in 1913.[3] The winter of
1916 and 1917 had been dubbed 'the turnip winter' because they
were the only kind of food in plentiful supply and by 1918 fish
had vanished almost completely from German tables thanks to the
British blockade. These privations spoke of a nation that could not
even sustain herself let alone subdue others and adding to this sense
of despondency was the sight of thousands of soldiers arriving
home crippled, maimed, disfigured, blinded or badly wounded,
while news of the Sixtus Affair confirmed that Germany's own
allies had no faith in a final victory.

October 1918 saw a frantic scramble to transform the government
in preparation for peace talks. The American President, Woodrow
Wilson, made it clear in the middle of the month that the United
States would not negotiate with 'the power which has hitherto
controlled the German nation'. Whether he meant the army or the
monarchy was unclear. Initially, many people assumed the former,
perhaps because they could not quite believe that a foreign head
of state would dare mandate the complete realignment of another
country's political system in line with his own. Prince Maximilian
von Baden, a distant cousin of the Kaiser known for his liberal
politics, was appointed Chancellor, and immediately set about
trying to reform the German political system by strengthening
the Reichstag, in the hope that such a move would please the
Allies by limiting the high command's influence at home. Despite
von Baden's appointment, there were some in Germany who
believed that President Wilson would not accept peace terms if the
Hohenzollern monarchy itself was left intact. Supremely confident
in his own abilities, President Wilson looked at the carnage of the
Continent and assumed that the whole old European system had
been rotten to its core. If it was all swept away, the future would be
bright; progress, to President Wilson's mind, was an inevitability.
Few political demands in history can have had such devastating
long-term results. The Empress was livid and railed against 'the
audacity of the parvenu across the Sea who thus dares to humiliate
a princely house which can look back on centuries of service to
people and country'.[4]

When General von Hindenburg bristled at President Wilson's
demands for change, von Baden went to the Kaiser and demanded

that he put an end to the military's interference in government. Goaded into action by his cousin and finally aware of the full extent of the trouble facing the Crown, Wilhelm II quarrelled with Ludendorff and made it clear that his resignation, if tendered, would be welcomed. On 26 October, far too late, General Ludendorff lost power. 'I have separated the Siamese twins,' remarked the Kaiser.[5] It is often assumed that he was talking about the army and the government, but it is equally possible that he was making a joke about the inseparable Ludendorff and von Hindenburg. In this atmosphere of unrest, anger on the streets reached a fever pitch as riots and disturbances swept Germany and the naval personnel stationed at Kiel mutinied. The Spartacists too were on the street, hoping to bring about a revolution similar to Russia's; that was to be expected, but it was desertion by his beloved navy, his pride and joy, that really broke Wilhelm II's spirits. He left Berlin to spend some time at army headquarters at Spa. As with Nicholas II, it was a poor decision that removed him from the capital at a vital moment. He was too far away to be involved in any of the decisions being made as the First World War unravelled and the monarchy with it.

The mood within the imperial entourage as it made its way to Spa was surreal, its connection to reality tenuous at best. Wilhelm's friend Albert Ballin thought that abdication was the only way forward: 'I don't think the emperor would be very sad when he could now make a noble gesture and withdraw into private life.' But he thought that many of those close to Wilhelm would prevent him from doing so – 'with certainty the empress will strike up a hefty resistance' – and even some of Wilhelm's long-suffering courtiers were still nurturing the fantasy that by staying close to the army the Kaiser could hold on to power.[6] Reports from the high command confirmed that the army's loyalty was now as suspect as the navy's and that the overall consensus was that Wilhelm must abdicate. The chairman of the left-wing Social Democrats, Friedrich Ebert, told the Chancellor, 'The mood of the people pushes the responsibility on to the emperor, it doesn't matter whether they are right or wrong. The important matter for the people is that they can see the supposed guilty parties removed from their positions. For this reason the emperor's abdication is necessary if the masses are to be hindered from going over to a revolutionary position.'[7] Any suggestion that he abdicate in favour of the Crown Prince was rejected on the grounds that the son was now even more unpopular than his father. Some, like Albert Ballin and Chancellor von Baden, thought that if they acted quickly the Crown Prince's eldest son, twelve-year-old Wilhelm, could be proclaimed Wilhelm III with a regency approved by the Reichstag, but as communications broke down between Spa and Berlin, the chance to save the monarchy was lost. In the Reichstag, the Chancellor's attempts to paint a picture of a future which contained the monarchy were met with derisive cries of 'Too late! Too late!'[8] In Berlin, crowds burst into the royal palaces and ransacked the imperial family's rooms, further aggravating the Empress's heart problem.

Squirming against fate and wasting precious time, Wilhelm offered to stand down as German Emperor but not as King of Prussia. Some of his courtiers thought that this might just about be possible, but it was a fantasy from which they were all rudely jolted on 9 November when the Chancellor announced Wilhelm's removal from power in a speech given to the Reichstag. In a cabinet meeting on the previous day, one of the Chancellor's allies, Philip Scheidemann, told his colleagues, 'The abdication is no longer the subject of the discussion. The revolution has broken out. Sailors from Kiel have grabbed power in Hamburg and Hanover as well. Gentlemen, it is no longer the moment for discussion, we must act. We do not know whether we shall be sitting in these chairs tomorrow.'[9] As in Russia, power had not so much been seized as picked up off the floor.

The news was brought to Wilhelm at half past two in the afternoon while he was relaxing in a garden at a house near the army headquarters in Spa. The general who told him was shaking with shock to the point that his teeth were chattering. Hearing that he had been deposed, Wilhelm screamed, 'Treachery! Treachery, shameless, outrageous treachery!'[10] The Crown Prince, who was present, stalked off and climbed into his chauffeur-driven car to be whisked away without saying goodbye. If he still had dreams of salvaging his own career at the expense of his father's, they were as misplaced as they were unlovely.

Wilhelm walked back inside and collapsed into an armchair. He lit a cigarette, which turned into nervous chain smoking as those around him struggled to comprehend the speed with which the Hohenzollern monarchy had been destroyed. Von Hindenburg told him that he needed to flee. 'I could not take responsibility for Your Majesty to be dragged back to Berlin by mutinous troops to be delivered as a prisoner to the revolutionary government.'[11] The general's chilling words made it clear to Wilhelm that any return to the heartlands of his former empire was impossible. He became hysterical, at one point claiming that he wanted to shoot himself. When some of his entourage suggested that there would be still be some loyal troops who would be willing to fight at Wilhelm's side, he refused to consider it. The diehard courtiers argued that even if such a gesture failed, it would be more honourable than simply accepting revolution so meekly. 'A king has no right to send his men to death to assuage his personal vanity,' Wilhelm said later. 'It would have meant the sacrifice of valuable lives, merely to provide me with a spectacular exit.'[12] Bowing to von Hindenburg's advice for the last time, Wilhelm boarded the imperial train which made for the border with neutral Holland. In the early hours of the morning of 10 November, the Kaiser became a political refugee. As he crossed the frontier, his only request was for a cup of strong English tea. Two weeks later, Augusta Victoria joined him and for the first time in her life, she hugged him in public. She brought her little dachshund, Topsy, with her.

At the same time, a similar fate was befalling Karl and Zita in Austria. Their summer had not proceeded with the same sense of impending and inevitable gloom that had characterised Wilhelm's. A state visit to Constantinople to meet with Austria-Hungary's Ottoman ally, the seventy-three-year-old Sultan Mehmed V, had been judged a great success thanks to Karl's politeness and Zita's gracefulness. The Ottoman court had been particularly impressed with the Empress's magnificent diadem and when the young couple returned to Vienna their train was covered in flowers from Turkish well-wishers. A visit to Pressburg (now Bratislava) on the same day that the Romanovs were to be murdered in Yekaterinburg saw large crowds surging forward to cheer the Emperor, the Empress and their two eldest children. Zita was revitalised by their adoration, but her husband remained subdued. On their journey back to Vienna, he warned Zita 'against forming any illusions. He knew that, however much the ordinary people waved and cheered, the empire could not go on much longer without peace abroad and reform at home.'[13]

In the last week of September, the news that Bulgaria was surrendering to the Allies confirmed that the war's end was in sight and that all the Central Powers would soon be entering into peace talks, weakened and vanquished. One of his ministers told Karl what he already knew about the Bulgarian news, 'This has knocked the bottom out of the barrel.' Zita, who was with her husband when he heard the news from Bulgaria, told her biographer years later, 'The Emperor was not really surprised. We knew that Ferdinand [the Tsar of Bulgaria] had been fishing in all waters for months past, especially towards the Americans ... For him [Karl], the collapse of Bulgaria only made it even more urgent to start peace talks up with the Western powers while there was still something to talk about.'[14] On 4 October, Austria-Hungary dispatched a telegram to President Wilson restating the empire's interest in peace talks and reminding him of its previous attempts to do so. That same day, the ex-Tsar of Bulgaria, Ferdinand, arrived in Austria-Hungary expecting to be given access to one of the six estates he owned in Hungary in a private capacity. Also unpopular because of the privations of the war, 'Foxy Ferdinand', as he was known, took the chance missed by Wilhelm II and Nicholas II to abdicate in favour of his next of kin, the Crown Prince Boris, and by doing so saved the Bulgarian monarchy. Zita, whose eldest sister Maria Louisa had been Ferdinand's first wife until her death from pneumonia in 1899, had little affection for her former brother-in-law and in any case she could not afford to be seen fraternising with yet another relative who had harmed Austria-Hungary's war effort. Karl refused to grant the ex-Tsar permission to stay and the train was instead diverted to the German city of Coburg, where Ferdinand lived out the last thirty years of his life.

Twelve days later, on 16 October, Karl issued a manifesto promising to turn the empire into a federal state in which 'each racial component shall form its own state organisation in its territory of settlement'. He honoured his coronation oath by stipulating that these new reforms 'shall in no way effect the integrity of the lands of the sacred Hungarian Crown', but as one historian of the family has pointed out, the Emperor's last-ditch attempt to unite all the myriad nationalities behind the throne meant that 'he was trying to replant the roots of the monarchy in ground which was not just trembling under war but cracking open in defeat'.[15] The manifesto had cleverly included the phrase 'rights of self-determination', one of the key buzzwords bandied around by President Wilson's fourteen-point programme for accepting a peace deal with the Central Powers. However, the White House's response was unenthusiastic. It was not enough. The American government replied that 'the President is ... no longer able to accept mere "autonomy" for these peoples as a basis for peace but is obliged to insist that they, and not he, shall be the judges of what action on the part of the Austro-Hungarian government will justify their aspirations'.[16]

On 28 October, the Hapsburg Empire came apart at the seams when the Czech National Council quietly assumed control of the governor's residence in Prague and declared Czechoslovakian independence from Austria and Hungary without a shot being fired. Twenty-four hours later, the Croats, once so vociferous in their loyalty to the monarchy, did likewise once they realised that the ship was sinking and they would have to look after their own region in a potentially unfriendly post-war world. Two days later, the Slovenians did the same, to be followed by the Polish communities living in the northern part of the empire, and then the Ukrainians and Romanians on the eastern frontier. Hungary, hoping to save her own borders in the event of a defeat, had her cabinet formally absolved of their oaths of loyalty to the House of Hapsburg so that they could at least claim to be behaving honourably when they abandoned it. The next day, all Hungarian troops serving in the Hapsburg military received an order from their new government to lay down their arms and come home. Over the course of ninety-six hours, the empire had simply ceased to exist.

As the death throes of the Hapsburg monarchy continued, large crowds roamed the streets of Vienna. The Emperor spent sleepless nights, waiting by the telephone for news from the Allies of a peace offer, clinging to the belief that it must surely come, even though it was clear the Allies could not make an offer unless all the major powers, including the United States, supported it, which they were unlikely to do if the monarchies remained intact. Perhaps those around the Kaiser and the Emperor should have remembered that President Wilson could not vouch for how his allies would behave and what demands they would make at the peace talks, even if Germany and Austria became republics, but everybody is wise in hindsight and who knows how anyone might react or function when faced with a situation as awful as the chaos of the First World War.

News of what had happened to the Romanovs had leaked into central Europe. The Soviet government's deliberate policy of misinformation meant that very few knew for certain exactly what had taken place and there were rumours that the Tsarina and her children had been moved to a place of safety, but the story that they had all perished was circulating as well and Zita was 'naturally very worried about the safety of my children'.[17] The red flag of socialism could be seen in demonstrations visible from the palace windows and cries of 'Long live the republic!' grew louder once Wilhelm II's deposition became public knowledge.

Zita, true to form, was withering in her assessment of the Kaiser's fall from power: 'To put it mildly, it wasn't considered exactly an inspiring example. But as we always knew that he was under the thumb of his generals, this, after all, seemed the natural end. They had just packed him off.'[18] Despite her fears of a second Yekaterinburg, she was watching those around her closely and she, alone of all the royals at the time, seems to have grasped the possibility that they were being fed misinformation. One division of troops loyal to the Crown would have been enough to restore order on the streets of Vienna, where the protesters were loud but neither particularly numerous nor well-organised. Karl was visibly moved when twenty young cadets from the Military Academy arrived at the palace and asked permission to lay down their lives for the preservation of the monarchy. Zita discovered later that the commander of the Salzburg garrison had wanted to join the cadets and offered to march on Vienna to support the Emperor, but the municipal authorities in the capital had refused. High-ranking republicans made use of Allied pressure and unrest on the streets to press ahead with their agenda and in parliament even the right-wing Christian Social Party believed that nothing could be done to save the monarchy in the event of military defeat. The empire it had created had vanished. What use could there be for the Hapsburgs now?

Admirals, generals and courtiers were calling to the Schönbrunn Palace to pay their respects to the Emperor. Etiquette remained inviolable to the last. The Hungarian Admiral Nicholas Horthy sobbed as he discussed the uprisings and ultimately became so hysterical that the Emperor asked the Empress to say a few words of consolation to him. In their presence, he held up his hand and vowed, 'I will never rest until I have restored Your Majesty to his thrones in Vienna and Budapest!'[19] But on 11 November, less-welcome visitors stood before the Emperor in the form of Chancellor Heinrich Lammasch and Edmund von Gayer, the Minister of the Interior, who arrived with a document that would remove Karl from political office. The strange document ironically advertised the weakness of the republican position, implicitly confirming the Empress's belief that it was a question of access to support and not a lack of support in itself which doomed the Hapsburg monarchy. What they were proposing to the Emperor was not an abdication but rather a renunciation; it spoke of the temporary and not the permanent. By signing it, Karl would simply agree to temporarily set aside his political rights until the peace settlement was negotiated. The monarchy would go into abeyance; it was not, at least at this stage, being abolished.

As the two men came into the Emperor's study, the Chancellor was so overcome with fear that Karl would not sign it, and thereby encourage a civil war led by the 'red hordes' similar to Russia's, that he grabbed the Emperor, manhandled him and begged him to sign it. Karl angrily shook him off, at which point Zita misunderstood what they were proposing and took the document for an outright abdication. She lost all of her usual elegance and flew into a rage. In that moment, she revealed herself to be a Bourbon to her marrow when, according to the Emperor's press secretary, she flung herself at her husband and cried, 'A sovereign can never abdicate. He can be deposed … All right. That is force. But abdicate – never, never, never! I would rather fall here at your side. Then there would be Otto. And even if all of us here were killed, there would still be other Hapsburgs!'[20] Karl explained to her that it was a temporary renunciation and she calmed down. Believing that it was best for Austria when it came to negotiating with the Allies and seeing no way to rule in defiance of political consensus, without the army and without the empire his family had ruled over for centuries, Karl removed a small metallic pencil from his pocket and signed *Karl* at the bottom of the page.

The cabinet were invited to take their leave of the Emperor as protocol and propriety demanded. Even those who had counselled for the renunciation, like the Chancellor, were visibly upset as Karl shook their hands and thanked them for their service to the vanished empire. Officials from the Swiss and Dutch embassies arrived with an offer to escort the Emperor and his family safely out of Austria and to guarantee his private properties, but Karl politely refused on the grounds that since he had not been deposed he had no reason to leave Austria. Instead, he would move his family to their hunting lodge at Eckartsau, near Austria's new borders with Hungary and Czechoslovakia.

Years later, the Empress described their leave-taking from the beautiful Schönbrunn later that day.

The Emperor and I went with our children to the chapel, where we said a short prayer that we might one day return here. After that, we went up to the so-called Hall of Ceremonies, where all those who had still remained behind were gathered. We said goodbye to them and thanked them one by one.

   Then down the stairway to the small inner courtyard below where the cars were waiting. Along the side of the arcades, drawn up in two ranks, were our cadets from the military academies, with tears in their eyes, but still perfectly turned out and guarding us to the end. They had really lived up to the motto the Empress Maria Teresa had given them: 'Allzeit Getreu' ('Loyal for Ever').

   It was dark by now, and a misty autumn night … The Emperor and I and all the children except Karl Ludwig [Karl and Zita's fifth child, born in March 1918][21] squeezed into the back of one car with Count Hunyády at the front. In the next one came the infant Karl Ludwig and the children's nurses ... We did not risk driving out the main gate in front of the palace. Instead we continued parallel with the main building along the broad gravel path that leads to the eastern side gate. We slipped out of this and left the capital by a special route. Late that night – without any trouble or incidents – we arrived at Eckartsau.[22]

Earlier that day, the war had ended, at the eleventh hour of the eleventh day of the eleventh month, when Germany surrendered to the Allies. Four years and millions of lives lost had all been in vain. At Eckartsau, the Hapsburgs spent a miserable and isolated Christmas. Zita hunted out food stuff to give to the servants as presents, while old gifts from state visits were used to hide the fact that the family could not afford new ones. The Emperor's paternal grandmother, Maria Annunciata of Bourbon and the Two Sicilies, had died of tuberculosis when she was twenty-eight and some of her children and grandchildren had weak lungs. On top of that, the Spanish influenza pandemic was sweeping the globe, killing nearly 5 per cent of the world's population, and Karl and all his children were hit by it. Years later, Zita described Christmas 1918 as 'rather a sombre festival – especially as the Emperor, who was anyway suffering from repeated heart attacks and overstrain, had gone down with a severe attack of the Spanish influenza ten days before [Christmas] and was now really ill. All the children caught it as well; some mildly, it is true, but some severely – Karl Ludwig, for example, who was then barely eighteen months old, very nearly died.'[23]

In Vienna, the socialist movement had formed the pro-communist Red Guard and there were lively fears for the imperial family's safety because of it. Zita's brother Sixtus asked for an audience with King George V at Buckingham Palace and it was granted. In the presence of both King George and Queen Mary, Sixtus pointed out that after what had happened to the Romanovs, nobody could be sure of what might befall the Hapsburgs. What if a communist revolution succeeded in Austria as it had in Russia? The King's guilt over his failure to help his cousins made itself clear when he agreed to Sixtus's request for help, despite the fact that Karl had led an enemy power. He promised Sixtus, 'We will immediately do what is necessary.'[24] And this time, he kept his word.

Lieutenant-Colonel Edward Lisle Strutt, a Catholic aristocrat who had studied in Austria as an undergraduate, gone skiing with the Archduke Franz Ferdinand at St. Moritz and been decorated for his bravery in the war by his own government, as well as those of Belgium, France and Romania, was dispatched to meet the Emperor and Empress at Eckartsau. He was granted an audience with Karl first, for even here in penurious internal exile, the rituals of court life were observed. He found Karl still dressed in a military uniform and wearing his medals 'with quite a good-looking, well-bred but weak face'. They spoke to each other in French and German and Strutt concluded that 'the Emperor's appearance describes his character; an eminently lovable, if weak, man, by no means a fool, and ready to face his end as bravely as his ancestress, Marie Antoinette'.[25] They discussed the possibility of the Emperor being evacuated to Switzerland, but Karl was reluctant and he quite rightly pointed out that, legally, the new republic now being proclaimed in Vienna had no right to exist as it violated the terms by which he had signed his act of renunciation. Under such circumstances, he could not leave.

With no decision about the family's future reached, Strutt was shown in to meet the Empress, who was wearing a long and elegant black dress and 'her wonderful pearls'. Strutt thought she looked

pale and ill. About medium height and with a slim figure, she looked younger than her age, twenty-six. The first impression I had was of extraordinary strength of character, softened by her own remarkable charm. Determination was written in the lines of her square little chin, intelligence in the vivacious brown eyes, intellect in the broad forehead half hidden by masses of dark hair. Without extraordinary claims to beauty, the Empress could always attract attention in a crowd. As I entered the room, I realised that she must share with the Queens of the Belgians and Romania the honour of being one of the three great royal women of the war.

His infatuation with the Empress did not preclude him from noticing that she felt the humiliation of their demotion 'more deeply than her husband', but that 'no more an affectionate and devoted couple that these two could possibly be found'.[26] The two struck up an immediate rapport and Zita showed herself willing to listen to his advice.

The new republican government told the British that the Emperor could only stay in Austria if he abdicated fully, in which case he could remain as a private citizen. If he chose not to abdicate, he must go abroad. If he chose to stay without abdicating, they would arrest him. Strutt discussed the situation at length with Zita and he advised her that her husband should leave without abdicating, then return later once everything had calmed down. The long-term future of republicanism in Austria did not look good. Many were unhappy at the prominence given to the radical Left in the new regime and the joke that the revolution had somehow created a republic without republicans captured something of the government's fragility. Zita initially recoiled at the idea of fleeing, but when Strutt told her, 'A dead Hapsburg is no good to anyone, whereas a live one, with a family, may yet be,' she gave in. Karl, brought around by his wife's entreaties and pacified by the knowledge that he would not have to abdicate, made but one condition to Strutt – 'Only promise me that I shall leave as emperor and not as a thief in the night.'

On 25 March 1919, the imperial family attended Mass for the Feast of the Annunciation and then boarded the imperial train, reassembled for one final journey. As the Hapsburgs left the local church, a crowd burst into the imperial national anthem. Veterans gathered to escort Karl to the train, and as it pulled off from the platform Strutt heard a low groan rise from the spectators. The train rattled across the length of Austria, on board was Zita's mother, Maria Antonia, whom Strutt thought looked like an over-decorated Christmas tree, having fled wearing most of her jewels, with her two pet dogs, from whom she refused to be separated. During the journey, Karl turned to Strutt and said quietly, 'After seven hundred years ...' The sentence hung in the air, its unspoken conclusion louder in its silence. At 3.45 p.m. on the following afternoon, the train crossed into Switzerland. Later, as they settled into life in exile, Karl wrote a letter to King George thanking him for all his help in getting his family out of Austria safely, but he concluded it with the forlorn wish, '*Dieu veuille Vous épargner de voir jamais dans l'avenir, ce que j'ai dû voir auprès moi.*'[27] – 'That God may spare you from ever seeing in the future what I had to see before me.'

Epilogue

'She's too short to be Tatiana'

The world that was birthed in the final years of the First World War was very different to what had come before. The peace treaties signed at Versailles, Saint-Germain-en-Laye, Neuilly-sur-Seine, Sèvres and Trianon stripped the former Central Powers of many of their most coveted possessions and inflicted upon them a peace perceived as so humiliating that it left a bitterness that grew stronger with each passing year. The sheer viciousness of the treaties made Woodrow Wilson's criminal idiocy in demanding the abolition of the central European monarchies as a condition for peace seem even more malignant in the eyes of the vanquished. The Kaiser and the Emperor had gone into exile on the assumption that it was the only way to save their countries from a punitive post-war settlement exactly like the one offered in 1919. Looked at in this light, it is just about possible to make the case that two of the most powerful governments in history came to a premature conclusion on the word of a lie or, if inclined to charity, a promise that could not be guaranteed by the man making it.

That the central European monarchies came to an end far too soon is difficult to dispute when one looks at what followed. The removal of centuries of stability coupled with the desensitising experiences of the war enabled horrific violence on the streets of Berlin, Munich, Budapest and Vienna. The rise of Nazism in the former Second Reich and then into the Hapsburg heartland of Austria through the *Anschluss* of 1938 created one of the most appalling regimes in human history. In the former Russian Empire, a holocaust of violence had already taken place during Lenin's consolidation of power, in which millions were murdered and many more fled abroad to wander Europe and the wider world as émigrés. The argument that the gulags and purges of Stalinism were somehow an aberration from the purer communism of Lenin and Trotsky is a popular one, but it is entirely incorrect. The wanton cruelty, the amoral viciousness and the depraved, random disregard for, as Trotsky put it, 'the papist-Quaker babble about the sanctity of human life' had all existed and flourished from the moment the Bolsheviks came to power in 1917. Stalin may have carried it to new heights, but the precedent had already been established. In the shadow of the Holocaust, *Kristallnacht*, the Red Terror and the gulags, it is therefore baffling that the pre-war monarchies are still habitually represented as somehow similarly unworthy, equally but differently repugnant.

Yet to argue that the collapse of the Romanov, Hapsburg and Hohenzollern monarchies was, on the whole, a negative sequence of events for Europe and that their destruction opened a Pandora's Box of instability and extremism from which millions perished and the Continent was plunged into a century of ideological conflict is not the same as saying that they were entirely innocent of the tragedies which befell them in 1918 or their subjects after 1914. The emperors made truly terrible mistakes, chief among which was their failure to prevent the war. Nicholas II and Wilhelm II both wanted peace, but they felt they were unable to stop the groundswell of opinion in their armed forces and people that hoped for war after Franz Ferdinand's death in Sarajevo. The monarchs' private desire for peace is not so much an excuse as it is an indictment – they both knew the wiser course to take, but at the crucial moment they allowed themselves to be outmanoeuvred or pressured into making a decision that they knew or feared to be wrong. Both the Kaiser and the Tsar believed in the sacred mission of kingship, in the divine right and corresponding responsibilities of sovereigns, and so by their own moral standards they bear a large share of blame for what happened.

Their inability to rein in the more jingoistic factions in their governments and armed forces is indicative of a wider problem facing the pre-deluge monarchies, namely their failure to successfully control the forces and attitudes unleashed by nationalism. In the Austrian case, that failure was born from a principled rejection of nationalism's key tenets, and it is because of this that the empire of Franz Josef was one of the very few continental states which refused to enact anti-Semitic legislation or to allow anti-Semitic initiatives to be put in place in its armed forces. That there was a popular culture of anti-Semitism in Austria at the time is indisputable, but equally the throne's opposition to it, as to all forms of overly aggressive partriotism, was often clearly expressed, in direct contrast to how the courts in Germany and Russia behaved.

Where the Hapsburgs struggled, like Canute, to turn back the tide of nationalism, the Romanovs and the Hohenzollerns identified themselves with it in the strongest possible terms. Over the course of the twentieth century, the symbiosis between monarchy and nation has been perfected by the British Crown, but it proved more troublesome for their Prussian and Russian cousins. Nationalism was the dragon that the monarchies tried and failed to tame. The elevation of the nation was problematic in an era which increasingly held that a community could be validated primarily by its superiority to others. For centuries, monarchies had flourished in an international arena in which dynasty trumped locality. Most royals were the product of marriages and family networks that crossed multiple borders – Wilhelm II was half-English, the Tsarina Alexandra was half-German and the Empress Zita was in the unenviable position of being a French-descended, Italian-born and British-educated woman at a time when her adopted homeland was at war with all three. The Crown Princess Cecilia's intercession with the Kaiser to allow her Russian cousin Irina to go home safely from her honeymoon was the first of numerous incidents during the First World War in which royals were accused of putting their foreign connections, now transformed from useful into suspicious by the outbreak of hostilities, above national interests. Xenophobia struck at the royal houses of Europe throughout the First World War, pitting patriotism against the throne with devastating consequences.

A closer analysis of the imperial regimes might also shake the belief that their downfall was part of the natural progression of history, in which the war acted as a catalyst for a political inevitability. These assessments are particularly prevalent in the historiography of Imperial Russia and Austria-Hungary, but the problems facing the supposedly backward Russia in terms of how its people's living standards were negatively affected by the war were not so different to the tribulations that occurred in the industrialised and prosperous German Reich. The war was simply too large in scope and too awful in its impact for any nation to endure it without great suffering. There were many problems in the three central European empires before 1914, but there are problems in all great nations at any point in history and the strains of the First World War turned what had been manageable into something unmanageable. What happened to the Romanov, Hapsburg and Hohenzollern empires was not so much a catastrophe waiting to happen but rather a trauma that could occur to any nation faced with a great and terrible war.

Above all, however, to study the history of the fallen monarchies of the First World War is to be confronted by the awesome and terrifying power of luck in the shaping of the human journey. It is not fashionable to speak of happenstance and coincidence as having the same influence over history as the grand and unstoppable long-term processes that reduce even the most powerful individuals to pieces floating along the surface of a strong-flowing river. The inevitability of the dialectic, as Marxists might like to call it, between rulers and ruled producing the implosion of the old-world hereditary empires looks increasingly untenable when one examines at the events that unfolded between 1914 and 1918. At any moment, the course might have been altered and the final act rendered very different. The assassination at Sarajevo and the circumstances of all three emperors' renunciations of their thrones are moments of aching frustration because of the number of variables that could have saved the monarchies and in doing so spared Europe decades of terror and dictatorship.

The exoneration or the excoriation of the German, Russian and Austro-Hungarian monarchies for their actions in the final four years of their rule is ultimately a matter of personal preference and interpretation. A monarchist could look at this story and legitimately see in its depths the supreme validation of their creed, while an opponent could see it as a tragicomedy of the folly of a dying class who had no place in the modern world and who were ultimately destroyed by the forces that they had so incompetently mishandled. Another observer might simply find it fascinating; the personal aspect is certainly compelling.

Refugees from modernity, exiles from time, the deposed and scattered royals tried to adjust to the bright and alien environment of the 1920s, with varying degrees of success. Labelled a war criminal along with the rest of his immediate family by the Treaty of Versailles, Wilhelm II was protected by the asylum granted to him by the Dutch government. The Dutch Queen Regnant, Wilhelmina, was so angered by Allied demands for extradition that she summoned their ambassadors to her presence and roundly lectured them on the inviolable nature of sanctuary in neutral and peaceful nations.

On 18 July 1920, Wilhelm's youngest son, Prince Joachim, blew his own brains out after a period of deep depression brought on by the breakdown of his marriage, mounting financial problems and his unhappiness at the political situation. The shock of losing her youngest son hastened his mother's decline, which had started with her heart attack in the last year of the war. The Empress died at Doorn, their picturesque home in the Netherlands, on 11 April 1921. Wilhelm accompanied her coffin as far as the German border, but he refused to set foot on republican soil and so he did not witness the tens of thousands who turned up to line the route of the railway line that bore Augusta Victoria back to be buried in the grounds of the Sanssouci Palace, as per her request.[1] Wilhelm lived for another twenty years and remarried shortly after the Empress's death to an aristocratic widow, Princess Hermine von Schönaich-Carolath, whom he met when her young son wrote him a childish but heartfelt letter of condolence after the Empress's death.

Like many members of the old elite, Princess Hermine was initially very sympathetic to the emergent National Socialist movement in Germany. She and some of Wilhelm's surviving sons even attended a few of the party's notorious rallies and she encouraged Wilhelm to meet with Hermann Göring after he implied that the movement might consider a restoration of the monarchy once it was in power. It was a bluff, like so many of the Nazis' moves in the early 1930s, but unlike General von Hindenburg, now the venerable President of the German republic, Wilhelm II was not taken in and he

distrusted the Nazi party intensely. For much of the 1920s he had
sunk further and further into the petty and vile anti-Semitism of
the post-war years, apparently forgetting all of his pre-revolution
Jewish friends and occasionally murmuring that the Eulenburg
scandal, the collapse of the monarchy and the Armistice had all
been the result of an international Jewish conspiracy, but when he
heard the news of *Kristallnacht* in 1938, he remarked, 'For the first
time I am ashamed to be a German.'[2] By that point, his wife had
also turned against the regime and his daughter-in-law Cecilia, still
living in Germany, had been open about her repugnance from the
beginning. However, the Crown Prince, ever a source of trouble,
had joined the movement, a decision which heightened his father's
feelings of disappointment in him.

When the Second World War started, the Netherlands was
occupied by the Wehrmacht and Wilhelm was thrilled to see the
German armies take Paris, something they had failed to do in 1914.
It felt to him like a settling of old scores. However, he remained
privately hostile to Adolf Hitler and the feeling was reciprocated.
Fifteen princes of the imperial line signed up to serve in the
Nazi armies in 1939, but Hitler increasingly saw the monarchist
movement as a threat. The princes' service in the Wehrmacht
showed that the Hohenzollerns were never likely to coalesce as
a principled form of opposition to Nazism in the way the House
of Hapsburg had, but the Führer remained uneasy. When the
ex-Crown Prince's eldest son was killed in action in 1940, thousands
turned up to his funeral and Hitler was so incensed by this display
of royalism that he ordered all Hohenzollerns to cease serving in
the German military and banned any further public exhibitions of
neo-monarchism. The Kaiser's stepson Ferdinand was arrested for
publicly criticising the government, while his son Prince Eitel was
banned from attending a reunion of his old regiment from the First
World War.

Despite the totalitarianism facing them, or perhaps because of
it, the monarchist old guard in Germany were ever more brazen
in showing their contempt for their country's corporal-turned-
dictator; when Otto von Bismarck's granddaughter, Countess
Hannah von Bismarck-Schönhausen, was invited to launch a new
warship bearing her grandfather's name, she tartly replied that she

had already christened a warship with the family's name during the reign of His Imperial Majesty and she saw no reason why she should repeat the task. At Prince Wilhelm's funeral, which had so raised Herr Hitler's heckles, the ninety-year-old Field Marshal von Mackensen, who had served the Kaiser devotedly on the Eastern Front and whose son Hans had been the companion of his fourth son Augustus Wilhelm, heard that a former colleague had been banned from serving in the Third Reich's war effort because the Nazi high command thoroughly disapproved of him, to which the *ci-devant* Field Marshal shouted, 'In that case I can only congratulate you with all my heart!'[3] When the Kaiser passed away in 1941 at the age of eighty-two, he expressly prohibited both the display of National Socialist symbols and that his body should be brought back for burial in a non-monarchist Germany. Today, the Kaiser's body rests in a lovely red-brick mausoleum in the grounds of Huis Doorn, his final home. His will stated that the body was to be exhumed and taken back to Germany in the event of a restoration of the Prussian monarchy.

For most of his twenty-three years in exile, Wilhelm II had behaved with a resigned dignity that was marred only by his conspiracy-theorist views and his constant inability to accept any of the blame for what befell him in 1918. 'I am a broken man,' he said early on in his exile, 'what can I do with my life now? There is no more hope, the only thing which remains for me is despair.' As he lay dying in 1941, the nurse attending him comforted him by saying, 'Your Majesty, it is better above. With the Most Supreme Lord it is better for us than on earth.' Wilhelm replied, 'I am ready ...'[4] From his own self-imposed relocation to Coburg, the ex-Tsar Ferdinand of Bulgaria summed up the royal attitude to years in the post-war wilderness: 'Kings in exile are more philosophic under reverses than ordinary individuals; but our philosophy is primarily the result of tradition and breeding, and do not forget that pride is an important item in the making of a monarch. We are disciplined from the day of our birth and taught the avoidance of all outward signs of emotion. The skeleton sits forever with us at the feast. It may mean murder, it may mean abdication, but it serves always to remind us of the unexpected. Therefore we are prepared and nothing comes in the nature of a catastrophe. The main thing in life is to support any condition of bodily or spiritual exile with dignity. If one sups with sorrow, one need not invite the world to see you eat.'⁵

Similar sentiments were echoed by Ferdinand's estranged brother-in-law Karl, who died at the age of thirty-four on the island of Madeira after a cold turned into bronchitis and then severe pneumonia, the same progression of illness that had killed the much-older Franz Josef in 1916. Karl died as Mass was being celebrated in the next room, with a crucifix pressed against his lips, while a pregnant Zita held his hand and prayed. On their wedding day, the devout Karl had told Zita, 'Now we must help each other get to Heaven.'⁶ That shared sense of Christianity had sustained them through the heartbreak and strain of the war and their exile afterwards. Yet Christian resignation did not mean surrender, as least as far as the Hapsburgs were concerned. Karl had never accepted the legality of his deposition and in 1921 he had even smuggled himself back into Hungary in an attempt to reclaim the Crown of Saint Stephen, a venture which failed when Admiral Horthy reneged on his tear-stained oath of 1918 to restore the monarchy, because in the interim he had acquired so much power for himself.

Karl's death meant the Hapsburg claim passed to his eldest son Otto, who did not pursue the vacant throne with quite the same vigour as his father. He retained his pre-war title of Crown Prince rather than elevating himself to *de jure* Emperor; he did become Head of the House of Hapsburg, a position he held until renouncing it in old age in favour of his son Karl in 2007. A vocal opponent of Nazism, Otto became heavily involved in Austrian expatriate and Allied movements designed to highlight the outrages perpetrated by the Third Reich even before the Second World War. Zita, likewise an opponent, had to move her large family to the safety of Canada for most of the war, where one of her daughters, the Archduchess Charlotte, moved south to find work and pursue her beliefs by becoming a welfare worker in New York's East Harlem.

After 1945, Otto von Hapsburg became an enthusiastic supporter of what eventually became the European Union, seeing in its dilution of national independence a reimagining of the Hapsburg dynasty's centuries-long commitment to a central authority that ameliorated the strength of national borders and competing identities. He was a revered figure in the European Parliament, but he also had some flashes of his mother's spirit. In 1988, when the Northern Irish Protestant fundamentalist politician Ian Paisley began to heckle Pope John Paul II as he addressed the parliament, citing the Book of Revelation and holding up a placard that called the Pope the Anti-Christ, several delegates turned on him, including an enraged Crown Prince Otto, who was one of those who attempted to punch Reverend Paisley in the face.

The Empress Zita endured a sixty-seven-year-long widowhood, dying in Switzerland in 1989 at the age of ninety-six. She lived long enough to see the communist system that had swallowed up so much of the old Hapsburg Empire after 1945 begin to crumble. To someone who saw herself as the protectress of the Hapsburgs' eight-century-long legacy, it must have seemed as if the Continent's grand experiment with communism had lasted little more than a blink of an eye. In 1989, the body of the Dowager Empress Zita, who had once been reviled as 'the Italian Schemer', was taken for burial in the same Capuchin crypt and via the same route where, seventy-three years earlier, she had walked behind the coffin of the Emperor Franz Josef. In 2011, the body of her son Otto was granted similar honours.

By the time the Empress Zita passed away, the Austrian republic had relaxed some of its more vindictive and patently illegal restrictions on the former ruling family. In the 1920s, they had seized almost every bit of property owned by any Hapsburg, even if it was owned entirely in a private capacity, and frozen their assets, including funds set up by Franz Josef made through investments to provide for his relatives in the specific circumstances of exile. The Czechoslovakian and Hungarian governments had done the same, leading to the eviction of Franz Ferdinand's three children from their home at Konopischt on grounds that are still being contested in the European courts. The children themselves struggled in the outside world. Due to his opposition to Nazism, Franz Ferdinand's eldest son, Maximilian, whose success in his school exams had been toasted the night before the tragedy in Sarajevo, was arrested after the *Anschluss* and spent years as an inmate at Dachau concentration camp. After his liberation and the end of the Second World War, the Austrian government returned Artstetten Castle, where his parents were buried, to the family and piece by piece the anti-Hapsburg laws were rescinded. Nor was Maximilian the only Hapsburg to fall victim to the mid-century dictatorships. The family's opposition to totalitarianism saw the Archduke Albrecht emerge from years in the Nazi work camps blind in one eye and with half his body completely paralysed as a result of torture inflicted by the Gestapo, while his brother Wilhelm was kidnapped off the streets of Vienna by the Red Army in 1947, flown to the USSR, interrogated, beaten, sentenced to twenty-seven years' hard labour and left to die in a Soviet prison.

The years of exile brought flight from communism and fascism, stolen jewels, controversial marriages, feuds and court cases, but of all the strange tragedies that befell the royal houses in exile, perhaps none was quite so famous or more puzzling than the Anastasia affair, which began after the Romanovs' missing bodies gave rise to the story that one or more member of the family might have survived the massacre. In 1921, the story rapidly began to centre on the figure of the Grand Duchess Anastasia thanks to the claims made by a patient at the Dalldorf mental asylum in northern Germany. The young woman had been brought there after she attempted suicide by jumping off the Bendler Bridge into the Landwehr Canal in Berlin. A fellow sufferer, Clara Peuthert, read a newspaper piece that speculated on the possible survival of some of the Tsar's family and she noticed a similarity between her companion and the Grand Duchess Tatiana, whose photograph accompanied the article. The anonymous suicide survivor did not deny Clara's speculations. As the rumours spread out from Dalldorf, eventually one of the Tsarina's surviving ladies-in-waiting, Baroness Sophie Buxhoeveden, who, like 500,000 other refugees from the Russian Revolution, had since made Germany her home, came to Dalldorf to see the girl for herself.

The patient cowered beneath her bed sheets and refused to meet the baroness's eye or answer any of her questions. Losing her patience, the baroness reached forward and yanked the poor girl out of bed before turning witheringly to the doctors and declaring, 'She's too short to be Tatiana.' At five feet two inches, she was far too short to be Tatiana, but she was just the right height for the shortest of the imperial sisters, Anastasia. Defending herself later, the woman pointed out, 'I never said I was Tatiana.'[7] Others had made the mistake and she simply had not corrected them. As interest in the resurrected Grand Duchess Anastasia grew, the longest court case in European history, ending only in February 1970, was fought to determine if she had any legal right to call herself a Romanov. In the meantime, she used a variety of pseudonyms, including Anna Tchaikovsky and Anna Anderson, as her claims split the exiled monarchist community.

One of her most high-profile supporters was Princess Xenia, the real Anastasia's second cousin. Strikingly beautiful, Xenia was two years younger than the Grand Duchess Anastasia and the girls had last met during the tercentenary celebrations of 1913, when Anastasia was twelve and Xenia was only ten. During the war, Xenia and her elder sister, Princess Nina, had lived in England and, not having any safe way to get home, they never returned to Russia or were reunited with their father, Grand Duke George, who was one of those executed by the Bolsheviks in 1919. Nina married another émigré, Prince Paul Chavchavadze, and they had a son together, David, who later went on to serve in the CIA. Xenia married an American millionaire, William Bateman Leeds, the heir to a tin-mining fortune, and she was living in New York, dividing her time between a luxurious apartment on the city's Upper East Side and a summer house on Long Island, when Anna Tchaikovsky arrived in Manhattan in 1927.

When she and the would-be Anastasia first met, in the Fifth Avenue drawing room of another sympathetic socialite, Anna Jennings, Xenia watched as 'Anna Tchaikovsky' extended her hand to a guest and was so impressed by the naturalness of the gesture that she became convinced that only a fellow Romanov could be capable of such unaffected majesty. Despite her husband's misgivings about how the rest of the Romanovs would take it, Xenia Leeds insisted upon providing sustenance and shelter for 'Mrs Tchaikovsky', who had come to New York through the generosity of some of her other supporters and hoped to stay. Later, the two women drifted apart because Xenia's husband found Anna's instability and demanding nature too difficult to bear, but

Mrs Leeds' support for her claim never wavered and she testified in her favour during subsequent court cases.

But Xenia Leeds's belief in Anna Tchaikovsky, or Anna Anderson, highlighted one of the running themes in those who endorsed her. On the surface, the roll call looked very impressive – cousins, fellow Romanovs, childhood playmates and celebrated émigrés like the composer Sergei Rachmaninoff – but when examined more closely, their credibility as witnesses was nearly always problematic. Xenia Leeds and her sister, Nina Chavchavadze, had not been regular playmates with the imperial children; as members of the same extended family, they met socially at various stages in their childhood, but it was hardly a close relationship. Added to that, Nina and Xenia's residence in England during the First World War meant that they had last seen Anastasia when she, and they, were very young. Xenia herself conceded that she would be hard-pressed to correctly identify her second cousin twelve years after they had last met as children, rather she insisted that her identification rested on knowing a fellow royal when she met one. The lifelong support of Gleb Botkin, son of the doctor who had perished at the Romanovs' side in Yekaterinburg, was certainly a boon, but Gleb's claims to have been best friends with the Romanov siblings during their shared childhood at Tsarskoe Selo is not borne out by what we know of their schedule. They played together very infrequently and the memories undoubtedly featured more in Gleb Botkin's head than they would have in the Romanovs'. In contrast, those who did not believe that she was Anastasia were often fewer in number but far more credible, including the real Anastasia's godmother, the Grand Duchess Olga Alexandrovna, Prince Felix Yussopov, now living in peripatetic exile with Paris as his base, Anastasia's French tutor Pierre Gilliard and one of her nannies, Alexandra Tegleva.

DNA tests carried out after the pretender's death in 1984 ascertained that she was not a Romanov and had far more probably been Franziska Schanzkowska, a Polish factory worker who disappeared in 1920.[8] For decades in Yekaterinburg, visiting communist party youth delegates were still being taken down into the cellar where the family had been murdered to pose next to the bullet-sprayed walls for commemorative photographs, while students at the KGB academies were told early in their training that the Soviet government had always known that the Grand Duchess Anastasia had died with the rest of her family in 1918.[9] Then came a public unveiling of the remains of five of the seven Romanovs murdered at Yekaterinburg after the fall of the Soviet Union, their ceremonial reburial in the family's necropolis in Saint Petersburg in 1998 and then the discovery in 2008 of the missing two bodies in a nearby secondary burial site, where the Bolsheviks had attempted to incinerate them. All the bodies were rigorously tested by DNA samples provided by some of the Romanovs' surviving relatives, including Prince Philip, Duke of Edinburgh, the husband of Queen Elizabeth II. However, the mystery had by then been enshrined in plays, novels, an Oscar-winning movie starring Ingrid Bergman and Yul Brynner, television shows, dolls, memorial websites and musicals in both stage and animation, with the Grand Duchess's name transliterated into its Americanised pronunciation of *Anna-stay-zee-a* rather than the English *Anna-stahz-ee-a* that she and her mother would have used.

The details of Anna Anderson's decades-long insistence that she was the last surviving member of Nicholas II's immediate family are still debated, with most of the remaining questions now focussing on trying to ascertain whether or not, with her history of mental illness, she actually believed her own delusions – whether, as John Klier and Helen Mingay suggested in their wonderful study of the mystery, 'the second undoubtedly believed she was the first. And, truly, she kept alive the memory of that other Anastasia. Without her there would be no films, no books, no romantic legend. The two Anastasias represent the two faces of the twentieth century. One century that really existed, full of war and the slaughter of the innocents. The second is the century we longed to have, of peace and family pleasures, and the dreams of any little girl who could close her eyes and become a princess.'[10] Or, as Felix Yussopov insisted, Anna Anderson was nothing more than a 'nervous, hysterical, vulgar and common ... adventuress, a sick hysteric and a frightful play actress ... [one] would recoil in horror at the thought that this frightful creature could be the daughter of our Tsar!'[11]

Either way, the posthumous fame of Anastasia Romanov helped preserve her family in a modern legend where she and her three sisters became the most celebrated victims of Russian communism's political violence. It could be argued that they were only four among millions of similar victims, but the young women's prominence as members of the imperial family meant that we know so much more about the intimate details of their lives than we do about most of those who lost their lives in the chaos unleashed by the First World War. We know what books they liked to read, their favourite bath scents, their pet peeves and their happiest memories, and in this knowledge we are able to more fully appreciate the humanity of all those who perished in similar ways. In death as in life, they have become symbols with which millions may identify and empathise, and through which wider points may be illuminated. In his study of Lady Jane Grey, the late Eric Ives justified the posthumous fascination with a sixteenth-century princess who, in comparison to her other relatives, achieved very little beyond a particularly tragic and premature death: 'The pages of history are asterisked with names which defy the erosion of time. Jane Grey is one such, but strangely so. Truth to tell she counted for little ... Undeniably, there is the macabre attraction of the girl sacrifice. She died Jane Dudley, but is universally remembered as Jane Grey, Ariadne chained to the rock. All this and more. But the fundamental justification for remembering Jane is the justification for remembering Anne Frank centuries later. They speak for the multitude of brutality's victims who have no voice.'[12] The same might very well be said for the Romanov sisters.

The ruling houses of the Edwardian period hover in our cultural imagination as a glittering prologue to the coming carnage of the First World War. They are girls in white linen dresses, men in immaculate military uniforms, in an era without weekends that birthed the Fabergé eggs, private yachts the size of small ocean liners, the first moving pictures of royalties' private lives, beautiful jewels, winning smiles, grand opera houses and waltzes that all speak of a society of haunting loveliness and facile grace. From sepia-toned photographs they stare at us from the other side of the impenetrable gulf created by what happened after 1914. The waltzes drown out the other sounds of that epoch – the misery of the factories, the rapid production of ever more deadly military hardware and the cheers of crowds hungry for war. The story of the emperors of the First World War is a grand political narrative, as well as an arresting sequence of personal dramas. It is by turns touching and frustrating, uplifting and appalling, an inspiration and a warning. The courage and dignity with which many of them met their ultimate fates is still a source of wonder and inspiration for their modern-day admirers, of which there are many – indeed, as of 1981, devotees. Nicholas II, his wife and their children were all canonised by the branches of the Russian Orthodox Church at various stages after 1981 as Passion-Bearers, a category of saint which specifically recognises that the person died in a Christ-like manner with their faith sustaining them on the path to death, but which differs from a martyr, who was explicitly killed for their faith. Also canonised was Alexandra's estranged sister, the Grand Duchess Elisabeth (known as Ella in the family), who was murdered by the Cheka later on the same day as her younger sister. Ella, who had founded and joined a convent in her widowhood, had been under house arrest in the nearby town of Alapaevsk, and she was taken out to an abandoned iron mine where she was beaten and then thrown in. With her was Sister Barbara Yakovleva, a nun from her convent, and several other Romanovs who had been caught and transported to the region – the poet and the Tsar's cousin, twenty-one-year-old Prince Vladimir Paley, the Grand Duke Sergei Mikhailovich, his secretary Feodor Kemez, and three Romanov brothers, Prince Ivan, Prince Constantine and Prince Igor, who ranged in age from thirty-two to twenty-four. They were all badly beaten and then thrown down the mine, with two hand grenades tossed in after them. The guards could hear the Grand Duchess and the others singing hymns, even after the second grenade, so they stuffed the entrance with wood and set it on fire. The White armies took the town and recovered the bodies a few days later, something which they did not manage to do in the more efficient killing fields at Yekaterinburg. The body of the Grand Duchess Elisabeth was transported for burial to the Russian Orthodox church of Mary Magdalene in Jerusalem.

In 2004, Pope John Paul II beatified Emperor Karl not just for the piety with which he greeted death in Madeira but also for his attempts to end the war, because, in the Pontiff's words, 'The decisive task of Christians consists in seeking, recognising and following

God's will in all things. The Christian statesman, Karl of Austria, confronted this challenge every day ... From the beginning, the Emperor Karl conceived of his office as a holy service to his people. His chief concern was to follow the Christian vocation to holiness also in his political actions. For this reason, his thoughts turned to social assistance. May he be an example for all of us, especially for those who have political responsibilities in Europe today!'[13] Beatification, which entitles Karl to the prefix of 'Blessed', is often a prelude to full canonisation and a committed lobby of Catholics, Austrian conservatives and royalists are working towards making Karl a member of the Catholic confraternity of saints. In the Ural Mountains, the places where the Romanovs' bodies were hidden in July 1918 have been marked by fields of lilies, and there are churches dedicated to each of the seven members of the imperial family. The house where they were slaughtered, torn down by Boris Yeltsin acting on the orders of the Soviet government in 1977 when it began to become a focal point of surreptitious pilgrimage, has been replaced by a sumptuous commemorative cathedral – The Church on Blood in Honour of All Saints Resplendent in the Russian Land. Thousands progress there every year, to the fields and the church, to partake of the 'Romanov Golgotha' and the symbiosis perceived as existing between the martyred royals and all subsequent victims of Russian communism. Flowers are still left in the Hapsburg crypt at the Capuchin church and in Germany the Kaiser's legacy is hotly debated as the study of the Second Reich emerges from the shadow of the more popular and more terrifying history of the Third.

Looking back on the years leading up to the revolutions, Felix Yussopov was moved to write a universal truth, 'Our memories are sometimes full of light and sometimes dark with shadow. In an eventful life some are sad and some are gay, some are pleasant, while others are so tragic that one's sole desire is never to recall them.'[14] Yet to forget or dismiss the story of the central European monarchies of 1914 is ill-advised. For better or for worse, whether it is to caution or to vindicate, to study as a historical epic or a biographical tragedy, the fall of the imperial families after 1914 is a tale worthy of interest and remembrance not just because it matters in the way that all history matters, but because it moves us with its extraordinary tragedy, and so perhaps the most appropriate final word in this study of their story are the words of the sixteen-year-old Grand Duchess Anastasia, penned to a family servant as an armoured train bore her away to a place of exile and death: 'Goodbye. Don't forget me.'

Notes

Prologue

1. The opening quote from Lady Elizabeth Bowes-Lyon, the future Queen Consort, can be found in William Shawcross (ed.), *Counting One's Blessings: The Selected Letters of Queen Elizabeth the Queen Mother* (London, 2013), p. 50. The story of the announcement at Windsor and the weekend at the Marchioness of Milford Haven's house is in Princess Marie Louise's memoirs, *My Memories of Six Reigns* (London, 1957), pp. 185–9.

1 The Russian, German and Austro-Hungarian Monarchies in 1913

1. Winston Churchill, *The World Crisis* (London, 1923), i. 107.
2. Orlando Figes, *A People's Tragedy: The Russian Revolution, 1891–1924* (London, 1996), p. 13.
3. Popular confidence in the size of Russia's military as the best guarantor of victory ensured that the defeat in the Crimean War (1853–1856) had largely been forgotten or ignored by 1904. For a particularly good history of the Russian army in this period see Bruce W. Menning's *Bayonets Before Bullets: The Russian Imperial Army, 1861–1914* (Indiana University Press, 1992).
4. Dominic Lieven, *Nicholas II: Emperor of All the Russias* (London, 1993), p. 148.
5. Much has been written on Imperial Russia's path towards industrialisation. An interesting account and one which I am indebted to is Tim McDaniel's *Autocracy, Capitalism and Revolution in Russia* (University of California Press, 1988).
6. E. J. Bing (ed.), *The Letters of Tsar Nicholas and Empress Marie* (London, 1937), p. 188.
7. *Letters of Tsar Nicholas and Empress Marie*, pp. 197–201.
8. Lieven, *Nicholas II*, p. 150.
9. Lieven, *Nicholas II*, p. 154.
10. Lieven, *Nicholas II*, p. 153.
11. Ascher, p. 139. *The New York Times*' report on 25 August 1906 incorrectly

stated that Natalia Stolypin had died as a result of her wounds; a correction was printed on 26 August 1906, when it was confirmed that she was in a critical state but had been moved to the Calmeyer Hospital.

12. Stolypin's career has received thorough treatment in Abraham Ascher, *P. A. Stolypin: The Search for Stability in Late Imperial Russia* (Stanford University Press, 2001). For a more negative appraisal of his legacy, see Figes, pp. 221–32, and for the wider debate, Judith Pallott, 'Modernization from Above: The Stolypin Land Reform' in J. Pallott and D. J. B Shaw (eds), *Landscapes and Settlement in Romanov Russia, 1613–1917* (Oxford University Press, 1990), pp. 165–94; D. A. J. Macey, 'Government Reactions and Peasant Reforms' in R. B. McKean (ed.), *New Perspectives in Modern Russian History: Selected Papers from the Fourth World Congress of Soviet and Eastern European Studies, Harrogate, 1990* (London, 1992), pp. 133–73. For the Russian peasantry's lifestyle and economic aspects in the late Tsarist period, H-D. Löwe, *Die Lage der Bauern in Russland, 1880–1905* (St Katharinen, 1987), a painstakingly researched account which presented the aforementioned study concerning the average peasant's diet under Nicholas II, and Esther Kingston-Mann and Tim Mixter (eds), *Peasant Economy, Culture and Politics in European Russia, 1800–1921* (Princeton University Press, 1991), were both invaluable.
13. Robert K. Massie, *Nicholas and Alexandra* (London, 1968), p. 215.
14. *Ibid.*
15. Count Vladimir Kokovstov, *Out of My Past: The Memoirs of Count Kokovstov*, trans. Laura Matveev (Stanford University Press, 1935), p. 283.
16. Figes, p. 12.
17. Meriel Buchanan, *The Dissolution of an Empire* (London, 1932), p. 36.
18. Letter from Maria, Duchess of Saxe-Coburg, to her daughter, Crown Princess Marie of Romania, dated 17–19 February 1914, quoted in Helen Rappaport, *Four Sisters: The Lost Lives of the Romanov Grand Duchesses* (London, 2014), p. 209.
19. Pierre Gilliard, *Thirteen Years at the Russian Imperial Court* (New York, 1921), p. 205.
20. Haemophilia can appear in families with no prior history and vanish over the course of several generations, hence Queen Victoria's incredulity when her son Leopold, the future Duke of Albany, was diagnosed with it in 1853 and why there have been no cases of the disease in the European royal houses since Alexei's generation.
21. Massie, p. 161.
22. Figes, p. 13.
23. Greg King and Sue Woolmans, *The Assassination of the Archduke: Sarajevo 1914 and the Murder that Changed the World* (London, 2013), p. 150.
24. Coryne Hall, *Little Mother of Russia: A Biography of the Empress Marie Feodorovna* (London, 1999), p. 261.
25. See in particular the work of John C. G. Röhl for the argument that Wilhelm's anti-Semitism played a significant role in preparing Germany for Nazism. For an excellent counterargument see Christopher Clark, *Kaiser Wilhelm II: A Life in Power* (London, 2009), pp. 350–6.

26. Clark, *Wilhelm II*, p. 171.
27. A wonderful introduction to, and assessment of, Wilhelmine foreign policy can be found in Clark, *Wilhelm II*, pp. 167–217 and Paul Kennedy, 'The Kaiser and German *Weltpolitik*: Reflexions on Wilhelm II's place in the making of German foreign policy' in John C. G. Röhl and Nicolaus Sombart (eds), *Kaiser Wilhelm II: New Interpretations* (Cambridge University Press, 2005), pp. 143–68.
28. Clark, *Wilhelm II*, p. 174.
29. In 1900, Philipp was elevated to become Prince zu Eulenburg. For ease of reference in such a short précis of his career, I have used the title of count, which he possessed when his influence with Wilhelm began. On the debate over Wilhelm II's love life, see in particular Nicolaus Sombart, 'The Kaiser in his epoch: Some reflexions on Wilhelmine society, sexuality and culture' in Röhl and Sombart (eds), pp. 305–11 for the argument that he was a homosexual and pp. 287–311 for the wider context. Tyler Whittle, *The Last Kaiser: A Biography of William II, German Emperor and King of Prussia* (London, 1977), pp. 89–91, tentatively suggests that Wilhelm may have been bisexual but that Eulenburg was the only man with whom he seems to have been romantically linked. For the opposing view see Clark, *Wilhelm II*, p. 104–5 and the English translation of John C. G. Röhl, *Young Wilhelm: The Kaiser's Early Life, 1859–1888* (Cambridge University Press, 1998), pp. 453–64, which contains updated information on Wilhelm's youthful heterosexual romances.
30. For Otto von Bismarck's assessment of the two men's relationship and for an excellent overview of the eventual downfall of Philipp zu Eulenburg, see James D. Steakley, 'Iconography of a Scandal: Political Cartoons and the Eulenburg Affair in Wilhelmine Germany' in Martin Baumi Duberman, Martha Vicinus and George Chauncey (eds), *Hidden from History: Reclaiming the Gay and Lesbian Past* (New York, 1990). For Christopher Clark's assessment that the relationship was platonic see Clark, *Wilhelm II*, p. 104.
31. Letter from the Crown Princess Victoria of Prussia to her mother, Queen Victoria, dated 28 April 1863, quoted in Roger Fulford (ed.), *Dearest Mama: Private Correspondence of Queen Victoria and the Crown Princess of Prussia, 1861–1864* (London, 1968), p. 203–4.
32. I am grateful to Rose Morgan for discussions on the best way to translate '*liebchen*'. It is an older term, with words like 'darling' also being possible comparable words in English. The existence of the missing dossier and the defence's attempts to find it are confirmed in a letter from Maximilian Harden to Friedrich von Holstein, dated 31 May 1908, and quoted in Norman Rich and M. H. Fisher (eds), *The Holstein Papers*, (Cambridge University Press, 1957), iii. 532. For zu Eulenburg and Count Kuno von Moltke's relationship, see the letters between Baron Axel von Varnbüler and von Moltke quoted in Isabel V. Hull, 'Kaiser Wilhelm II and the "Leibenberg Circle"' in Röhl and Sombart (eds), pp. 193–220, which also gives an excellent assessment of zu Eulenburg's political beliefs and Maximilian Harden's motives in targeting him.
33. Röhl, *Young Wilhelm*, p. 454.

34. Letter from Count Philipp zu Eulenburg to Hubertus, Prince von Bismarck, dated 5 August 1886, quoted in Clark, *Wilhelm II*, p. 105.

35. Clark, *Wilhelm II*, p. 240.

36. Giles MacDonagh, *The Last Kaiser: William the Impetuous* (London, 2000), p. 455. Shaw also thought that the Kaiser had one of the best intellects of any of the leaders of 1914.

37. Timothy Snyder, *The Red Prince: The Fall of a Dynasty and the Rise of Modern Europe* (London, 2008), p. 250.

38. In 1573, the feast day's name was changed to the Feast of the Holy Rosary. Between 1716 and 1913 it was celebrated on the first Sunday of every month, but it then reverted to its original date of 7 October.

39. Of the Hapsburg kings of an independent Spanish kingdom, Philip II (d. 1598) married his double first cousin, Princess Maria Manuela of Portugal (d. 1545), his second cousin Mary I, Queen Regnant of England and Ireland (d. 1558), Princess Elisabeth of France (d. 1568) to whom he was not closely related, and after her death the Archduchess Anna of Austria (d. 1580), his niece. Philip III (d. 1621), offspring of the latter marriage, married his first cousin once removed, Archduchess Margaret of Austria (d. 1611). Their son, Philip IV (d. 1665), married Princess Elisabeth of France (d. 1644), to whom he was not closely related, and then Archduchess Mariana of Austria (d. 1696), his niece. As a result of his immediate ancestors' marriages, their son Carlos II had genes more homozygous than if his parents had been siblings. He married his second cousin, Marie Louise of Orléans (d. 1689) and after her death Maria Anna of Neuberg (d. 1740), to whom he was not related. Both marriages were childless and the Spanish line of the Hapsburg family died out with him.

40. Edward Crankshaw, *The Fall of the House of Habsburg* (London, 1983), p. 14.

41. Count Egon Caesar Corti, *Vom Kind Zum Kaiser* (Graz, 1950) p. 332.

42. Crankshaw, p. 51.

43. Redlich Josef, *The Emperor Franz Josef* (London, 1929), p. 51.

44. Adolf Schwarzenberg, *Prince Felix zu Schwarzenberg* (New York, 1946), p. 11.

45. Crankshaw, p. 54.

46. Joan Haslip, *The Lonely Empress: A Biography of Elisabeth of Austria* (New York, 1965), p. 334.

47. Haslip, *The Lonely Empress*, p. 177.

48. For the best discussion of Ludwig's sexuality and his so-called 'secret diary' see chapter 15 of Christopher McIntosh, *The Swan King: Ludwig II of Bavaria* (London, 1982), pp. 153–9.

49. *Ibid.*

50. The Archduchess Maria Valerie, diary, 22 December 1898; Lieven, *Nicholas II*, p. 195.

51. Andrew Wheatcroft, *The Habsburgs: Embodying Empire* (London, 1995), pp. 288–90, for the theory that the Hapsburgs' style of government nurtured the artistic productivity of turn-of-the-century Vienna.

52. *The Daily Telegraph*, 7 January 1899; Marguerite Cunliffe-Owen, *The*

Martyrdom of an Empress (London, 1899), pp. 274–82; *The New York Times*, 10 November 1898.

2 Sarajevo, 28 June 1914

1. Interview given by the Dowager Empress Zita to author Gordon Brook-Shepherd on 7 March 1977, quoted in Gordon Brook-Shepherd, *The Last Empress: The Life and Times of Zita of Austria-Hungary, 1892–1989* (London, 1991), p. 23.
2. Jean-Paul Bled, *François-Ferdinand d'Autriche* (Paris, 2012), p. 96.
3. Archduchess Isabella and her husband, Archduke Friedrich, had eight daughters but tragically the fourth girl, the Archduchess Natalie, died at the age of fourteen in 1898. Franz Ferdinand's quote regarding the ball at the Larisch is quoted in King and Woolmans, p. 43.
4. King and Woolmans, p. 58.
5. King and Woolmans, p. 57.
6. King and Woolmans, p. 101.
7. Wladimir Aichelburg, *Archduke Franz Ferdinand and Arstetten Castle* (Vienna, 2000), p. 33.
8. King and Woolmans, p. 115.
9. King and Woolmans, p. 145.
10. Gerd Höller, *Franz Ferdinand von Österreich-Este* (Graz, 1982), p.226.
11. A. J. P. Taylor, *The First World War: An Illustrated History* (London, 1974), p. 13.
12. King and Woolmans, p. 218.
13. M. Ljuba Jovanović, 'The Murder of Sarajevo', *Journal of the British Institute of International Affairs* (March 1925), p. 31.
14. Dolph Owings, *The Sarajevo Trial* (Chapel Hill, 1984), p. 56.
15. Vladimir Dedijer, *The Road to Sarajevo* (New York, 1966), p. 388–9.
16. King and Woolmans, p. 189.
17. David James Smith, *One Morning in Sarajevo* (London, 2008), p. 175.
18. There are several versions and translations of what the Archduke said, but the variations are very slight and there are no significant differences in any of the surviving accounts.
19. *Neue Freie Presse*, 29 June 1914.
20. Theodor von Sosnosky, *Franz Ferdinand der Ezherzog Thronfolger* (Munich, 1929), p. 218–19.
21. Baron Andreas von Morsey, 'Konopischt and Sarajevo', *Berliner Monatshefte* (June 1934), p. 499.
22. Erika Bestenreiner, *Franz Ferdinand und Sophie von Hohenberg: Verbotene Liebe am Kaiserhof* (Munich, 2004), p. 251.
23. Rudolf Kiszling, *Erzherzog Franz Ferdinand von Österreich-Este* (Graz and Cologne, 1953), p. 303.
24. Baron Albert von Margutti, *The Emperor Francis Joseph and His Times* (London, 1921), p. 138–9.
25. Count Egon Caesar Corti and Hans Sokol, *Der alte Kaiser* (Vienna, 1955), iii. 412–14.

26. Interview given by the Dowager Empress Zita to Gordon Brook-Shepherd on 23 April 1968, quoted in Brook-Shepherd, p. 30.
27. Daisy, Princess of Pless, *Daisy, Princess of Pless: By Herself* (New York, 1929), pp. 145–6.
28. King and Woolmans, p. 208.

3 The Early War Years in Austria-Hungary and Germany

1. King George V, diary, 28 June 1914.
2. *L'Osservatore Romano*, 30 June 1914.
3. Maurice Paléologue, *An Ambassador's Memoirs* (London, 1923–5), i. 12–13.
4. Paléologue, i. 14.
5. *Ibid.*
6. *Ibid.*
7. Lieven, *Nicholas II*, p. 198.
8. David Fromkin, *Europe's Last Summer: Why the World went to War in 1914* (London, 2004), p. 188.
9. The Grand Duke Nicholas Nikolaevich (1856–1929), a grandson of Tsar Nicholas I on his father's side, hereafter referred to by the more Russian version of his Christian name, Nikolai, to differentiate him from Emperor Nicholas II. The Romanov family usually referred to him as 'Nikolasha' for the same reason.
10. Paléologue, i. 22–3.
11. Virginia Cowles, *The Last Tsar and Tsarina* (London, 1977), p. 149.
12. Margaret MacMillan, *The War That Ended Peace: How Europe Abandoned Peace for the First World War* (London, 2013), p. 563.
13. Walther Rathenau, *Notes and Diaries*, Hartmut Pogge von Strandmann and Caroline Pinder Cracraft (eds) (Oxford University Press, 1985), p. 153.
14. MacDonagh, p. 378.
15. John C. G. Röhl (ed.), *1914: Delusion or Design* (London, 1973), p. 87.
16. MacDonagh, p. 363–4.
17. MacDonagh, p. 367.
18. *Ibid.*
19. Brook-Shepherd, p. 34.
20. From a transcript written by the Dowager Empress Zita in May 1981 for Gordon Brook-Shepherd about the wartime court, quoted in Brook-Shepherd, p. 39.
21. *Ibid.*
22. *Ibid.*, p. 37.
23. Wheatcroft, p. 287.

4 Nicholas II's Wartime Leadership and the Rise of Rasputin

1. Andrei Maylunas and Sergei Mironenko (eds), *A Lifelong Passion: Nicholas and Alexandra, Their Own Story* (London, 1997), p. 418.
2. Greg King, *The Last Empress: The Life and Times of Alexandra Feodorovna, Tsarina of Russia* (London, 1995), p. 233.

3. Anna Vyrubova, *Memories of the Russian Court* (New York, 1923), p. 105–6.

4. Cowles, p. 151.

5. Baroness Sophie Buxhoeveden, *The Life and Tragedy of Alexandra Feodorovna, Empress of Russia* (New York, 1928), p. 192.

6. Rappaport, *Four Sisters*, p. 93.

7. Robert Wilton, *The Last Days of the Romanovs* (London, 1920), p. 220.

8. Rappaport, *Sisters*, p. 119.

9. *The Letters of the Tsaritsa to the Tsar, 1914–1916* (London, 1987), Bernard Pares (intro.), p. 41. Hereafter referred to as *Letters*.

10. Buxhoeveden, p. 193.

11. *Letters*, p. 41.

12. *Letters*, p. 53.

13. Tsuyoshi Hasegawa, *The February Revolution of Petrograd, 1917* (University of Washington Press, 1981), p. 48.

14. Lieven, *Nicholas II*, p. 214.

15. *Ibid*.

16. Lili Dehn, *The Real Tsaritsa* (London, 1922), p. 40.

17. See chapter 1, page 26 for a description of the Spala incident.

5 Total War and the Marginalisation of the Kaiser

1. Count Theobold von Bethmann-Hollweg, *Betrachtungen zum Weltkrieg* (Berlin, 1921), p. 20.

2. Paul Herre, *Kronprinz Wilhelm: Seine Rolle in der deutschen Politik* (Berlin, 1954), p. 55; Diana Preston, *Wilful Murder: The Sinking of the Lusitania* (London, 2002), p. 335.

3. MacDonagh, p. 371.

4. MacDonagh, p. 367.

5. Alfred von Tirpitz, *Erinnerungen* (Leipzig, 1920), p. 462.

6. Clark, *Wilhelm II*, p. 321. The story of the Kaiser's conversation with his dentist is told in Arthur N. Davis, *The Kaiser as I Knew Him* (New York, 1918), p. 11–12.

7. The *Mauretania* and *Olympic* served mainly as troop transport ships. The *Aquitania* and *Britannic* became hospital ships and in that service the *Britannic* sank after hitting a German mine in the Mediterranean in 1916. The other three re-entered commercial service after the Armistice.

8. Preston, p. 246.

9. Preston, p. 247.

10. This has been contested by Preston, pp. 478–86, who persuasively argues that the torpedo was the main cause of the damage because of the angle and point of impact, and that if the *Lusitania* had been carrying the suspected amount or kind of munitions, the second explosion would in fact have been much louder and more damaging.

11. MacMillan, p. xix.

12. MacDonagh, p. 381.

13. Clark, *Wilhelm II*, p. 321–2.

6 The Death of Franz Josef and the Accession of Karl

1. Antonia Fraser, *Marie Antoinette: The Journey* (London, 2002), p. 3.
2. Brook-Shepherd, p. 41.
3. *Ibid.*
4. Members of the imperial line are still entitled to burial in the Capuchin crypt and the same beautiful ceremony is adhered to. Visual recordings of it during the funeral of Karl and Zita's son, Crown Prince Otto, in 2011 are currently available online.
5. Brook-Shepherd, p. 45.
6. Cases of false diagnoses of famous syphilitics include King Henry VIII of England (1491–1547), who certainly did not suffer from it, and the Emperor Franz Josef, who allegedly transmitted it to his gorgeous wife Elisabeth.
7. *Neue Freie Presse*, 22 November 1916.
8. Arturo Beeche and David McIntosh, *Empress Zita of Austria, Queen of Hungary (1891–1989)* (London, 2005), p. 8.
9. Brook-Shepherd, p. 55.
10. Countess Catherine Károlyi, *A Life Together* (London, 1966), p. 169.
11. Brook-Shepherd, p. 84–5.
12. Brook-Shepherd, p. 50.

7 The Assassination of Grigori Rasputin

1. Margaretta Eager, *Six Years at the Russian Court* (Bowmanville, 2011), p. 52.
2. Rappaport, *Four Sisters*, p. 280.
3. Massie, *Nicholas and Alexandra*, p. 283.
4. Sir John Hanbury-Williams, *The Emperor Nicholas as I Knew Him* (London, 1922), p. 239.
5. Vyrubova, p. 105.
6. Lieven, *Nicholas II*, p. 215.
7. Lieven, *Nicholas II*, p. 218.
8. Lieven, *Nicholas II*, p. 220.
9. Hall, p. 272.
10. Lieven, *Nicholas II*, p. 221.
11. Gleb Botkin, *The Real Romanovs* (London, 1932), p. 125.
12. Hall, p. 273.
13. Prince Felix Yussopov, *Lost Splendour* (London, 1953), p. 193.
14. Yussopov, *Lost Splendour*, p. 194.
15. *Letters*, p. 170.
16. Cowles, p. 173.
17. Paléologue, ii. 166.
18. Lieven, *Nicholas II*, p. 224.
19. Lieven, *Nicholas II*, p. 224–5.
20. Peter Bark, 'Vospominaniya', *Vozrozhdenie* (July 1966), p. 78.
21. Vladimir Purishkevich, *The End of Rasputin* (Ann Harbor, Michigan, 1985), p. 73.
22. Yussopov, *Lost Splendour*, p. 157.
23. For discussions of Felix Yussopov's sexuality, see Greg King, *The Murder of*

Rasputin: The Truth About Prince Felix Youssoupov and the Mad Monk who Helped Bring Down the Romanovs (London, 1996), pp. 88–90, 103–5.

24. Yussopov, *Lost Splendour*, p. 86.
25. *Letters*, p. 294.
26. Yussopov, *Lost Splendour*, p. 88.
27. King, *The Murder of Rasputin*, p. 110–11.
28. Hall, p. 252.
29. Yussopov, *Lost Splendour*, p. 149.
30. King, *The Murder of Rasputin*, p. 116.
31. King, *The Murder of Rasputin*, p. 128.
32. Prince Felix Yussopov, *Rasputin: His Malignant Influence and Assassination* (New York, 1927), p. 68.
33. Figes, p. 289.
34. *Letters*, p. 458
35. *Letters*, p. 461.
36. Massie, *Nicholas and Alexandra*, p. 362.
37. Rappaport, *Four Sisters*, p. 277.
38. Rappaport, *Four Sisters*, p. 279.
39. *Ibid*.
40. Massie, *Nicholas and Alexandra*, p. 362.

8 The February Revolution and the Fall of the Russian Monarchy

1. For an especially illuminating overview of the circumstances preceding this, see Thomas Fallows, 'Politics and the War Effort in Russia: The Union of Zemstvos and the Organization of the Food Supply, 1914–1916', *Slavic Review*, (1978), pp. 70–90.
2. Hasegawa, p. 48.
3. Grand Duke Alexander Mikhailovich of Russia, *Once a Grand Duke* (London, 1932), p. 314–5.
4. Mikhail Rodzianko, *The Reign of Rasputin* (London, 1927), pp. 252–4.
5. See in particular the letter quoted in Mark Steinberg and Vladimir Khrustalëv, *The Fall of the Romanovs: Political Dreams and Personal Struggles in a Time of Revolution* (Yale University Press, 1995), p. 73.
6. Rodzianko, p. 263.
7. Steinberg and Khrustalëv, p. 67.
8. Steinberg and Khrustalëv, p. 68.
9. Steinberg and Khrustalëv, pp. 73–6.
10. Steinberg and Khrustalëv, p. 76–7.
11. Figes, p. 321.
12. Sir Bernard Pares, *The Fall of the Russian Monarchy* (London, 1939), p. 451.
13. Cowles, p. 196.
14. Steinberg and Khrustalëv, p. 88–9.
15. Cowles, p. 196.
16. Gilliard, p. 195.
17. Pares, *Monarchy*, p. 468.
18. Paléologue, iii. 265–6.

19. Protocol of talks between deputies of the State Duma Alexander Guchkov and Vasily Shulgin, and Nicholas II in Pskov, concerning an act of abdication from the throne, cited in Steinberg and Khrustalëv, pp. 97–8.

20. Pares, *Monarchy*, pp. 468–9.

21. Grand Duke Alexander, p. 287.

22. Hall, p. 282.

23. Hall, p. 283.

24. The account of the meeting is given by the Grand Duke Paul's widow in Princess Olga Paley, *Memories of Russia* (London, 1924), p. 61.

25. Dehn, p. 165.

26. Rappaport, *Four Sisters*, p. 291.

27. Rosemary and Donald Crawford, *Michael and Natasha: The Life and Love of the Last Tsar of Russia* (London, 1997), p. 305.

28. See Crawford and Crawford, p. 302.

29. Crawford and Crawford, p. 300.

30. R. H. Bruce Lockhart, *Memoirs of a British Agent* (London, 1932), p. 160.

31. Varying translations of Mikhail's renunciation are offered. For instance, see Steinberg and Khrustalëv, p. 105.

32. Crawford and Crawford, p. 360.

33. Steinberg and Khrustalëv, p. 77.

34. Gilliard, p. 214–5.

35. Rappaport, *Four Sisters*, p. 303

36. Count Paul Benckendorff, *Last Days at Tsarskoe Selo*, trans. Maurice Baring, (London, 1927), p. 43.

37. Vyrubova, p. 212.

9 The Triumph of Military Government in Imperial Germany

1. Christopher Clark, *Iron Kingdom: The Rise and Downfall of Prussia, 1600–1947* (London, 2007), p. 268.

2. Alexandrine of Mecklenburg-Schwerin (1879–1952) was Queen Consort of Denmark from 1912 to 1947. She was also Queen Consort of Iceland from 1918 to 1944, between Iceland's Act of Union with Denmark and the plebiscite which established an independent republic. Like her sister Cecilia, Queen Alexandrine was opposed to Nazism and she and her husband King Christian X became symbols of Danish independence and opposition during the Second World War.

3. Despite the popularity of the eugenics movement in Wilhelmine Germany, the Crown Prince posed for official photographs with his daughter Alexandrine and she was very much counted as a full member of the imperial family. There is some debate over Alexandrine of Prussia's life after the collapse of the monarchy. From the ages of sixteen to eighteen, she was privately educated at a school for students with special needs, the Trüpersche Sonderschule in Thuringia, but it is not true, as is sometimes stated, that she was institutionalised when she turned twenty. Surviving photographs taken at a family wedding show the Princess standing next to her eldest brother Wilhelm in what appears to be the Wehrmacht uniform, which he did not adopt until

the outbreak of the Second World War in 1939. I am grateful to the wonderful Antonia Ede for her help in identifying the uniforms and fashions. In the photograph, both Alexandrine and her younger sister Cecilia are wearing dresses from the second half of the 1930s, after Alexandrine turned twenty. It is inconceivable that an institutionalised person would have been allowed out for events like this or at all. Therefore, it seems clear that the story she was institutionalised in 1935 or 1936 is erroneous. She died in 1980 at the age of sixty-five, having spent most of her life living in Bavaria.

4. Roger Chickering, *Imperial Germany and the Great War, 1914–1918* (Second edition, Cambridge University Press, 2004), p. 91.

5. Proclamation, 'Der Kaiser an die deutsche Flotte. Dank für die Sieger vom Skagerrak', 5 June 1916.

6. German arms had actually been imported into Ireland before the war by both nationalists, who wanted to see some form of Irish political independence, and loyalists, who were extremely hostile to the idea and wanted to preserve full legislative union with Britain. The guns were ironically enough bought from the same factory, but smuggled into Ireland through the southern port of Dun Laoghaire for the nationalists and the northern town of Larne for the loyalists. In 1916, the separatists had been very keen to harness German support and negotiations had been ongoing via the German embassy in Washington DC. This was what led to the *Aud*'s failed mission. See Russell Rees, *Ireland, 1905–1925* (Newtownards, 1998), pp. 203–5.

7. For a useful introduction to the developments surrounding the Sinn Féin Ard Fheis of 1917, when the main body of Irish separatism officially endorsed republicanism, see Rees, pp. 222–230. For the nationalist suggestion of offering an Irish throne to Prince Joachim, see Desmond FitzGerald, *Desmond's Rising: Memoirs, 1913 to Easter, 1916* (Dublin, 2006), p. 143.

8. No English-language study of the attempt to create an independent Finnish kingdom in 1918 exists. For those versed in Finnish, a good account is contained in volume 3 of Ohto Manninen (ed.), *Itsenäistymisen vuodet 1917–1920* (Helsinki, 1992), an excellent study of Finland's first three years after secession from the Russian Empire.

9. The intended crown was not made until a replica was cast using the original plans in the 1990s by the goldsmith Teuvo Ypyä. It consisted of heraldic roses, as well as coats of arms of the different provinces of Finland around its base and it was surmounted by an orb cast in blue and white, the national colours, with the country's traditional heraldic lion on top. This replica is now stored in a museum in the Finnish town of Kemi.

10. Clark, *Wilhelm II*, p. 322.

11. *The Times*, 21 April 1917.

12. Piers Brendon and Philip Whitehead, *The Windsors: A Dynasty Revealed, 1917–2000* (London, 2000), p. 17.

13. MacDonagh, p. 388.

14. The story was first reported in a German biography in 1931, but its details were confirmed by the Dowager Empress Zita in a private interview with Brook-Shepherd, cited in Brook-Shepherd, p. 64.

10 The Sixtus Affair and the Attempts to End the War

1. Count Ottokar von Czernin, *In the World War* (New York, 1920), p. 161.
2. Brook-Shepherd, p. 63.
3. For monarchism's fluctuating fortunes under the Third Republic, see Kevin Passmore, *The Right in France from the Third Republic to Vichy* (Oxford University Press, 2013).
4. Georges de Manteyer, *The Austrian Peace Offer, 1916–1917* (London, 1921), p. 39.
5. Brook-Shepherd, p. 69.
6. *Ibid.*
7. Brook-Shepherd, p. 70.
8. Brook-Shepherd, p. 71.
9. Brook-Shepherd, p. 72.
10. Brook-Shepherd, p. 100.
11. The Empress Zita, diary, 14 April 1918.
12. Hugo Hantsch, *Graf Berchtold* (Vienna, 1979), ii. 816.

11 The Murder of the Romanovs

1. Pavel Bykov, *The Last Days of Tsardom* (London, 1934), p. 33.
2. Cowles, p. 201.
3. Paul Bulygin and Alexander Kerensky, *The Murder of the Romanovs* (London, 1935), p. 122.
4. Alexander Kerensky, *The Crucifixion of Liberty* (London, 1934), p. 167–8.
5. Benckendorff, p. 76.
6. Benckendorff, p. 74.
7. Benckendorff, p. 76.
8. Bulygin and Kerensky, p. 15.
9. Rappaport, *Four Sisters*, p. 303.
10. Massie, *Nicholas and Alexandra*, p. 434.
11. Rappaport, *Four Sisters*, p. 302.
12. Massie, *Nicholas and Alexandra*, p. 433.
13. Rappaport, *Four Sisters*, p. 307.
14. Frances Welch, *The Romanovs and Mr Gibbes: The Story of the Englishman who Taught the Children of the Last Tsar* (London, 2002), p. 18.
15. Edward, Duke of Windsor, *A King's Story* (New York, 1947), p. 131.
16. King George V's mother, Alexandra of Denmark, and Nicholas's mother, the Empress Marie, were sisters; his father, King Edward VII, and Alexandra's mother, the Grand Duchess Alice of Hesse-Darmstadt, were also siblings. Lord Bertie's letter excoriating the Empress is quoted in Bilyugin and Kerensky, p. 117.
17. Brendon and Whitehead, p. 16.
18. Massie, *Nicholas and Alexandra*, p. 439.
19. Bilyugin and Kerensky, p. 120.
20. Massie, *Nicholas and Alexandra*, p. 446.
21. Bilyugin and Kerensky, p. 129.

22. Colonel Evgeny Kobylinksy, *The Last Days of the Romanovs* (London, 1920), p. 183.
23. Welch, *Gibbes*, p. 68.
24. Rappaport, *Four Sisters*, p. 322.
25. Welch, *Gibbes*, p. 68.
26. Rappaport, *Four Sisters*, p. 350.
27. Massie, *Nicholas and Alexandra*, p. 456–7.
28. Gilliard, p. 256.
29. Figes, p. 637.
30. For Robespierre's reaction to Marie Antoinette's trial see the modern reprinting of the letters of Helena Maria Williams, *Letters Written in France* (Calgary, 2001), p. 173.
31. Interview given by Vasili Yakovlev to the *Izvestia* newpaper, 16 May 1918.
32. *Ibid.*
33. *Ibid.*
34. Helen Rappaport, *Ekaterinburg: The Last Days of the Romanovs* (London, 2008), p. 1.
35. Telegraph from the Ural Regional Soviet to Vladimir Lenin and Yakov Sverdlov, 28 April 1918, in Steinberg and Khrustalëv, p. 249.
36. Telegram from Yakov Sverdlov to the Yekaterinburg Regional Committee of the Bolshevik Party, 29 April 1918, in Steinberg and Khrustalëv, p. 251.
37. Telegram from Vasily Yakovlev to Yakov Sverdlov, 29 April 1918, in Steinberg and Khrustalëv, p. 252.
38. *Ibid.*
39. Interview given by George Gibbes to Greg King, May 1989, quoted in Greg King and Penny Wilson, *The Fate of the Romanovs* (London, 2003), p. 140.
40. *Ibid.*
41. Baroness Sophie Buxhoeveden, *Left Behind: Fourteen Months in Siberia during the Revolution, December 1917 – February 1919* (London, 1919), p. 69.
42. King and Wilson, p. 141.
43. Rappaport, *Four Sisters*, p. 367.
44. Buxhoeveden, *Left Behind*, p. 73.
45. Valentin Speranski, *'La Maison à Destination Special': La Tragédie d'Ekaterinbourg* (Paris, 1929), p. 158–9.
46. King and Wilson, p. 76; Figes, p. 641.
47. Harrison Salisbury, *Black Night, White Snow: Russia's Revolutions, 1905–1917* (New York, 1977), p. 152.
48. Figes, p. 641–2.
49. King and Wilson, p. 241–2.
50. Speranski, p. 55.
51. Speranski, p. 57. My thanks to Catherine Maxtone-Parker for her help in translating some of Speranski's remarks.
52. King and Wilson, p. 243.
53. Countess Hendrikova's execution and the survival of Baroness Buxhoeveden led to a suspicion that the baroness betrayed her employers by providing the Ural Soviet with information about them, specifically that they had jewels

sewn into their undergarments to provide for themselves in exile. Although this theory has been repeated in some modern accounts of the monarchy's downfall, there is not much evidence for it. If Baroness Buxhoeveden had told the Soviet about the Romanov women's jewel stash, it is curious that this information was not factored into the plans on how to kill them and that the discovery of the jewels on their victims came as such a surprise to the executioners afterwards. To argue that the countess perished for her loyalty while collaboration saved the baroness is to accredit the Red Terror with a logic it did not possess; a further discussion of the random and capricious nature of early communism's attack on the aristocracy can be found in Douglas Smith, *Former People: The Destruction of the Russian Aristocracy* (London, 2013).

54. Empress Alexandra Feodorovna, diary, 11 July 1918.
55. Rappaport, *Four Sisters*, p. 375.
56. Cowles, p. 216.
57. My own views are that Lenin knew what was going to happen to Nicholas II's family and that the order to kill them came from the central Soviet government in Moscow. The logistics of the execution itself were clearly left to the Ural Soviet, but it is nearly inconceivable that Moscow was not consulted about such a momentous decision. Trotsky's recollection that Lenin announced the news a few days after the event without surprise corroborates the view that the latter had known about the plan to kill the Romanovs beforehand, not simply approved of it afterwards. Robert Service, *Lenin: A Biography* (London, 2010), pp. 363–366, agrees and argues that the order was given personally by Lenin but delivered through Sverdlov.
58. John Klier and Helen Mingay, *The Quest for Anastasia: Solving the Mystery of the Lost Romanovs* (London, 1996), p. 46.
59. Deciphered telegram from Alexander Beloborodov to Nikolai Gorbunov, 17 July 1918, in Steinberg and Khrustalëv, p. 337.
60. Steinberg and Khrustalëv, p. 362.
61. Steinberg and Khrustalëv, p. 359.
62. Steinberg and Khrustalëv, p. 360.

12 The End of the War and the Fall of the Monarchies

1. MacDonagh, p. 399.
2. Erich Ludendorff, *Ludendorff's Own Story: August 1914 – November 1918; the Great War from the siege of Liège to the signing of the Armistice as viewed from the headquarters of the German army* (New York, 1920), p. 421.
3. David Welch, *Germany, Propaganda and Total War, 1914–1918* (London, 2000), p. 122.
4. Maurice Baumont, *The Fall of the Kaiser*, trans. E. Ibbetson James (London, 1931), p. 3–4.
5. Clark, *Wilhelm II*, p. 340.
6. MacDonagh, p. 404.
7. MacDonagh, p. 408.
8. MacDonagh, p. 412.

9. MacDonagh, p. 408.

10. MacDonagh, p. 412.

11. *Ibid.*

12. MacDonagh, p. 413.

13. Brook-Shepherd, p. 109.

14. Interview given by the Dowager Empress Zita to Gordon Brook-Shepherd on 9 October 1978, quoted in Brook-Shepherd, p. 111.

15. Brook-Shepherd, p. 114.

16. Brook-Shepherd, p. 115.

17. Brook-Shepherd, p. 121.

18. Interview given by the Dowager Empress Zita to Gordon Brook-Shepherd on 9 October 1978, quoted in Brook-Shepherd, p. 127.

19. Brook-Shepherd, p. 129.

20. These are the words recorded by the Emperor's press secretary, Karl Werkmann. In an interview with Gordon Brook-Shepherd in 1978, the Dowager Empress Zita confirmed that the gist of his account was accurate, although she could not remember if the exact wording was correct.

21. The Empress mentions the baby Archduke Karl Ludwig in two of her quotes. The first time she references him as being an infant when leaving with them in the motorcade from the palace, and he was indeed born in March 1918. However, in her quote about the Christmas where most of her family caught the Spanish influenza, Zita said that Karl Ludwig was barely eighteen months old at the time. Her maths is wrong, but it's possible that because she was giving this information in an interview to Gordon Brook-Shepherd decades after it took place that she'd simply added up Karl Ludwig's age incorrectly; he was nine months when the influenza pandemic hit Austria.

22. Brook-Shepherd, p. 132.

23. Spanish influenza did not originate in Spain. Its king, Alfonso XIII, was another monarch who caught the disease and survived. Wartime censorship in the United Kingdom, France and the United States meant that the press were unable to report the full extent of deaths caused by the pandemic, however no such restrictions were in place in Spain, which gave rise to the erroneous impression that the country had suffered more than the others, hence the pandemic's nickname. Zita's recollection of Christmas 1918 is quoted in Brook-Shepherd, p. 136.

24. Account of the audience given by Prince Sixtus of Bourbon-Parma, quoted in Brook-Shepherd, p. 137.

25. Brook-Shepherd, p. 140.

26. *Ibid.*

27. I am grateful to Claire Handley for her help with the translation of the Emperor's letter.

Epilogue

1. The Empress was buried in an 'Antique Temple' in the park grounds of Sanssouci, an eighteenth-century retreat built on the orders of King Friedrich the Great. Initially, the temple was intended to be a museum but

during Wilhelm II's reign plans had been made to convert it into a chapel for the court's use. Augusta Victoria was the first member of the House of Hohenzollern to be laid to rest there. The body of her youngest son, Prince Joachim, who had committed suicide in 1920, was moved to rest alongside hers later. Her second son, Prince Eitel Friedrich, was buried there as well in 1942, as was her grandson Prince Wilhelm when he was killed in the Second World War. During the Soviet Union's occupation of Germany after the Second World War, Wilhelm II's second wife, the Dowager Empress Hermine, died in the communist-controlled East in 1947 and she too was buried at Sanssouci, meaning that both of Wilhelm II's consorts are now buried in the same place. The mausoleum is closed to the public.

2. Clark, *Wilhelm II*, p. 355.
3. The story about Countess Hannah von Bismarck-Schönhausen's refusal to launch a ship for the Nazi regime was recounted by Cecilia, Countess von Sternberg, to the author Tyler Whittle and referenced in Whittle, p. 339 n. Field Marshal von Mackensen at Prince Wilhelm's funeral, see Whittle, p. 340.
4. MacDonagh, p. 416–17, 459.
5. Theo Aronson, *Crowns in Conflict: The Triumph and Tragedy of European Monarchy, 1910–1918* (London, 1986), p. 175.
6. James Bogle and Joanna Bogle, *A Heart for Europe: The Lives of Emperor Charles and Empress Zita of Austria-Hungary* (Leominster, 2000), p. 35.
7. Klier and Mingay, p. 95.
8. Klier and Mingay, p. 223.
9. Klier and Mingay, p. 234.
10. Klier and Mingay, p. 235.
11. King, *The Murder of Rasputin*, p. 237–8.
12. Eric Ives, *Lady Jane Grey: A Tudor Mystery* (Oxford, 2009), p. 293.
13. *The Beatification of Five Servants of God*, the Vatican website, 3 October 2004. The beatification of the late Emperor was not without controversy, although criticisms voiced in the English-language newspapers which suggested Karl was a murderous or incompetent buffoon hardly seem particularly fair, likewise suggestions that he was simply beatified to solidify conservative political-religious opinion in modern Austria. For the contrary view, see Ian Traynor, 'Pope to beatify "buffoon" who was Austria's last emperor', *The Guardian*, 18 January 2004.
14. The opening quote to chapter XXI of Yussopov, *Lost Splendour*.

Bibliography

Newspapers and Periodicals

Izvestia, Moscow
L'Osservatore Romano, Vatican City
Neue Freie Presse, Vienna
The Daily Telegraph, London
The Guardian, London
The New York Times, New York
The Times, London

Books and Journals

Aichelburg, Wladimir, *Archduke Franz Ferdinand and Artstetten Castle* (Vienna, 2000)

Albertini, Luigi, *The Origins of the War of 1914* (Oxford University Press, 1956)

Alexander Mikhailovich, Grand Duke of Russia, *Once a Grand Duke* (London, 1932)

Aronson, Theo, *Crowns in Conflict: The Triumph and the Tragedy of European Monarchy, 1910–1918* (London, 1986)

Ascher, Abraham, *P. A. Stolypin: The Search for Stability in Late Imperial Russia* (Stanford University Press, 2001)

Baden, Prince Maximilian von, *The Memoirs of Prince Max of Baden*, trans. W. M. Calder (London, 1928)

Bark, Peter, 'Vospominaniya', *Vozrozhdenie* (July 1966)

Barkai, Haim, 'The Macro-Economics of Tsarist Russia in the Industrialization Era: Monetary Developments, the Balance of Payments and the Gold Standard', *Journal of Economic History* (1973)

Baumont, Maurice, *The Fall of the Kaiser*, trans. E. Ibbetson James (London, 1931)

Beeche, Arturo and David McIntosh, *Empress Zita of Austria, Queen of Hungary (1891–1989)* (London, 2005)

Beller, Steven, *Francis Joseph* (London, 1996)

Benckendorff, Count Paul, *Last days at Tsarskoe Selo*, trans. Maurice Baring (London, 1927)

Benedict, Heinrich, *Monarchie der Gegensätze* (Vienna, 1947)

Bestenreiner, Erika, *Franz Ferdinand und Sophie von Hohenburg: Verbotene Liebe am Kaiserhof* (Munich, 2004)

Beutler, Gigi, *The Imperial Vaults of the PP Capuchins in Vienna* (Vienna, 2007)

Bing, E. J. (ed.), *The Letters of the Tsar Nicholas and Empress Marie* (London, 1937)

Bled, Jean-Paul, *François-Ferdinand d'Autriche* (Paris, 2012)

Bogle, James and Joanna Bogle, *A Heart for Europe: The Lives of Emperor Charles and Empress Zita of Austria-Hungary* (Leominster, 2000)

Botkin, Gleb, *The Real Romanovs* (London, 1932)

Boyer, J. W., 'The End of an Old Regime: Visions of Political Reform in Late Imperial Austria', *Journal of Modern History* (1986)

Brendon, Piers and Philip Whitehead, *The Windsors: A Dynasty Revealed, 1917 –2000* (London, 2000)

Bridge, F. R., *From Sadowa to Sarajevo: The Foreign Policy of Austria-Hungary, 1866–1914* (London, 1972)

Brook-Shepherd, Gordon, *The Last Empress: The Life and Times of Zita of Austria-Hungary, 1892–1989* (London, 1991)

Bruce Lockhart, R. H., *Memoirs of a British Agent* (London, 1932)

Buchanan, Meriel, *The Dissolution of an Empire* (London, 1932)

Bülow, Prince Bernhard von, *Memoirs of Prince von Bülow* (Boston, 1931)

Bulygin, Paul and Alexander Kerensky, *The Murder of the Romanovs* (London, 1935)

Buxhoeveden, Baroness Sophie, *Left Behind: Fourteen Months in Siberia during the Revolution, December 1917 – February 1919* (London, 1919)

Buxhoeveden, Baroness Sophie, *The Life and Tragedy of Alexandra Feodorovna, Empress of Russia* (New York, 1928)

Bykov, Pavel, *The Last Days of Tsardom* (London, 1934)

Cassels, Lavender, *The Archduke and the Assassin* (New York, 1985)

Cavendish-Bentinck, William, 6th Duke of Portland, *Men, Women and Things* (London, 1938)

Cecil, Lamar, *Albert Ballin: Business and Politics in Imperial Germany, 1888–1918* (Princeton University Press, 1967)

Cecil, Lamar, *Wilhelm II: Emperor and Exile* (University of North Carolina Press, 1996)

Chickering, Roger, *Imperial Germany and the Great War, 1914–1918* (Second edition, Cambridge University Press, 2004)

Churchill, Winston, *The World Crisis* (London, 1923)

Clark, Christopher, *Iron Kingdom: The Rise and Downfall of Prussia, 1600–1947* (London, 2007)

Clark, Christopher, *Kaiser Wilhelm II: A Life in Power* (London, 2009)

Cook, Andrew, *The Murder of the Romanovs* (Stroud, 2011)

Corti, Count Egon Caesar, *Elisabeth, Empress of Austria* (Yale University Press, 1936)

Corti, Count Egon Caesar, *Vom Kind Zum Kaiser* (Graz, 1950)

Corti, Count Egon Caesar, and Hans Sokol, *Der alte Kaiser* (Vienna, 1955)

Cowles, Virginia, *The Last Tsar and Tsarina* (London, 1977)

Crankshaw, Edward, *The Fall of the House of Habsburg* (London, 1983)

Crawford, Rosemary and Donald Crawford, *Michael and Natasha: The Life and Love of the Last Tsar of Russia* (London, 1997)

Cunliffe-Owen, Marguerite, *The Martyrdom of an Empress* (London, 1899)

Davis, Arthur N., *The Kaiser as I Knew Him* (New York, 1918)

de Manteyer, Georges, *The Austrian Peace Offer, 1916–1917* (London, 1921)

Deák, István, *Beyond Nationalism: A Social and Political History of the Habsburg Officer Corps, 1848–1918* (Oxford, 1992)

Dedijer, Vladimir, *The Road to Sarajevo* (New York, 1966)

Dehn, Lili, *The Real Tsaritsa* (London, 1922)

Duberman, Martin Baumi, Martha Vicinus and George Chauncey (eds), *Hidden from History: Reclaiming the Gay and Lesbian Past* (New York, 1990)

Eager, Margaretta, *Six Years at the Russian Court* (Bowmanville, Ontario, 2011)

Edward, Duke of Windsor, *A King's Story* (New York, 1947)

Eisenmerger, Victor, *Archduke Franz Ferdinand* (London, 1928)

Epkenhaus, Michael, *Tirpitz: Architect of the German High Seas Fleet* (Washington DC, 2008)

Erdödy, Count Tamás, *Habsburgs Weg von Wilhelm zu Briand* (Leipzig, 1932)

Fallows, Thomas, 'Politics and the War Effort in Russia: The Union of Zemstvos and the Organization of the Food Supply, 1914–1916', *Slavic Review* (1978)

Fenyvesi, Charles, *Royalty In Exile: The Inside Story of the Ex-Majesties of Europe* (London, 1981)

Feuerlicht, Roberta Strauss, *The Desperate Act: The Assassination of Franz Ferdinand at Sarajevo* (New York, 1968)

Figes, Orlando, *A People's Tragedy: The Russian Revolution, 1891–1924* (London, 1996)

Fischer, Fritz, *Germany's Aims in the First World War* (New York, 1967)

FitzGerald, Desmond, *Desmond's Rising: Memoirs, 1913 to Easter, 1916* (Dublin, 2006)

Fraser, Antonia, *Marie Antoinette: The Journey* (London, 2002)

Fromkin, David, *Europe's Last Summer: Why the World Went to War in 1914* (London, 2004)

Fuller, William C., *The Foe Within: Fantasies of Treason and the End of Imperial Russia* (Cornell University Press, 2006)

Fuller, William, *Strategy and Power in Russia, 1600–1914* (New York, 1992)

Gilliard, Pierre, *Thirteen Years at the Russian Imperial Court* (New York, 1921)

Hall, Coryne, *Little Mother of Russia: A Biography of the Empress Marie Feodorovna* (London, 1999)

Hanbury-Williams, John, *The Emperor Nicholas as I Knew Him* (London, 1922)

Hantsch, Hugo, *Graf Berchtold* (Vienna, 1979)

Hasegawa, Tsuyoshi, *The February Revolution of Petrograd, 1917* (University of Washington Press, 1981)

Haslip, Joan, *The Lonely Empress: A Biography of Elizabeth of Austria* (New York, 1965)

Haslip, Joan, *The Emperor and the Actress: The love story of Emperor Franz Josef and Katharina Schratt* (London, 1982)

Hauser-Köchert, Irmgard, *Imperial Jewellers in Vienna* (Firenze, 1990)

Herre, Paul, *Kronprinz Wilhelm: Seine Rolle in der deutschen Politik* (Berlin, 1954)

Herring, George C., *From Colony to Superpower: US Foreign Relations since 1776* (Oxford, 2008)

Herzer, Manfred, *Magnus Hirschfeld: Leben und Werk eines jüdischen, schwulen und sozialistischen Sexologen* (Hamburg, 2001)

Hewitson, Mark, 'Germany and France before the First World War: A Reassessment of Wilhelmine Foreign Policy', *English Historical Review* (2000)

Höller, Gerd, *Franz Ferdinand von Österreich-Este* (Vienna, 1982)

Hull, Isabel, *The Entourage of Kaiser Wilhelm II, 1888–1918* (Cambridge University Press, 2004)

Ives, Eric, *Lady Jane Grey: A Tudor Mystery* (Oxford, 2009)

Jászi, Oscar, *The Dissolution of the Habsburg Monarchy* (University of Chicago Press, 1929)

Jelavich, Barbara, 'What the Habsburg Government Knew about the Black Hand', *Austrian History Yearbook* (Houston, 1991)

Josef, Redlich, *The Emperor Franz Josef* (London, 1929)

Jovanović, M. Ljuba, 'The Murder of Sarajevo', *Journal of the British Institute of International Affairs* (March 1925)

Károlyi, Countess Catherine, *A Life Together* (London, 1966)

Kennan, George, *Siberia and the Exile System* (New York, 1891)

Kerensky, Alexander, *The Catastrophe* (London, 1927)

Kerensky, Alexander, *The Crucifixion of Liberty* (London, 1934)

King, Greg, *The Last Empress: The Life and Times of Alexandra Feodorovna, Tsarina of Russia* (London, 1995)

King, Greg, *The Murder of Rasputin: The Truth about Prince Felix Youssoupov and the Mad Monk who Helped Bring Down the Romanovs* (London, 1996)

King, Greg and Penny Wilson, *The Fate of the Romanovs* (London, 2003)

King, Greg and Sue Woolmans, *The Assassination of the Archduke: Sarajevo 1914 and the Murder that Changed the World* (London, 2013)

Kingston-Mann, Esther, and Tim Maxter (eds), *Peasant Economy, Culture and Politics in European Russia, 1800–1921* (Princeton University Press, 1991)

Kiszling, Rudolf, *Erzherzog Franz Ferdinand von Österreich-Este* (Graz and Cologne, 1953)

Klier, John and Helen Mingay, *The Quest for Anastasia: Solving the Mystery of the Lost Romanovs* (London, 1996)

Kobylinsky, Evgeny, *The Last Days of the Romanovs* (London, 1920)

Kokovstov, Count Vladimir, *Out of My Past: The Memoirs of Count Kokovstov*, trans. Laura Matveev (Stanford University Press, 1935)

Kramer, Alan, *Dynamic of Destruction: Culture and Mass Killing in the First World War* (Oxford University Press, 2008)

Lerman, Katherine A., *The Chancellor as Courtier: Bernhard von Bülow and the Government of Germany, 1900–1909* (Cambridge University Press, 1990)

Lieven, Dominic, *Russia and the Origins of the First World War* (Basingstoke, 1987)

Lieven, Dominic, *Nicholas II: Emperor of all the Russias* (London, 1993)

Löwe, Heinz-Dietrich, *Die Lage der Bauern in Russland, 1880–1905* (St Katharinen, 1987)

Ludendorff, Erich, *Ludendorff's Own Story: August 1914 – November 1918; The Great War from the Siege of Liège to the Signing of the Armistice as Viewed from the Headquarters of the German Army* (New York, 1920)

MacDonagh, Giles, *The Last Kaiser: William the Impetuous* (London, 2000)

MacMillan, Margaret, *The War that Ended Peace: How Europe Abandoned Peace for the First World War* (London, 2013)

McDaniel, Tim, *Autocracy, Capitalism and Revolution in Russia* (University of California Press, 1988)

McDonald, D. M., *United Government and Foreign Policy in Russia, 1900–1914* (Cambridge University Press, 1992)

McIntosh, Christopher, *The Swan King: Ludwig II of Bavaria* (London, 1982)

McKean, R. B. (ed.), *New Perspectives in Modern Russian History: Selected Papers from the Fourth World Congress of Soviet and Eastern European Studies, Harrogate, 1990* (London, 1992)

McLean, Roderick R., *Royalty and Diplomacy in Europe, 1890–1914* (Cambridge University Press, 2001)

Manninen, Ohto (ed.), *Itsenäistymisen Vuodet 1917–1920* (Helsinki, 1992)

Marie Louise of Schleswig-Holstein, Princess, *My Memories of Six Reigns* (London, 1957)

Massie, Robert K., *Nicholas and Alexandra* (London, 1968)

Maylunas, Andrei and Sergei Mironenko, *A Lifelong Passion: Nicholas and Alexandra, Their Own Story* (London, 1997)

Menne, Bernhard, *Blood and Steel: The Rise and Fall of the House of Krupp*, trans. G. H. Smith (New York, 1938)

Menning, Bruce W., *Bayonets before Bullets: The Imperial Russian Army, 1861–1914* (Indiana University Press, 1992)

Millard, Frank, *The Palace and the Bunker: Royal Resistance to Hitler* (Stroud, 2012)

Morris, Edmund, *Theodore Rex* (New York, 2001)

Morton, Frederic, *Thunder at Twilight: Vienna, 1913–1914* (New York, 1989)

Mosse, W. E., 'Stolypin's Villages', *Slavonic and Eastern European Review* (1964–5)

Nolan, Michael E., *The Inverted Mirror: Mythologizing the Enemy in France and Germany, 1898–1914* (New York, 2005)

Owings, Dolph, *The Sarajevo Trial* (Chapel Hill, NC, 1984)

Paléologue, Maurice, *An Ambassador's Memoirs* (London, 1923–1925)

Paley, Olga, Princess, *Memories of Russia* (London, 1924)

Pallot, J. and D. J. B. Shaw (eds), *Landscape and Settlement in Romanov Russia, 1613–1917* (Oxford University Press, 1990)

Palmer, Alan, *Twilight of the Habsburgs: The Life and Times of the Emperor Francis Joseph* (New York, 1994)

Pares, Bernard, *The Fall of the Russian Monarchy* (London, 1939)

Pares, Bernard (intro.), *The Letters of the Tsaritsa to the Tsar, 1914–1916* (London, 1987)

Passmore, Kevin, *The Right in France from the Third Republic to Vichy* (Oxford University Press, 2013)

Pless, Daisy, Princess of, *Daisy, Princess of Pless: By Herself* (New York, 1929)

Preston, Diana, *Wilful Murder: The Sinking of the Lusitania* (London, 2002)

Purishkevich, Vladimir, *The End of Rasputin* (Ann Harbour, Michigan, 1985)

Radzinsky, Edvard, *Rasputin: The Last Word*, trans. Judson Rosengrant (London, 2000)

Rappaport, Helen, *Ekaterinburg: The Last Days of the Romanovs* (London, 2008)

Rappaport, Helen, *Four Sisters: The Lost Lives of the Romanov Grand Duchesses* (London, 2014)

Rathenau, Walther, *Walther Rathenau: Industrialist, Banker, Intellectual, and Politician: Notes and Diaries, 1907–1922*, Hartmut Pogge von Strandmann and Caroline Pinder Cracraft (eds) (Oxford University Press, 1985)

Rees, Russell, *Ireland, 1905–1925* (Newtownards, 1998)

Regan, John M., *Myth and the Irish State* (Irish Academic Press, 2013)

Remak, Joachim, *Sarajevo: The Story of a Political Murder* (New York, 1959)

Remak, Joachim, 'The Healthy Invalid: How doomed was the Habsburg Empire?', *Journal of Modern History* (February, 1969)

Rich, David Alan, *The Tsar's Colonels: Professionalism, Strategy, and Subversion in Late Imperial Russia* (Cambridge University Press, 1998)

Rich, Norman and M. H. Fisher (ed.), *The Holstein Papers* (Cambridge University Press, 1957)

Rodzianko, Mikhail, *The Reign of Rasputin* (London, 1927)

Röhl, John C. G., *Germany without Bismarck: The Crisis of Government in the Second Reich, 1890–1900* (London, 1967)

Röhl, John C. G. (ed.), *1914: Delusion or Design?* (London, 1973)

Röhl, John C. G., *The Kaiser and His Court: Wilhelm II and the Government of Germany* (Cambridge University Press, 1996)

Röhl, John C. G., *Young Wilhelm: The Kaiser's Early Life, 1859–1888* (Cambridge University Press, 1998)

Rummel, Rudolph, *Lethal Politics: Soviet Murder and Mass Genocide since 1917* (Rutgers University, 1990)

Salisbury, Harrison, *Black Night, White Snow: Russia's Revolutions 1905–1917* (New York, 1977)

Schorske, Carl E., *Fin-de-Siècle Vienna: Politics and Culture* (New York, 1981)

Schuselka, Franz, *Deutsche Worte eines Oesterreichischers* (Hamburg, 1843)

Schwarzenberg, Adolf, *Prince Felix zu Schwarzenberg* (New York, 1946)

Shawcross, William (ed.), *Counting One's Blessings: The Selected Letters of Queen Elizabeth the Queen Mother* (London, 2013)

Service, Robert, *A History of Modern Russia: From Nicholas II to Putin* (London, 2003)

Service, Robert, *Lenin: A Biography* (London, 2010)

Smith, David James, *One Morning in Sarajevo* (London, 2008)

Smith, Douglas, *Former People: The Destruction of the Russian Aristocracy* (London, 2013)

Snyder, Timothy, *The Red Prince: The Fall of a Dynasty and the Rise of Modern Europe* (London, 2008)

Sondhaus, Lawrence, *Franz Conrad von Hötzendorf: Architect of the Apocalypse* (Boston, 2000)

Speranski, Valentin, *'La Maison à destination special': La Tragédie d'Ekaterinenbourg* (Paris, 1929)

Stannard, Martin, *Evelyn Waugh: The Early Years, 1903–1939* (London, 1990)

Steinberg, John W., *All the Tsar's Men: Russia's General Staff and the Fate of the Empire, 1898–1914* (Baltimore, 2010)

Steinberg, Mark and Vladimir M. Khrustalëv, *The Fall of the Romanovs: Political Dreams and Personal Struggles in a Time of Revolution* (Yale University Press, 1995)

Stephanie, Crown Princess of Austria and Hungary, *I Was to Be Empress* (London, 1937)

Taylor, A. J. P., *The First World War* (London, 1974)

von Bethmann-Hollweg, Count Theobold, *Betrachtungen zum Weltkrieg* (Berlin, 1921)

von Czerin, Count Ottokar, *In the World War* (New York, 1920)

von Margutti, Baron Albert, *The Emperor Francis Joseph and His Times* (London, 1921)

von Morsey, Baron Andreas, 'Konopischt and Sarajevo', *Berliner Monatshefte* (June 1934)

von Sosnosky, Theodor, *Franz Ferdinand der Erzherzog Thronfolger* (Munich, 1929)

von Tirpitz, Alfred, *Erinnerungen* (Leipzig, 1920)

Vyrubova, Anna, *Memories of the Russian Court* (New York, 1923)

Welch, David, *Germany, Propaganda and Total War, 1914–1918* (London, 2000)

Welch, Frances, *The Romanovs and Mr Gibbes: The Story of the Englishman who Taught the Children of the Last Tsar* (London, 2002)

Wheatcroft, Andrew, *The Habsburgs: Embodying Empire* (London, 1995)

Whittle, Tyler, *The Last Kaiser: A Biography of William II, German Emperor and King of Prussia* (London, 1977)

Williams, Helena Maria, *Letters Written in France* (Calgary, 2001)

Wilton, Robert, *The Last Days of the Romanovs* (London, 1920)

Yussopov, Prince Felix, *Rasputin: His Malignant Influence and Assassination* (New York, 1927)

Yussopov, Prince Felix, *Lost Splendour* (London, 1953)

Zweig, Stefan, *The World of Yesterday* (London, 2011)

Index